GENERATION SPACE:
A LOVE STORY

by
Anna Leahy & Douglas R. Dechow

www.GenerationSpace.com

stillhouse
press

CRAFT PUBLISHING FOR ARDENT SPIRITS

Fairfax, VA

I believe the most important stories today reveal the connection between the personal and the historical; that is, they reveal how individual lives reflect the most important aspects of the broader culture around us. Good storytelling is the best form of understanding and education. *Generation Space* will appeal to a broad range of readers and will be a very human and compelling contribution to our understanding of how we all have been influenced by rapid technological change.

    —Kristen Iversen, author of *Full Body Burden*

Weaving together personal narratives while telling a broader cultural story, Anna Leahy and Doug Dechow have written a book that is as delightful as it is instructive. The *Challenger* shuttle exploded on my eighth birthday, and in curious ways it seems that my life has been framed and punctuated by space travel; after reading this book, I understand why. If I've never felt comfortable with the label Generation X, it's because I'm more accurately a member of Generation Space. Exploring linguistic subtleties and technological details, ranging across scientific anecdotes and poetic insights, *Generation Space: A Love Story* is truly an adventure, and a discovery.

    —Christopher Schaberg, author of *The End of Airports*

In this engaging and deeply reported memoir, Anna Leahy and Douglas Dechow capture the unique mixture of nostalgia, hope, and derring-do that surrounds humanity's successful attempt to puncture the veil of space. *Generation Space* is a book that will resonate with the children of that Apollo era and one that asks the urgent question that few seem willing to answer in the 21st century: where do we go from here?

    —Tom Zoellner, author of *Train*

Generation Space is an engaging tale of two love affairs: the authors' love for one another and America's fascination with lunar landings and interplanetary travel. Like twin moons in similar orbits, the stories become inseparable. Kudos to Anna Leahy and Douglas R. Dechow for reminding us of all the reasons we constantly reach for the stars.

    —Dinty W. Moore, author of *Between Panic & Desire* and *Dear Mister Essay Writer Guy*

Generation Space presents a unique and personal history of the American space program, focusing not so much on NASA's already well-documented pioneers or the iconic astronauts and technicians of the moon landings, but on what came after...the space journeys of the past few decades, journeys that have retained the fascination, romance and adventure of their more widely publicized Mercury, Gemini, and Apollo predecessors. Told in alternating chapters by the married couple Anna Leahy and Doug Dechow, a poet and a scientist, this fascinating history is interwoven skillfully with the story of their partnership, shared passion, and personal explorations. "Following the shuttles reminded me that I'd had childhood dreams, that life is full of potential," writes Dechow. *Generation Space* is likewise inspiring.

    —Gordon McAlpine, author of *Woman with a Blue Pencil* and *The Misadventures of Edgar & Allan Poe* series

This book is great fun—an entertaining love story by two writers whose prose makes you feel you are in marvelous company, as you move from Leahy's perspective to Dechow's, and the whole thing is full of what I like to call knowledge-bearing sentences: the story of our involvement and fascination with space, and space travel, through their eyes, and in light of their love of each other. A sweet ride all the way.

    —Richard Bausch, author of *Before, During, After* and *Something Is Out There*

SECOND STILLHOUSE EDITION, APRIL 2017

stillhouse press

Stillhouse Press
4400 University Drive, 3E4
Fairfax, VA 22030
www.stillhousepress.org

Stillhouse Press is an independent, student-run nonprofit press based
out of Northern Virginia and established in collaboration
with the Fall for the Book festival.

Library of Congress Control Number: 2016951542
ISBN-10: 0-9969816-1-3
ISBN-13: 978-0-9969816-1-3

Cover design by Douglas J. Luman
Interior layout by Kady Dennell

Printed in the United States of America.

This publisher is a proud member of

[clmp]

TABLE OF CONTENTS

INTRODUCTION
WHEN YOU WISH UPON A STAR
BOTH

Yet for me the first great joy of traveling is simply the luxury of leaving all my beliefs and certainties at home, and seeing everything I thought I knew in a different light, and from a crooked angle.

— Pico Iyer

Ours has never been a conventional love story. We first met on Valentine's Day of 1989, months after space shuttle *Discovery*'s return-to-flight mission following the *Challenger* accident. We became a couple on Thanksgiving of that same year, as *Discovery* orbited two hundred miles overhead on a secret mission. At the time, we had no idea that we'd meet four of the astronauts who flew those missions.

We've been wanderers, looking together for our place in the universe. America's love affair with space exploration has never been conventional, either. Like NASA, we've belonged many places, in our case seven states and even more cities and apartments. In the 1990s, we moved to the DC-area and spent hours upon hours at the National Air and Space Museum, the world's busiest museum, where we touched a Moon rock with our own fingers. We wended our way through graduate degrees and jobs, and, all the while, the shuttle hummed in the background of our lives, for us and for our whole generation.

Pico Iyer, a visiting writer at our university, wrote, "And we travel, in essence, to become young fools again—to slow time down and get taken in, and fall in love once more." In 2008, we traveled to new jobs at a university—one of us a poet-professor and the other a scientist-turned-librarian—in Southern California, the birthplace of the space shuttle. Only then, in refreshing foolishness, did we let ourselves get taken in and fall in love again, both with each other and with the Space Age.

The song "When You Wish Upon a Star" claims that it doesn't matter who you are for your dreams to be fulfilled, that fate intersects with desire in unlikely ways that make all the difference. We wondered whether the reality of our adulthood could match the dreams of our childhood, when we'd wished upon a star. *Generation Space* chronicles the intertwined love stories of us as a couple and of a culture that has fallen for space and space exploration.

Only months after we'd settled into our home in California, on Saturday, November 29, 2008, space shuttle *Endeavour* had been orbiting Earth for more than two weeks. Thunderstorms and crosswinds that day made landing at Kennedy Space Center on the eastern edge of Florida too dangerous. NASA didn't want *Endeavour* to wait a couple of days for better weather there.

Despite the weather predictions, NASA would decide whether a Kennedy landing would be okay when the time came for the deorbit burn, the point at which *Endeavour*—orbiting upside-down and tail-first—would fire its engines against the direction it was traveling to slow down and begin its fall through Earth's atmosphere. Once deorbit burn occurred, there was no stopping descent, no changing their minds. NASA hoped for the best, planned alternatives, and, once committed, saw its plan through. Even though no one expected good enough weather for a safe return to Florida, NASA had two separate times on Sunday at which they could give the "go" for the deorbit burn to land at Kennedy.

Meanwhile, NASA had a backup plan: landing at Edwards Air Force Base in California, where the military has long done flight testing and which was home to NASA's Dryden Flight Research Center (renamed for Neil Armstrong since then). For the initial three years of the Shuttle program, Edwards had been the first-choice landing site, but landing shuttles where they launched saved money. Edwards became the backup in 1984, with landings there uncommon and expensive because they required the shuttle to be strapped to the top of a 747 and ferried back to Florida for its next launch. A "no go" at Kennedy would mean that *Endeavour* would land in its California birthplace, not far from where we'd moved only three months earlier.

"We should go see the shuttle land tomorrow." A lark, but the idea gripped us. That quick exchange began our path to this book.

That Sunday, the two of us woke before 9:00 a.m. to hang on words from the local radio and stalk CNN for updates. We checked websites for NASA's updates. We hadn't wished this hard for bad weather since we longed for snow days in our Midwestern childhoods.

For the shuttle, a complete orbit of Earth took about ninety minutes, and California highway speed limits top out at seventy miles per hour. The situation called to mind a story problem from our grade-school textbooks. Because *Endeavour* circled Earth almost twice between a final "no go" for Florida and a "go" for California, we would have enough time for the drive to Edwards.

At Edwards, only one possible landing time existed: 1:25 p.m. We became giddy, then worried that our anticipation had the power to clear clouds and calm winds across the country in Florida.

By 9:30 a.m. in California, the first landing opportunity for Kennedy was a "no go." Two missions earlier, in March, *Endeavour*'s first opportunity at Kennedy was called off for weather, with better conditions ninety minutes later. By 10:50 a.m. our time, we would know whether the second chance in Florida was also a "no go." We dressed quickly and then paced from kitchen to living room and back.

The crew on *Endeavour* had serviced and repaired two rotary joints for the solar arrays of the International Space Station. These joints allow the solar panels, which provide power, to rotate to track the Sun as the space station circles the globe. These arrays of two-sided panels create the illusion of rectangular wings, and they give the otherwise clunky, modular object an elegance, making it look as if the station is floating instead of zipping at almost five miles per second—roughly 17,500 miles per hour—around Earth. The solar panel arrays are why anyone can look up on the right night at the right time and see overhead a spark of light—Sun reflecting off panels—that contains human beings. We have an app on our phones so that we can catch glimpses together.

That Thursday had been Thanksgiving, the day that we've celebrated as our own anniversary, when we first kissed and admitted to falling in love with each other. The crew of *Endeavour* and the residents of the space station—one Russian among the Americans—ate a traditionally American holiday dinner, complete with turkey, stuffing, and yams. An out-of-this-world celebration of togetherness.

On Sunday, the astronauts woke to the song "Gonna Fly Now" and waited to be told where they would land. We waited alongside, as they circled Earth roughly 250 miles above us. We printed out driving directions from our house in Orange to Edwards Air Force Base.

By 11:00 a.m., both Florida landing times were "no go." We had roughly two-and-a-half hours to get to Edwards. We grabbed soda and protein bars and jumped into our car. We guided each other; we played to our strengths. The shuttle was coming to California; we would greet it.

In reality, we hadn't planned ahead well. We had to stop for gas on the way out of town, taking valuable minutes needed at the other end of our journey. Though we saw on the map an entrance with public access to the Air Force Base, we didn't know where to go from there. In addition, because the mountains lie between our home and the landing site, no direct path existed. The two of us rushed against NASA's clock with anticipation instead of information.

Driving in our aging Saturn, we saw what boom and bust meant in the early days of the nation's economic collapse. A couple of hours from the established suburbs surrounding Los Angeles, looming signs pointed to deals on large houses, many of which had never been occupied and some of which hadn't even been finished and stood abandoned. A gas station and one fast food restaurant survived in front of a strip mall that displayed mostly empty storefronts. SUVs buzzed around the equivalent of a few blocks, but the surrounding land looked empty for miles, as if this place were a social experiment or a town quarantined. We'd never before seen somewhere indefinitely half-accomplished. We did not say aloud then what this meant to us: this unnerving landscape echoed NASA's announcement that shuttles would stop flying; it echoed the abandonment of manned space exploration. Space exploration remained half-accomplished too; we haven't yet set foot on Mars.

We drove on, headed onto a crest above Rogers Dry Lake. With landing time approaching quickly, we pulled off where a dozen other cars had formed a haphazard line on the side of the road. We walked a few steps in one direction, then in another. We didn't see many people at this juncture, so there must have been somewhere else more suitable. Tiny lizards scurried through the underbrush. We saw the runway in the distance below and didn't have time to search for a better location.

"Is that west?" We traced our fingers along a possible flight path. We pondered aloud. "We came in from the north. The ocean is over there?"

That sunny November day in the California desert, we had no map of the blue sky, no coordinates. Our hats and hands shaded our eyes. Another couple in our proximity guessed at a direction from which the shuttle would appear, and our eyes followed their gestures. We both scanned the horizon, our minds focused on the singular task.

We heard the first sonic boom, air ripping apart then slapping back together as the shuttle passed through it faster than the speed of sound. Then, immediately after, the second boom. The startling rhythm of a shuttle landing. But we didn't see the vehicle. When a jet flies overhead, its engines emit a sensory cue so that ears, then eyes, orient us toward the aircraft's flight path. The over-in-an-instant double bang of the shuttle's sonic boom wasn't enough visceral information; our minds didn't keep up with the shuttle's path.

"Where is it?" We heard each other's desperation. "Do you see it?"

How far away was the orbiter when we heard the booms? We didn't know. We should have. We'd read about the shuttle and how it works. How steep was the final glide? Seven times steeper than for an airliner, we'd read. The orbiter slowed, dropped below the speed of sound. From this distance, how big was it supposed to look? We'd lost perspective. Gear dropped with fifteen seconds left. Landing was imminent. But we couldn't catch a glimpse. Our eyes searched ocean of sky, glanced over mottled lakebed. We wanted to know this orbiter personally.

In days to come, we said, "We drove to Edwards to see the shuttle land." A semantically true statement that let friends think we saw wheels touch down, chute opening behind to slow the most complex machine ever built. Later, we learned that *Endeavour* didn't land on the main runway, which was being upgraded at the time. So even if we'd known the shuttle's usual path, we didn't know to look for the shorter, temporary Runway 4 Left. At a military base, runways aren't marked for spectators. Our mistakes that day prepared us for the launches that we did see.

That day in 2008, *Endeavour*—a real-life spaceship—stood small in the distance, in front of a clump of buildings. We saw it with our own eyes. "I'm a scientist and I know what constitutes proof," Douglas Adams wrote in *So Long, and Thanks for All the Fish*. "But the reason I call myself by my childhood name is to remind myself that a scientist must also absolutely be like a child. If he sees a thing, he must say that he sees it, whether it was what he thought he was going to see or not." Hours earlier, this object had flown beyond Earth's atmosphere. We squinted to make out the orbiter's contours. We felt like children, fascinated, curious.

We leaned into each other, our hands coming to rest in familiar places, physically reminding ourselves—*pinch me!*—that we were in this place overlooking a space shuttle, that we shared this experience, including our mistakes. Love can't be explained so much as it must be lived. That shuttle-bolt out of the sky imparted inexplicable clarity we'd never before felt about the long-term future: we wanted to build our lives together, and we wanted space exploration to continue. Our hearts were in these two dreams.

As we stared at *Endeavour*, a small group of vehicles approached the orbiter. One truck hosed away whatever toxic materials and fumes surrounded the orbiter. The astronauts usually crawled out within an hour of wheel-stop. At Edwards, no press waited for comments, and spectators like us were far away. Shortly after landing at Edwards, the crew could be eating Mexican food at a renowned local restaurant.

We left too soon. As far away as we were from the tarmac, we couldn't have discerned one astronaut from another. Of the seven astronauts we didn't see that day, four flew on the last three Shuttle flights. We saw those four astronauts up close and in person in the years that followed, in the years that we followed Shuttle's end and made this book.

In our photographs of *Endeavour* that day, it is a white speck you'd need to know to look for and trust that it is what we say it is. The real proof that we were there and saw a space shuttle rests in each other. The Thanksgiving trek to the desert was a shifting point in our lives. The result: we married in Las Vegas the following Thanksgiving, a year after this unexpected epiphany and twenty years after we'd first kissed, and we reoriented our lives around the end of Shuttle a year after that. We let our longings lead us.

We have come to understand that those of us born after Sputnik in 1957 and before the first space shuttle mission in 1981 are Generation Space. It's an alternative way to understand the slice of time into which the two of us were born and the transition in the United States from post-WWII Baby Boomers to supposedly well-educated, change-hungry, racially heterogeneous Gen Xers. The two of us were born into Apollo a few years before the Moon landing and were in high school when the shuttle first took flight in 1981, twenty years to the day after Yuri Gargarin had become the first human in space. We were in college when *Challenger* broke apart in 1986, and much of Generation Space was in grade school or high school then, watching knowing that a school teacher had perished before their eyes. We grew up thinking travel to Mars was inevitable, perhaps not far off in the future. To understand Generation Space offers one way to understand the legacy and potential we leave to Millennials as well.

Our Space Age love story is a way to understand history, culture, technology, and each other more deeply. Even among the dedicated space reporters we met, few connected the minutia with which they were fascinated to their own lives or to cultural views and moods. News and science reporting provide important versions of the story, but our version explores who the two of us are, both as a couple and as part of a generation.

We made a pact to retain the joy we felt that day in the desert but never to be as clueless in our pursuit. Part of that pact became following the last space shuttle launches, knowing by experience in addition to reputation. In *Moby-Dick*, the classic tale of searching for one's whale—the object of one's obsession—Herman Melville writes, "there are a rabble of uncertain, fugitive, half-fabulous whales, which, as an American whaleman, I know by reputation, but not personally." We wanted to know our white whale personally. We became explorers together—witnesses and investigators—of Generation Space.

In *Generation Space: A Love Story*, we take turns as a poet and as a scientist-librarian, investigating where this generation has been and where we're going. While the two of us share many interests and experiences, we don't always think about ideas and information the same way. Each of us tells different parts—different chapters—of this story; each chapter is in the voice of one or the other of us. We intend this back-and-forth to encompass more than either of us can on our own and, thereby, to capture a body of thought and emotion for our generation.

To tell the story of the Space Age, we begin with Sputnik and the Mercury project, which occurred before we were born, and the Gemini and Apollo programs of our childhood. Then, we chronicle our experiences with Shuttle's end and how that led us to understand the Space Age, Generation Space, and our own personal relationship. We hope that readers will fall in love with the Space Age all over again, as we did, and, in doing so, understand this shared slice of history. In the end, we ponder whether—or, rather, when—we're going to Mars. We thought we'd be there already, but maybe that's a multigenerational story we've only begun to narrate.

CHAPTER I
IN THE BEGINNING
ANNA

> We know what we can see:
> that which reflects light, catches
> our eyes in the night,
>
> hits the mirror of our collective telescope.
>
> —Anna Leahy, from "The Visible Universe"

When my sister was in kindergarten (at the age when precocious Doug started browsing *Popular Mechanics*), she, like multitudes of kindergarteners in Catholic schools in 1972, made a holiday ornament for the family Christmas tree. Her teacher handed out toothpicks and foam the shape and size of golf balls. Brigid stuck a few toothpicks into the white polystyrene. Then, the teacher spray-painted it silver. Brigid sprinkled it with glitter. Behold, my sister had created the Star of Bethlehem.

At five years of age, my sister thought of stars as twinkle-twinkles that catch one's eyes in the night sky. She didn't know then that the twinkle we see is the result of a thermonuclear reaction that transforms hydrogen into helium. She didn't know about different kinds of stars—red giants, white dwarfs, pulsating stars—nor that the Sun is the star at the center of our solar system. The Star of Bethlehem may have been a planet or a comet, but my sister knew it as the "star of wonder, star of night." But when Brigid held her ornament by its thick velvet ribbon to show our mother what she'd made in school, our mother exclaimed with great pride, "You made Sputnik!"

That my mother recognized a spacecraft shows how deeply space exploration entered people's consciousness. My mother had been a history major and finished her law degree shortly after I was born. When my sister produced this marvel, my mother was a leader in state government and still a practicing Catholic. She had little interest in science, and it'd be decades before the Church acknowledged Galileo shouldn't have been imprisoned for saying Earth orbited the Sun. Still, my mother, like most of her generation, knew Sputnik when she saw it, even when it was meant to be something else.

On October 4, 1957, from the desert steppe of what is now Kazakhstan, the Soviet Union launched Sputnik. For the first time, something human-made reached beyond Earth's atmosphere and into space, circling there. At the time, my parents hadn't yet met. My father had graduated from college as an English major (like me) though he was the first in his family to go to college and was doing his requisite military service as an enlisted man; his number had come up in the draft, so he'd put off career and love. While the future astronauts were busy as military test pilots, he was stationed overseas at a depot with underground caves for maintaining ready-to-roll forces. East Germany—the Soviet Bloc—wasn't far from where he cleaned nuclear warheads. I imagine everyone there on alert, waiting to see whether Sputnik meant war.

Back home in the United States, as Howard E. McCurdy recalls in *Space and the American Imagination*, Sputnik became "the media event of the decade." That Sputnik weekend in 1957, in my mother-in-law's childhood home, the firstborn in a litter of kittens was named Sputnika in homage to the satellite that had captivated the world's attention. An odd choice on the Cold War home front in the Midwestern heartland. At the same time, in Pasadena, California—several times farther away from Illinois than Sputnik was from Earth—a young girl who'd grow up to be my husband's boss walked in the San Rafael hills, near a hub of American rocketry, to catch a nighttime glimpse of Sputnik as it passed overhead. Across the United States, people strained to see the Russian orb glittering in the infinite darkness.

Sputnik 1 was a gleaming, aluminum sphere weighing 184 pounds and studded with four radio antennae. *Sputnik* is a Russian word for *fellow traveler*. This particular companion, roughly the size of a beach ball, became the first stride in the Space Race that ran through the next decade into which I was born. Sputnik launched on a Friday.

By the following Monday, physicists at the Johns Hopkins University Applied Physics Laboratory hummed with the news. George Weiffenbach and William Guier, two physicists, grabbed a receiver and decided to try to pick up Sputnik's signals. The Soviets were broadcasting an accessible signal, proof to the world so that nobody could claim it a hoax. Even amateurs quickly picked up the satellite's radio signals.

Of course, there were tape recorders on hand. Weiffenbach and Guier began to wonder whether they could figure out the satellite's movement based on changes in the waveform of the signals. The Doppler effect explains why the sound of an ambulance siren seems to change in pitch as it gets closer, passes, and moves away, even though the siren emits the same patterned sound all along. The scientists surmised Sputnik's movements by listening to it like a siren. Within a few hours, they calculated both Sputnik's speed and course overhead.

Sputnik's ninety-two-minute orbit was elliptical, rather than a perfect circle, so that, at its most distant point—known as the apogee of its ellipsis—Sputnik was almost 600 miles away from Earth. The perigee—its closest point—was a mere 134 or so miles from the ground, roughly the distance between Philadelphia and Washington, DC. In order to remain suspended in its gravitational dance with Earth, Sputnik traveled at a speed of eighteen thousand miles per hour.

At first, my father surely didn't realize that what was going on overhead would change the future, that it had made real the space travel of the B-movies he liked. He rode the secret elevator into caves with three fellow soldiers, tossed his radiation detection badge into a bin every now and then, and dreamed of fried eggs and bacon. He did not realize Sputnik would change soldiering, nor his family's sense of security at home.

The following spring, a higher-up—probably running through national security scenarios—asked those scientists at Johns Hopkins another question: If you know the satellite's path and position, can you use the satellite to determine the location of a stationary receiver or user on the ground? That was a huge switch in perspective: not only could we get a satellite into space to learn about what's out there, but we could use it to find and track what's down here. Indeed, a transmitting object in space could tell us exactly where an object with a receiver was on the ground. Within three years, a year after my father was honorably discharged, the United States military was using satellites to aid submarine navigation on Earth. Years later, we have unmanned drones—a controversial development—navigated via satellite mapping and tracking.

In other words, those two physicists in 1957 spent a few hours understanding an idea that gave birth to Transit, the first satellite navigation system and the precursor to the Global Positioning System (GPS), an idea hatched in 1973. This system of satellite-based navigation was shared for civilian use in 1983, when it was called the Defense Navigation Satellite System. Today, GPS tells us when to make a turn, as if we can follow the second star to the right like Peter Pan and go straight on till morning. More than a thousand satellites now thread through space above us in low-Earth orbit.

When Sputnik launched, my mother was in high school. Children, including my mother, must have watched the satellite's trail in awe. Adults—parents, teachers, businessmen, national leaders, and soldiers like my dad—soon had a different reaction: fear. They'd grown up crouching under their school desks for nuclear attack drills (as I had for tornado drills), and, if the Soviets could put a satellite into space, they could put nuclear warheads on similar rockets and send them anywhere. In his book *Sputnik, Scientists, and Eisenhower*, James R. Killian, who advised the president about science, recounts what he'd thought at the time: "Sputnik I created a crisis of confidence that swept the country like a windblown forest fire. Overnight there developed a widespread fear that the country lay at the mercy of the Russian military machine."

Fear of and competition with the Soviets upped the stakes for the United States to get a satellite into orbit quickly. For Americans, second-best didn't jive with the previous decade's sense of self-satisfaction. This country had invented the atom bomb and won World War II with it. Though Russia had been on the winning side in that war, that nation had lost millions of its people, and her cities and industries had been devastated. When the Soviet Union tested its first atomic bomb, the United States responded by developing the bigger, badder thermonuclear bomb. The United States was not to be outdone. This country had been first in flight, with Orville and Wilbur Wright taking to the air in 1903. Chuck Yeager had been first to break the sound barrier, flying high above the desert in the blue, blue California sky in 1947. So, in space, an arena that was clearly an outgrowth of aviation, how had this country finished last in a two-nation race? Last, in the Cold War, could mean dead last.

The nation settled into the notion of mutually assured destruction. The effects were writ large across America, and I was born into it. Seemingly overnight, K-12 classrooms, for instance, refocused curricula to produce future engineers and scientists who would lead the United States to number one again. So-called *New Math* emerged to turn kids' attentions from abstract formulas to practical conundrums that could be solved mathematically. *If a couple leaves their house by 11:00 a.m. and travels at an average of 60 miles per hour over the mountains and through the desert—how long before we see a space shuttle land?* Though New Math had been discussed decades earlier, education expert Angela Walmsley points out that its popularity soared in part because "federal funds [...] became available through the United States National Defense Education act of 1958, partly as a result of *Sputnik*." Cause: Sputnik. Effect: me, as a fourth-grader sixteen years later, poring over frustrating story problems for hours.

It's not as if the United States hadn't been working on its own satellite. But the initial foray worsened the US position in the Space Race. On December 6, 1957, roughly two months after Sputnik, in a live nation-wide television broadcast from Cape Canaveral, viewers witnessed the catastrophic explosion of America's first attempted satellite launch, Vanguard Test Vehicle Three, or TV3. I think of the engineers that day and cringe; I can hardly imagine the pressure and disappointment as those in the blockhouse watching the launch saw it rise a few feet and then drop back to the ground in a hellfire.

Vanguard means on the forefront, on the cutting edge. That's what the United States wanted to reclaim from the Communists; for the Soviets, the term referred to the revolutionary working classes under Vladimir Lenin's rule. A Soviet newspaper called it "pshik," and the *London Daily Mirror* exclaimed, "OH DEAR!!!" As the lore goes, even Americans called the failed mission "Kaputnik," "Flopnik," and "Stayputnik." According to NASA history, haughty delegates to the United Nations from the Soviet Union offered US delegates technical assistance through their program to aid backward nations.

Vanguard was planned as part of the International Geophysical Year (IGY), an idea that emerged at a party in 1950 at physicist James Van Allen's home. By the time it began in 1957, this eighteen-month collaboration among researchers in sixty-seven nations included the Soviet Union and Communist Bloc countries. It was designed to better understand Earth—its landmasses, its oceans, its atmosphere, and even its relationship with the Sun. People wanted to see Earth as it really was, and they were going to do it together, as a planet. The IGY's idealistic planetary unity, though, was a thin veneer of civility over Cold War divisions.

And then Sputnik beat us.

Despite President Dwight D. Eisenhower's reticence to use military hardware for space exploration, especially during a year designated for international cooperation, the US satellite Explorer 1 rose from Florida's coast into orbit on January 31, 1958, atop a Jupiter C, the civilian version of an Army surface-to-surface missile. To my mind, the image of Explorer's success is a photograph of its builder William Pickering, its instrument designer Van Allen, and Wernher von Braun, the German rocket scientist responsible for the V-2 combat missile that had demolished London and Antwerp in Word War II. I look at that photograph now: three smiling men, arms raised to hoist a model of the eighty-inch Explorer 1 above their heads. All wore dark suits and ties, their white shirt cuffs revealed as they reached up. Van Allen stretched as if on tip toes between the two others, his fingertips on the model. The tall von Braun grasped the top third of the rocket firmly and smiled the widest. They liked building rockets; they liked being winners.

During the four months it collected data, Explorer made one of the most dramatic discoveries of the IGY: radiation counts varied with the satellite's distance above Earth. Data collected by Explorer 3, launched in March, confirmed that this planet is encircled by two distinct bands of charged particles spanning thousands of miles, named the Van Allen radiation belts for the man whose instruments detected them.

The universe became more visible. My interest in this discovery is as much about seeing my surroundings as a poet as it is about my genuine interest in science. It is as much about the connection between the scientific and artistic worldviews as it is about my and also Doug's way of looking at the world around us. As Leonard Schlain says in his book *Art & Physics*, "While their methods differ radically, artists and physicists share the desire to investigate the ways the interlocking pieces of reality fit together." When I see visual representations of these belts, I imagine Earth in its larger context, surrounded by a reverberation, a shadow of sorts stretched like a Slinky or a tire. There's more to beauty than words, despite my ability and desire to form ideas through language.

Vanguard, initially a debacle, got back into action on March 17, 1958 (more than five months after Sputnik 1 and about six weeks after Explorer 1). At three-and-a-quarter pounds, roughly sixty times smaller than Sputnik, the Vanguard satellite was a pipsqueak compared with Sputnik and Explorer. Soviet Premier Nikita Khrushchev called it *the grapefruit satellite.* Yet, of those three early missions to space—Sputnik, Explorer, Vanguard—only Vanguard is still up there. In fact, Vanguard 1, though quiet now, should circle the planet for two hundred years; Vanguard 3 may drift a hundred years after that. These satellites, built by human hands and launched before I was born, will outlast everyone now on Earth.

Eight years before I was born, Sputnik marked the beginning of the Space Age. Very little scientific data, however, was collected and relayed back to Earth by the three Sputnik spacecraft. They were mostly for show. Instead, information gathered through that space program led to improvements in guidance systems of intercontinental ballistic missiles. So, the events of the official year of global unity made more effective our ability to destroy each other.

Within a year of Sputnik's launch, the National Aeronautics and Space Administration, or NASA, was formed. Even the burgeoning *beatnik* counter-culture formed its name as a portmanteau of Beat Generation and Sputnik. My parents—in 1957, one was a teenager, the other, a young adult—knew a world before Sputnik, before NASA. I never did. I was born into this new way of seeing Earth and envisioning the future; I am Generation Space.

CHAPTER 2
LIGHT THIS CANDLE
ANNA

> Star sailor, history's tailor, spacefarer,
> how far you've needled your path through air,
> past blue halo, our circle of vapor,
> past the vast figure-eight of plasma swathes,
>
> how near to infinity and back.
> That happy past has gone by, is bygone,
> and then it came slapping back again,
> booming on boosters, rolling upside down,
>
> catching its breath as if overcoming
> dynamic forces requires only great
> inspiration. Will posterity shear
> gravity along the seam, trail a wake,
>
> wake us? The astronaut's trajectory
> has stitched the warp and weft of history.
>
> —Anna Leahy, "Trajectory"

In early May of 1961, more than four years before I was born and long before she deemed my sister's holiday ornament Sputnik, my mother, still a college student, was in a car accident. Bruised and sore, she lay in a hospital bed. When a nurse brought her personal effects from the Emergency Room, my mother noticed cash missing from her wallet. The nurse said that Chicago's police accepted such items as perks of the job and she was lucky all her jewelry was there. This was Mayor Richard

J. Daley's city, known not only for corruption that included the police but also for vote rigging in the presidential election of John F. Kennedy the year before. (My mother, much to her satisfaction, would later win as an Independent candidate to the Illinois Constitutional Convention against Daley's political machine.)

On the morning of May 5, a doctor came into my mother's room. He turned on the TV, and other physicians wandered in. My mother's room was one of few in the hospital to have a television set; it was crowded that Friday. Across the country, forty-five million people watched the same event: the first American in space.

While a quarter of the nation prepared to watch on television the launch of Alan Shepard inside his *Freedom 7* capsule, the beaches and roadways near Cape Canaveral were also crowded with the curious. This launch was the culmination of a two-year public spectacle. Since the first press-packed announcement of the hopeful spacefarers of the Mercury program—the Mercury Seven, as they were commonly called— these astronauts-in-training had never been far from the public eye. The Cold War American media fed the public's gaze.

The nightly news, which gained influence and power steadily through the 1960s, followed the popular story, but the most in-depth and detailed coverage appeared in newspapers and magazines. In fact, each of the seven astronauts was signed to an exclusive deal with *Life* magazine, which featured them on the September 14, 1959, cover, with the promise of a print version of today's reality show: "First-Person Reports by the Astronauts. Start of Continuing Exclusive Stories of Epochal Mission." Readers saw John Glenn in a spacesuit, Deke Slayton spinning on his back in a training simulator, and Alan Shepard testing the capsule seat molded to fit his body. Image after image of astronauts and their nuclear families were displayed for all of America to see. The public savored every tidbit about each homegrown space sailor.

That morning of the first launch of an astronaut, the blockhouse for Launch Complex-5, where the flight would be controlled and monitored, stood barely a hundred yards from the steaming, popping Redstone rocket. Atop that rocket, rising sixty-five feet into the Florida sky, a silver-suited Shepard sat in the *Freedom 7* spacecraft, growing more impatient by the moment. I've toured that blockhouse, which is now a part of a museum and has the aura of a mausoleum. Everything is entombed behind glass; you can see, but you can't touch. Each console contains an ashtray, many of which are pulled open and still hold a cigarette butt or two. Shepard may have been testy because it had been so long since his last cigarette.

In May, Florida is damp and hot. This blockhouse must have felt especially cramped and clammy that day, with 130 engineers, scientists, managers, and fellow astronauts—all with anxious hopes—crammed into the tiny area. I imagine Wernher von Braun, tanned with slicked-back hair, smoking incessantly while leaning to look at changing numbers on a monitor. The view of Shepard's rocket through thick safety glass would have been a thin-section, ever-so-brief view of the launch.

That morning, while the men in the blockhouse and television viewers across the United States waited, Alan Shepard's mercurial temperament turned snappish. He had to pee. The countdown had proceeded in fits and starts. Stoppages for cloud cover and a glitch in a power supply unit had turned the affair into a more-than-four-hour ordeal. His silver spacesuit—a Frankenstein-like wrapping of zippers and straps based on the Navy's Mark IV high-altitude flight suit—was designed for a very short flight, with no accommodation for bodily waste elimination. Chatter among the medical team, flight controllers, and engineers undoubtedly suggested, *Can he hold it?* If he could have, he surely would have. That's a skill I learned when I was a toddler, with my sister on the way and my mother unable to fathom two kids in diapers with a legal and political career underway. Shepard was a test pilot with an iron will, a Navy man, and one of the most private astronauts in the history of manned spaceflight. If he got out of the spacecraft to urinate, not only would the whole world find out, but the already-delayed launch would be delayed yet again. So he peed in his suit.

Finally, after all those hours, near the end of his patience, Shepard uttered one of the more famous one-liners of the Space Age: "Light this candle!" In full, he said, "Why don't you fix your little problem and light this candle?" I've seen the quote written in both forms—with a question mark, with an exclamation point—and, while the question mark is grammatically correct, the exclamation point is emphatically correct. He was ready to leave the ground.

A short burst of white smoke shot from the rocket's tail: the mission had begun. Shepard's launch vehicle, the Army's Redstone ballistic missile, was similar to the machine that launched Explorer 1, with modifications to make it a little safer for human flight. The rocket's rise began slowly. Gaining speed, to be sure, but America's first astronaut didn't disappear in the blink of an eye. My breath still catches when I watch that rise, that slight bend, even on my computer screen.

Freedom 7 burst through the atmosphere. It arced for a few minutes. It came rushing back down as planned. The astronaut was subjected to weightlessness, but he was strapped so tightly to his perfectly fitted seat that he didn't really experience it. Shepard's path into history was described as a ballistic, suborbital trajectory. Ballistic comes a Greek word meaning to throw, and Freedom 7, with Shepard nestled tightly inside, was thrown roughly 116 miles above Earth's surface and out over the Atlantic some three hundred miles downrange from Florida's coast, where he had begun. Shepard's trip lasted just over fifteen minutes.

The astronaut had little time to do much of anything during the flight. He demonstrated some control over the small spacecraft by firing hydrogen peroxide powered jets to change its pitch (nose up and down) and yaw (nose side to side). He glanced through the tiny window afforded the astronauts to discern what outer space looked like, but his vantage wasn't great. Freedom 7 was also equipped with a periscope, which extended out and above the spacecraft's side after it was beyond Earth's atmosphere. Shepard used that to look back at our world. He mentioned cloud cover and said, "What a beautiful view." But that view probably wasn't very beautiful. Tom Wolfe described Shepard's situation in his book The Right Stuff:

He knew he was in space, but there was no way to tell it!... He looked out the periscope, the only way he had of looking at the earth. The goddamned gray filter! He couldn't see any colors at all! He had never changed the filter! The first American to ever fly this high above the earth—and it was a black-and-white movie.

Despite the filter and physically limited view, Shepard kept his lack of clear and vibrant vision to himself. However it appeared, the perspective from space was an inherently beautiful view.

In my mother's hospital room, the hubbub was over more quickly than she'd expected. That's what she remembered: how fast it happened. Forty years later, I stood in the sand of Cocoa Beach, which I knew well from my favorite show as a five-year-old, *I Dream of Jeannie*, and its space program, its magic. Standing there myself, I looked in the direction Shepard's flight took. I've thought about his fifteen minutes and wondered if that's where Andy Warhol got his notion about fame, because, although he was famous before his flight—as all of the Mercury Seven were—that fifteen minutes of sitting on his back and talking over a radio made Shepard more famous than he could have imagined. There were parades for him in Los Angeles, Manhattan, and Washington, D.C. More television interviews. More meetings with heads-of-state. More, more, more, and the nation couldn't get enough.

When Shepard launched, it was the third scheduled attempt in four days. Even before that, launch day had been pushed back and back again for the better part of a year, as engineers worked on the man-rated version—approved for launching human beings into space—of the military's Redstone booster. If delays hadn't occurred, Shepard would have been the first human in space. He wasn't.

Instead, during those delays, Yuri Gagarin flew to space on April 12, 1961, less than a month before Shepard. The Soviet Union beat the United States in the Space Race—first with a satellite, then with a man. I visited the Soviet Union as a college student in 1986, shortly after the *Challenger* space shuttle accident, the Chernobyl nuclear power plant accident, and my father's death from cancer at age fifty-three. I was twenty-one years old, on the cusp of adulthood, the same age my mother was when she watched Shepard's flight in that upside-down year: the numbers nineteen and sixty-one are upside-down images of each other, and the year became topsy-turvy with Cold War tensions. That January, President Eisenhower had warned of what he called "the military industrial complex" of which he must have thought Shepard's flight was a part. Then, John F. Kennedy, on whom my mother pinned

her hopes for a more just world, became president, only to be faced with
the attempted overthrow of Cuba's communist dictator, Fidel Castro, in
the Bay of Pigs invasion days before the Soviets beat the United States
to space.

In May, Kennedy announced to the world that the United States
would put a man on the Moon by the decade's end. In June, he encouraged Americans to build nuclear fallout shelters, and, in October, the
Soviet Union tested a nuclear weapon that resulted in what remains, to
this day, the largest man-made explosion. By the end of that year, the
United States was involved in the Vietnam War, the conflict that, as a
child, I saw on the evening news. Spaceflight can't be disentangled from
these political goings-on.

Gagarin hadn't only been first into space in his *Vostok-1* spacecraft;
he'd also made a complete orbit around Earth, whereas Shepard merely
arced over the atmosphere for a few minutes. Gargarin felt "suspended";
weightlessness felt "somewhat unfamiliar." Did he feel upside-down?
Did my mother, thinking about it then? The event wasn't televised, and
the existing film is grainy and opaque. When the announcement of his
successful spaceflight was made, Gargarin became an instant international celebrity. Vostok means *dawn* or *east* in Russian. It certainly
signified the rise of something new, east of where the United States had
hoped.

A decade later, in 1971, it was revealed that Gagarin hadn't returned
all the way to the ground inside *Vostok-1*. Once the capsule returned to
the atmosphere, he ejected from the spacecraft and landed with a parachute. In the late 1950s, the Fédération Aéronautique Internationale
(FAI), the international agency founded in 1905 that certifies aviation
records, developed rules for certifying spaceflight. According to the FAI,
to qualify as a spaceflight, Gagarin had to return to Earth in his spacecraft. Though the nuances of these rules are petty, the Soviet Union
initially kept the details of Gagarin's bailout secret. To be fair—and to
my post-Cold War mind—a spaceflight is a spaceflight.

To orbit means to circle one object around another so that, as long as
enough speed is maintained, the circling object is actually falling without end. Earth has this sort of relationship with the Sun; the planets of

the solar system orbit the Sun in elliptical paths. Imagine Earth moving sideways parallel to the Sun. If this star exerted no gravitational pull, Earth would travel in a straight line and keep going. Instead, the Sun's gravity pulls on Earth; this pull is just strong and steady enough to curve the planet's path continually but not strong enough to draw it in fully.

With Gagarin, orbiting a celestial body became something people could do. To visualize a spacecraft's orbit around Earth, imagine a string around a globe following the path of the equator, then move that string up a little on one side of the globe and down on the other side. It's still a firm circle but now askew so that it crosses the equator instead of lining up around Earth's middle. Though it still forms a circle around a globe, when laid flat on a map or on NASA flight control's big screen, the orbit looks like an S laid on its side. When we change perspective—how we look at associations among objects or ideas—we see differently. A circle? Or an S? Which is the real path? Of course, when we see a globe or a map, we are not looking at the thing itself—not Earth as Gagarin and Shepard saw it from their vantage as the ground moving beneath them.

Latin is the language of science and medicine and the only one besides my native English that I've studied. In high school, I went over basic vocabulary, conjugations, and declensions; then I did the same in college, and again in graduate school. English words with Latin roots tend to sound mellifluous, though Latinate vocabulary can feel formal or intellectual. I turn to etymology when I'm thinking about meanings and relationships among meanings, as when I think about *orbit*, which means *ring* in Latin. Thinking about *ring* helps me see *orbit*. Language conveys perspective; without words and phrases, we cannot be sure how we perceive the world around us, nor exactly what we think.

When a spacecraft in orbit moves more slowly than Earth's surface curves below it, gravity pulls it into the atmosphere. For a satellite, this is a steady process of slowing and lowering called *decay*. The word is apt, as it comes from the Latin meaning *to fall from*. Falling is what the spacecraft has been doing all along, only now it's moving at a rate slower than Earth's surface is curving away from it, and the distance between the two closes. Colloquially, the word *decay* refers to a move away from a better condition, a process of loss. Orbit, then, is akin to a near-perfect state of being; orbital decay is a fall from that grace.

When its orbit decayed, Sputnik burned up in the atmosphere. John Glenn, who'd initially been frustrated not to be the first American in space, became famous as the first American to orbit Earth on February 20, 1962. When it was time to return, Glenn slowed his Mercury capsule by firing retrorockets, and then gravity pulled the capsule through the atmosphere. Glenn called what he saw out the window during reentry "a real fireball." A warning light indicated the capsule's protective heat shield might be loose, but there wasn't anything anyone could do as *Friendship 7* blazed through the atmosphere. The warning ended up a false alarm. He "felt like a falling leaf." Years later, a fictional character in the film *Serenity* would echo Glenn's words, saying, "I am a leaf on the wind. Watch how I soar." *Gravity*, from the Latin word for *heavy*, acts upon a spacecraft and a leaf in the same way. The parachute and landing bag both deployed as planned, and, less than a year after Gagarin's flight, *Friendship 7* splashed down in the Atlantic Ocean. The sky wasn't the limit anymore.

In sixty-five years, less than an average American's lifespan, the world went from having a single artificial satellite newly orbiting our own planet to having multiple satellites orbiting other planets as well as our own. In even fewer years, humans went from throwing a person beyond Earth's atmosphere for a once-around to living for months inside a permanent space station. Sputnik and Gagarin—and Shepard and Glenn (and Gus Grissom in between)—forever changed what human beings could do and see. They helped create the Space Age into which my husband and I—and a whole generation—were born. The world in which we came of age was fundamentally different than the one in which our parents grew up. As Generation Space, I had inklings we could touch the stars. Or at least set foot on Mars.

CHAPTER 3
SHIFTING PERSPECTIVES
DOUG

To see the earth as : truly is, small and blue and beautiful in that eternal silence where it floats, is to see ourselves as riders on the earth together, brothers on that bright loveliness in the eternal cold.

—Archibald MacLeish, *New York Times*

Just two months before I was born (roughly a year after Anna), *Star Trek* premiered in September 1966. This television show ran for only three years, so I never saw it in its original run, but by the time *Star Trek* ran in syndication, I was ready for all it offered my young, curious mind. I even watched the cartoon version on Saturday mornings in the early 1970s.

As a boy during the Apollo era, I wanted to explore new worlds and boldly go where no one had gone before, and *Star Trek* showed me how that would happen. Thus captivated, I uttered, "Live long and prosper." And I garnered a mail-order matched set of the holy trinity of gadgets: phaser (with pistol grip), communicator, and tri-corder. Any doubts about ordering from an ad at the back of a magazine were assuaged when my postal-carrier uncle hand-delivered the boxes full of plastic potential. I set my phaser to stun and, in a further attempt to replicate what I'd seen on television, built my own force field of sorts in the backyard with my buddy, Joey, using steel welding rods, nichrome wire, and a 9-volt battery from a science kit.

My father was an engineer and I gravitated to the character of the Scottish engineer played by James Doohan, a Canadian D-Day veteran. In a pair of drab grey coveralls that my grandmother festooned with a sew-on NASA patch and pilot's wings, I happily turned outdoor playtime into missions to the Moon, Mars, and beyond. America was in the midst of a romance with the Space Age, and I was exultant to be swept into it.

Even later, as an undergraduate engineering student, one of my favorite classes was Engineering Graphics. The perspective drawings that I produced in this class used parallel lines drawn to a vanishing point. It's a technique for convincing the human eye that an object is off in the distance. Perspective depends upon the mindset one brings to viewing a problem or issue. Popular culture and my own imagination were ahead of reality, searching for a perspective that would allow sense-making of a Space Age future, for humans rarely accomplish much without having imagined it first.

Five years before *Star Trek* premiered and I was born, April 1961 had been a bad month for President John F. Kennedy and the United States. The Bay of Pigs, in which CIA-backed counter-revolutionaries attempted to invade Cuba, became an international embarrassment. The Soviet Union had launched cosmonaut Yuri Gagarin into space before the United States could loft astronaut Alan Shepard beyond Earth's atmosphere. On May 25, 1961, less than three weeks after Shepard's foray into suborbital space—no American had yet orbited Earth—and sixteen years to the day before the film *Star Wars* would be released to my utter excitement as a ten-year-old, Kennedy went before Congress to discuss the "numerous and varied" proposals designed to combat "the adversaries of freedom." Those proposals included a Moon landing via the Apollo program, which had been concocted by the Eisenhower administration. The president stated emphatically, "this nation should commit itself to achieving the goal, before this decade is out, of landing a man on the moon and returning him safely to the earth."

After that speech, Project Mercury finally flew four orbital missions, and NASA added Project Gemini and additional astronauts to its roll. Gemini flew concurrently with the Apollo program's development and my own earliest development. Its missions tested human endurance and the wherewithal of equipment over the many consecutive days a Moon mission would demand, tried out spacewalking, and allowed engineers and astronauts to discern nuances of rendezvous and docking so that astronauts on the Moon's surface could return to the capsule to go home.

I imagine Frank Borman and Jim Lovell lifting off at the end of 1965, almost a year before I was born, on the fourth manned Gemini flight to spend almost two weeks together in the cramped crew compartment. They sweated for days, then unsuited. They rendezvoused within a foot of another manned Gemini spacecraft, then read books. Though each was married to his high school sweetheart, the most intimate, extended time they spent with another person was surely that flight. No Apollo flight would take as long. The Gemini program flew ten manned flights, the last a couple of weeks after I was born.

For the Greeks, Apollo was an all-occasion god adaptable to new functions, not only racing across the Sun. NASA adopted the name Apollo for the space program that would land the first human on the Moon. Apollo was also the Roman god of poetry. Perhaps I fell in love with Anna because we stayed up all night talking about poetry when I was still a college student. Is Anna Latin to my Greek, concurrently spoken, influencing each other, but distinct?

Apollo 1 was a tragedy. My own experiences with Murphy's Law and other, more obscure engineering dictums make me wonder whether some of us are assailed by misfortune for spates in our lives, the universe somehow conspiring against us. Odd mishaps had happened to Gus Grissom, the second American in space: his *Liberty Bell 7* capsule sank while he waited for rescue after his Mercury mission; he whacked his head and cracked his helmet visor when the spacecraft parachute deployed on Gemini 3. On January 27, 1967, Grissom and his Apollo 1 crewmates, Roger Chaffee and Ed White, were in the midst of a ground test when a fire started near Grissom's seat.

Of that fateful day, fellow astronaut Michael Collins wrote the following about getting the initial news in Houston:

> All I could think of was, My God, such an obvious thing and yet we hadn't considered it. We worried about engines that wouldn't start or wouldn't stop; we worried about leaks; we even worried about how a flame front might propagate in weightlessness and how cabin

pressure might be reduced to stop a fire in space. But right here on the ground, when we should have been most alert, we put three guys inside an untried spacecraft, strapped them into couches, locked two cumbersome hatches behind them, and left them no way of escaping a fire.

One astronaut inside Apollo 1—designated AS-204 at the time—reported the fire. Then, White said, "Fire in the cockpit." Communication continued for seventeen seconds. In ideal circumstances, escape took ninety seconds, but even in practice, they'd never done it that quickly. "Get us out." The fire burned so hot in the pure oxygen at the ground pressure of sixteen pounds per square inch and the hatches were so complicated that it took rescuers five long, desperate minutes to reach the men's bodies. The three astronauts were dead, right there on the ground. Though they suffered serious burns, their suits had protected them relatively well against the flames. The three men had died of asphyxiation. The fire had lasted less than thirty seconds.

That event was a failure in perspective. With their minds singularly focused on the dangers that travel in space presented, the engineers, scientists, and astronauts working against the clock to launch Apollo 1 had forgotten about myriad possible dangers on Earth.

Only days before his death, Grissom finished drafting his book *Gemini: A Personal Account of Man's Venture into Space*. There, he wrote, "The conquest of space is worth the risk of life." NASA mourned, redesigned the Apollo spacecraft, and moved on. I was just an infant then, handed the promise and risks of the Moon and Mars before I had my legs under me.

By 1968, cross-country road trips were common—my family grew into a station wagon—and travel to the Moon seemed possible, even probable. The film *2001: A Space Odyssey*, written by its director Stanley Kubrick and science-fiction writer Arthur C. Clarke, premiered on April 2. In this cult classic, the spacecraft *Discovery One*, with its crew and sentient computer, travels toward Jupiter to investigate a monolith. The next day in 1968, *Planet of the Apes*—a film in which an astronaut crew crash-lands on a planet inhabited by intelligent apes—was released. As powerful as traveling beyond the infinite had been in 2001, the ending of the original *Planet of the Apes* was just as shocking, recasting basic ideas of who we are and who we might become. Though I didn't see these films until later, their ideas set the vision for Generation Space: our future meant traveling beyond Earth even as most of us remained here.

The news of turbulent 1968 was also filled with the war in Vietnam and that year's Tet Offensive. In February, a now-iconic and Pulitzer Prize-winning photograph of a South Vietnamese police chief executing a Viet Cong officer in a plaid shirt hit the news. The Troubles—a political conflict steeped in religious and national divides—began in Northern Ireland. Civil rights rallies and sit-ins sprung up on university campuses in the United States, and two African-American athletes raised their arms in the black power salute on the medal podium at the Olympics. Polish students protested their government, and French students marched against capitalism. *Hair*, the musical about hippies and the sexual revolution, opened on Broadway. Yale University decided to admit women, and help-wanted ads divided by sex become illegal. Shirley Chisolm became the first African-American woman elected to Congress. In April, Martin Luther King Jr. was assassinated. In June, Bobby Kennedy was killed. Anna, who was not yet three years old, remembers her mother sitting in the rocking chair, watching the evening news, crying. The world in which our parents had hoped to raise us was precarious. I was too young to know what was happening.

On December 21, 1968, Apollo 8 launched. Imagination became reality. Its crew included three astronauts: Frank Borman, the only astronaut on the Apollo 1 investigation board; Jim Lovell, who'd go on to fly on the near-catastrophic Apollo 13 mission chronicled in the eponymous 1995 film; and Bill Anders, who was on his only spaceflight. The original mission called for carrying the Lunar Module, but it was not yet ready. NASA removed the lander from the critical list and made the engineering decision to go without that item so as not to delay the program. That end-of-decade deadline to land on the Moon loomed, and Apollo 8 was a necessary dry run.

At first, Lovell had trouble sighting the stars for navigation because of haze from the venting rocket. I'm sympathetic. Even as a Boy Scout, I too struggled with orienteering right here on Earth. I failed to orient myself with a simple compass and a very rough map of a campground that seemed designed to flummox me. Lovell used a sextant built into the spacecraft and precise calculations done by experts at the Massachusetts Institute of Technology. He and his crew would have to depend on his navigating if they lost communication with Earth. Lovell would later tell *Astronomy* magazine that Charles Lindbergh thought Apollo 8 was a lot like his solo crossing of the Atlantic Ocean; both expeditions navigated by the stars.

Borman had trouble sleeping and then became ill. To let Mission Control know about the astronaut's intestinal distress without letting the entire world in on the secret, the quick-thinking crew used a backchannel—a data storage system—instead of the usual communication channel. In hindsight, now that we've learned more about spaceflight's effects on the human body, it's clear that Borman was suffering from space sickness—a version of motion sickness much like what I suffered in the family station wagon— though, at the time, Borman was thought to have a twenty-four-hour stomach flu that cleared up.

Fifty-five hours into the mission, the crew broadcast images of Earth from space. Anders remarked, "We came all this way to explore the Moon, and the most important thing is that we discovered the Earth." For the first time, a person took a photograph of Earth in its entirety, half illuminated by the Sun. Our way of seeing—of being—changed in a split-second by that new glimpse. People saw Earth from a distance, through a human eye, and really saw it as a planet for the first time. From that distance, Earth was small enough to fit inside the frame, and that was humbling.

Shortly after their broadcast, these three men became the first people to experience the gravitational pull of another celestial body. The spacecraft had traveled far enough that the Moon's gravity had a greater effect on it than Earth's did. The three astronauts were weightless and free falling, and they were falling toward the Moon.

Lovell described the Moon's surface as "like plaster of Paris or sort of a grayish beach sand." Apollo 8 was the first manned mission to circle around the Moon, and the crew saw the backside—the dark, unlit side, the side always facing away from Earth—for the first time. Anders remembered the scene: "There were stars everywhere except this big black hole. It was blacker than pitch. That was the Moon. It made the hair stand up on my neck." They had travelled farther from Earth than any other human beings ever had.

As the spacecraft orbited the Moon, Anders shot the amazing "Earthrise" photograph. I imagine the extra care that Dick Underwood, the NASA chief who developed the seven rolls of film, must have taken, knowing that these images might change the way people see themselves. In the color photograph, the lunar surface provides a reference, with the blue-and-white Earth behind it in the blackness of space. In reality, the task was to look at the lunar surface, so Earth in the frame is happenstance. Interesting, too, is that the black-and-white shots were snapped by Borman and used the lunar surface as the horizon at the bottom of the frame. The color image by Anders was shot with the lunar surface vertical on the right side of the frame, though it's often shown rotated to shift the perspective so that Earth appears to be rising above the Moon.

For the first time, people saw what Earth looks like from another celestial body. Not as imagined by a movie or television show but as actual human eyes saw from beyond the Moon. With Earth fit into the frame, the darkness surrounding it seemed to me a glimpse at the universe even as it was a glimpse at humanity. The first time I saw that photograph, which I remember as being in the *World Book Encyclopedia*, I knew enough about the world around me, geometry, and distance that it left me grappling to reconcile that heavenly perspective with the one I had standing on Earth's surface. In the epigraph that begins this chapter, writer Archibald MacLeish captures my feelings: blue orb on which we live but also the eternal universe surrounding us.

That shift in perspective also allowed humanity, for a moment, to be two places at once, to switch places in the universe. The view flips *here* and *there*. Earth, for the first time, became a *somewhere else* in the frame instead of the *here* people take for granted all around, all the time.

On Christmas Eve, in the most widely viewed television broadcast to that date—the History channel says that *TV Guide* estimated one of every four of the 3.5 billion people on the planet watched this first message from this first journey around the Moon—Borman described the celestial body as "a vast, lonely, forbidding expanse of nothing." Then, each astronaut read from Genesis in the Bible. Though the United States has had a long, at times sticky, tradition of separation of church and state, and though an atheist did sue the government—futilely—over this broadcast, I think the astronauts turned to these words to recall a time before humans existed, words imagined as having come from a place removed from Earth, having come from somewhere else that we'd never known.

Shortly after that moving broadcast—through which I undoubtedly slept as a two-year-old—and some unplanned manual alignment with the stars, the astronauts headed back toward their home planet, toward the rest of humanity. Fellow astronaut Deke Slayton, who'd been grounded with a heart rhythm problem but who was in charge of astronaut selection, had left a holiday-style turkey dinner in the food locker. Reward for adventure. The bottle of brandy from Slayton remains unopened, or so they say. Perhaps it's a *tontine*, a prize for the last man standing.

On December 27, the Apollo 8 mission ended. Re-entry and splashdown went smoothly, though Borman was again ill, likely seasick as the command module bobbed in the water waiting for the rescue ship. That capsule is now on display at the Museum of Science and Industry in Chicago, where, as an adult, I first peered into it to visualize the three astronauts right there in their seats and yet on the other side of the Moon. That spacecraft made me feel, for a moment deep in my imagination, that I was both here and there, two places at once.

The political and cultural messages of 1968 were mixed, often contradictory, and fluctuated chaotically. *Star Trek* presented viewers with an optimistically multiracial, multicultural, and even multispecies vision, where humans and non-humans came together. The political reality was of young people across the world coming together, marching in the streets, challenging the perspective that they had inherited. Apollo gave Americans a way to see 1968 not as only a year of social and political crisis, but also as, ultimately, a year of hope for humanity and the future—Generation Space's future.

CHAPTER 4
THE GIANT LEAP
DOUG

[T]he men played a brilliant game of ideas and space: "You start with this gigantic rocket, the biggest Von Braun can build."

—James Michener, *Space*

After thousands of years of gazing up at the Moon, how did humans manage to travel there? Given the complexity of the task, how did humans possibly manage the journey through inhospitable space to the Moon within a dozen years of putting the equivalent of a steel basketball a few hundred miles above our parents' heads? In the years since my childhood engineering efforts—including the non-functional force field that Joey and I built in my backyard—I've learned how real engineers balance knowledge, effort, and imagination. I think of my father even now, in his seventies, tinkering with his company's machines. He was in school at the same time as the younger Apollo engineers, and I'm awed by how that cohort trusted that everything would work while also accounting for the statistical uncertainties— that something might not—all without the aid of the fast and ubiquitous computers I take for granted.

NASA spent almost $24 billion of the nation's money on human spaceflight between 1959 and 1973, with roughly $20 billion going to Apollo. A 2008 report from the Federation of American Scientists put Apollo's price tag at almost 100 billion current-year dollars. That's the kind of money Apple had in the bank in 2012, when it would've bought the big three US auto companies or paid for fifty-nine space shuttles, if the Shuttle program hadn't ended by then.

Not only the expenditure of dollars during Apollo was gargantuan. The program required huge numbers of people. At the project's height, in 1966—the year I was born—Apollo employed more than four hundred thousand civil servants, contractors, and university researchers to make sure the big hardware items could be built. How did NASA organize and manage all those people in the pursuit of a unified goal? In order to manage people in pursuit of an enormous goal, thinking shifted from object to process.

As a kid, while my younger brother was fascinated by taking apart and reassembling household items like the telephone, I was as interested in the larger context of how objects were made and how they changed the world. Between World War II and the Moon landing, when my father—part of the so-called Silent Generation born after World War I but before the Boomers—was growing up to become an engineer himself, a seismic shift in how we approach the engineering of large, complex things took place.

North American Aviation secured its reputation during World War II by rolling out its P-51 fighter—paper plan into aluminum flesh ready to fly—in just 117 days. North American's contributions to Apollo—the command module, the cabin for astronauts; the service module, the segment to which the capsule was attached that provided thrust, electricity, and storage; and the second stage of the Saturn V rocket, used to propel the spacecraft toward orbit—were produced in a new era but within an equally demanding timeframe. As I've learned from home renovation projects and a PhD dissertation, a timeframe—for Apollo, the end of the decade—is a constraint that changes process as well as product. While it was possible to manage design changes on a P-51 by writing them on the airplane's parts during production, that kind of dashed-off, person-to-person communication of information couldn't work on the more ambitious and complex Apollo program, with its growing cadre of contractors.

NASA had a goal and a deadline, two of the essential ingredients for the completion of any product, but engineers didn't know exactly how to accomplish that goal by that deadline. A team would gather to figure something out: *What if we did this to save weight? Yes—and if we did this, then maybe we could do that.* Suddenly, the Lunar Module had a different number of legs, no seats, and a new configuration of windows. Innovation happens when smart, ambitious, creative people come together. Neuroscientist Nancy Andreasen talks in her book *The Creating Brain* about circumstances in a cultural environment of creativity: a critical mass of creative people, freedom and novelty, a fair and competitive atmosphere, mentors and patrons, and economic prosperity. Apollo was that combination of circumstances; improvisation was how Apollo worked. But it's hard to coordinate improvisations among a lot of people and parts. Sometimes, as Anna and I have learned in twenty-some years as a couple, it's tricky to coordinate improvisation between just two people.

Apollo required focus on the people and processes that produced the complex set of objects needed to land a person on the Moon, not merely focus on an object to be made. Fortunately, in the years prior to Apollo, there had come new ways of thinking about organization of people and processes. In the 1940s, Ma Bell—the phone system of Generation Space, our parents, and their parents (it ran from 1877 to 1984)—had become so large that it was no longer predictable, even though behaviors of the individual pieces of the system were well understood. Bell Labs introduced *systems engineering* to tame the complexity. By the time I worked at Lucent Technologies in the late 1990s, Bell Labs had become its research arm and was said to have averaged a patent a day for the previous seventy years.

In the 1950s, as an outgrowth of building reliability into ballistic missiles, systems engineering was paired with *systems management*, corporate-speak for the organization of people and projects, for when managing the process of creating a thing became more difficult than understanding how the thing being created worked. It was a new way of doing big things and was fully embraced by NASA, emerging in time for Apollo.

Apollo was a symbiosis of human and machine. That's how the United States was able to reach the Moon within a decade. And that's one of the most lasting legacies of the Apollo program: the revolution in processes—in *how* technology is created. I like to think that, as a result of Apollo, Generation Space, too, embraced the thinking the Moon missions represent and has always harbored the potential to become more than the sum of our individual parts.

My first conscious memory: a flickering image of a single man clambering down the ladder of an insect-like spaceship and planting his oversized boots on the Moon, with the deep black of the universe beyond the white spacesuit. Now turned fifty, I wasn't yet three years old when Apollo 11 made it to the Moon on Sunday, July 20, 1969. My mother had plunked me in front of the family television set in the den that would become my bedroom a few years later. I sat in the middle of the carpeted floor with my parents, one of them cradling my brother behind me on the green upholstered couch, to watch the event along with an estimated five hundred and thirty million viewers worldwide. Somehow, I knew that the hazy black-and-white images of two men in gleaming spacesuits were important. There were people inside those bulky, bouncing spacesuits; I listened to their crackling voices. The Moon seemed a place I might visit someday. Upon that image of the Moon landing, everything I have experienced and know has been built.

The Apollo 11 mission had begun four days earlier from Kennedy Space Center in Florida. Inside the Command-Service Module were three men: Neil A. Armstrong, Michael Collins, and Edwin "Buzz" Aldrin. All had been to space before. Collins was on this crew only because he'd had back surgery that required him to switch places in the schedule with Jim Lovell, so Collins flew on Apollo 11 instead of Apollo 8. Once the spacecraft was orbiting the Moon, Collins stayed aboard, while Armstrong and Aldrin descended to the Moon's surface in the Lunar Module designated *Eagle*. Theirs were the feet I glimpsed from my television screen; theirs were the voices that made up the first building block of my consciousness.

During that descent, the guidance computer couldn't keep up with all the information and tasks and was emitting alarms to signal the information overflow. With what he later called "gun-barrel vision," Aldrin stayed calm as he input responses on the DSKY, the computer's display and keypad.

Years later, I touched the DSKY that had flown on Apollo 15; it had been mistakenly shipped to a NASA center for aircraft testing and purposefully not returned to Houston. The user interface of the DSKY has much more in common with an engineering calculator than with what we have come to think of as a computer interface, particularly touch- and gesture-based devices like smartphones and tablets. I found it humbling to think of Aldrin's professionalism in using the limited but focused interface in such a mission-critical context.

With fuel running low, Armstrong patiently scanned the surface for a flat place to land. Charlie Duke was serving as CAPCOM—capsule communications, the voice of Mission Control—back on Earth. At the time, he was anxious, though his southern drawl made him seem calm. When I talked with Duke in 2012 (we met him twice), he said, "It was a very exciting time, a very tense time in Mission Control. We were running out of gas." The whole world shared Duke's nervousness. When Armstrong announced, "The *Eagle* has landed," Duke responded, "You got a bunch of guys about to turn blue. We're breathing again."

After a few hours of preparation (instead of sleep that had been in the original flight plan), Armstrong and Aldrin emerged from the Lunar Module. Armstrong became the first person to set foot on another celestial body. His small step became history and what he deemed "one giant leap for mankind." Aldrin described the sight around him as "magnificent desolation." I remember thinking as a toddler that humans were *there*, somewhere else entirely.

The men got to work. Armstrong bagged up some Moon dust; they would gather almost fifty pounds of Moon matter on this excursion. They figured out how to walk on the fine powder with only one-sixth of the gravity to which they were accustomed on Earth. Armstrong sent photos back to Earth, in part so that engineers could see how the lunar module (abbreviated LM and pronounced *lem*) sat on the moon's surface. He showed the world his view; humanity saw what he saw. Again, our way of seeing—of being—shifted when we glimpsed the universe from the surface of another celestial body. Humanity was no longer confined to its cradle, its birthplace.

Once the camera was on its tripod, the astronauts planted the American flag. That Space Age moment became so iconic that, two decades later, as I sat around doing high school homework, there was cartoon Buzz on MTV with that flag, the Apollo mission recast in montage because MTV's creative director thought the launch of the video music channel was just as important to culture as the Moon landing. A collective memory reworked. In fact, the Video Music Award remains a statue version of Buzz with the flag.

While more than five hundred million people on Earth watched the Moon landing, Collins, orbiting a mere sixty-nine miles above the lunar surface—almost exactly the distance from my home in Orange to the I-5 beach city of Encinitas—and closer to the action than anyone else, could not see from the capsule *Columbia* what his crewmates were doing below on the surface. Collins has written eloquently about his sense of isolation in lunar orbit, and he was, by any meaningful definition, at that moment, a human being even more isolated than Adam in Genesis.

The men spent about two-and-a-half hours outside on the Moon, then returned to *Eagle,* closed the hatch, blasted off, and rendezvoused with Collins. They returned to Earth on July 24, were put into quarantine for three weeks in case they carried previously unknown space germs, then emerged to a worldwide celebration. They rode in parades in major cities—New York, Chicago, Los Angeles—ate a state dinner, received the Medal of Freedom, and embarked on a forty-five-day whirlwind tour of the world. The United States, despite having lost the early legs of the space race to the Soviet Union, had achieved the greatest feat in the history of humanity.

On December 7, 1972, less than four years after the first manned Apollo mission and when I was watching *Star Trek* in syndication, Apollo 17 lifted off, a bright burn in the night sky. Four days later, Gene Cernan and geologist Harrison Schmitt were driving on the Moon, kicking up dust onto their spacesuits because they'd broken a fender on the rover. They took three Moonwalks and measured gravity. When it was time to crawl back into the Lunar Module so that it could rendezvous with the Command-Service Module, Cernan paused to say, "America's challenge of today has forged man's destiny of tomorrow. And, as we leave the Moon at Taurus-Littrow, we leave as we came and, God willing, as we shall return, with peace and hope for all mankind."

But there has been no return. Instead, I ran into Cernan standing in line at a Southwest Airlines counter, waiting to fly just like the rest of us. As a kid, it hadn't occurred to me that there would be a time when the United States didn't have the wherewithal to fly me to space. I thought it was my destiny, and shows like *Star Trek* offered images of that possible future. The Apollo program, despite its unique success of putting humans on the Moon, ended abruptly. Its last three missions were ready to go, with hardware built and crews assigned. But President Richard Nixon decided that NASA needed different priorities. Early in 1970, Apollo 20 was canceled so that its Saturn V rocket could instead launch Skylab, a manned orbital science laboratory. After Skylab's launch was moved ahead of Apollo 18 and Apollo 19 in the schedule, those missions were canceled. I wasn't paying attention to politics then. I was waiting for Star Fleet Academy to open so that I could apply.

A government science program can be wrapped up quietly when money and political support—in a chicken-and-egg relationship—dries up. Boeing's Dyna-Soar space plane for the military was canceled in 1963, after six years of research and development and an expenditure of roughly five billion of 2016 dollars; construction of that spacecraft had just begun. The notion of Dyna-Soar was replaced with the Air Force's Manned Orbiting Laboratory—a spy in the sky—which was canceled six years later because, by then, the United States had figured out how to spy with unmanned satellites. In 1991, NASA canceled the X-33 and X-34 reusable space planes; some said they were too costly, while others pointed to design flaws.

Though not a space program, the Superconducting Super Collider was canceled in 1993, after $2 billion and digging fourteen miles of tunnel. As a physics major who later worked at a different particle accelerator in Illinois, I was dispirited by this short-sighted decision about science. In discussions about federal spending, some in Congress pitted the accelerator against a proposed space station, then known as Freedom, and said the nation can't take on too many big science projects at once. The United States gave up. Now, the Large Hadron Collider in Europe, with its discovery of the Higgs boson, is the physics project du jour.

Federal budget wrangling, though, rarely hinges on a this-or-that choice, and NASA's budget isn't all that big to be pitted against other worthwhile efforts. Apollo 11 astronaut Michael Collins made still-relevant points in his book *Carrying the Fire*, after Apollo was canceled:

Either cure cancer or fly in space. Either clean up the environment or fly in space. There doesn't seem to be a willingness to do all these things on a balanced basis. Furthermore, I think Americans are grossly misinformed about how much of their tax dollar goes into space. [...] My personal opinion is that canceling the space program would have little effect on [other] projects even if the money could be directly transferred.

Not much has changed since 1974. More than forty years later, NASA's budget still represents roughly one-half of one percent—just a half-penny on the dollar—of the federal budget.

When I was six years old, I carried around the blue plastic lunar rover toy that had come with a canister of Tang. One day—I want it to be April 1972, during the Apollo 16 mission—my grandmother confronted my space-obsessed self with her assertion that space exploration was a waste of money. She had lived through the Great Depression and believed in the War on Poverty that President Lyndon Johnson had waged. I wanted people to have what they needed too. Looking at the toy in my hand, though, I also wanted to be one of those white plastic astronauts sitting in the rover on the Moon—like Charlie Duke and John Young on Apollo 16. Of stepping out of the lunar module, Duke exclaimed, "Fantastic! Oh, that first step on the lunar surface is super." I wanted to experience that too.

In January 1972, Nixon had announced the future Shuttle program, the one I yearned to fly someday. I told my grandmother that we learned a lot by going to space and made new things here on Earth because of it. As I recall, I'd read an article, probably in *Popular Mechanics*, about spacesuit technology adapted to protect firefighters. Though I didn't call it a spinoff—that's what NASA calls it when they develop technology that then has commercial application—that's how I successfully convinced my grandmother of the need to go to space. In that moment, in that childhood conversation about space, I chose to define myself as a fact-based person, a person of reason, a person who might explore the universe.

Here's how physicist Neil deGrasse Tyson, the rock star of scientists, considers the choices we make: "America is a wealthy nation. Let's ask the question, 'What is going to space worth to you?' How much of your tax dollar are you willing to spend for the journey that NASA represents in our heart, in our minds, in our souls?" Space exploration has become a vital part of the story we tell about ourselves as Americans over this last century. Tyson asks us to rise above the either/or: "It's the entire portfolio of spending that defines a nation's identity. I, for one, want to live in a nation that values dreaming as a dimension of that spending. Most, if not all, of those dreams spring from the premise that our discoveries will transform how we live." I couldn't say it better myself, and I hear in this the same sentiment that I expressed to my grandmother all those years ago.

The Space Age my generation has lived transformed our lives. Along with sending men to the Moon, it has produced GPS; heart valves and a variety of other medical devices; and Tyvek, Velcro, and other materials we take for granted. Space exploration is never a waste. Even more importantly, when we see Earth as a small blue marble against the black void, we understand the precariousness of the world in the universe and the shortness of our individual existence—"Fragile," Apollo 11's Mike Collins has said. The Space Age shaped our individual and collective consciousness. Space exploration, like no other pursuit, makes us aware of *having* perspective, of being human in the universe, of not knowing exactly where we were, until we leave and look back.

Whose jaw doesn't drop to see the Moon's glow and shadows and think that people have stood on that otherworldly orb? We see differently because of Apollo. We see it as a place where generations may well live and work. Space exploration changes who we think we are and who we can become.

CHAPTER 5
COUNTDOWN AT THE CAPE
ANNA

> From a distance, two form one,
> a trick of perception of wishful thinking.
> Relationships are always trickier
> when you're up close, when you're in one.
>
> The distance between one another
> determines everything. Far enough, and
> it's as if you're all alone. You can do
> as you please with no good or ill effect.
>
> You may as well go your own way.
> In fact, admit it, you already have.
> Close enough, and attraction takes over,
> the allure toward each other, the circling,
>
> one around the other, the other around one,
> the ability to share planets and measure
> years the same way. Maybe he's a red supergiant,
> and you're a hot companion and blue.
>
> —Anna Leahy, from "Binary Star"

The United States *chose* to go to the Moon in 1969, when I was not yet four years old. The nation *chose* to develop orbital spaceflight and orbital science with the space shuttle, which started launching when I was in high school. We *chose* to work with nations around the globe to build a permanent space station; I was in my thirties then. By 2010, the then-penultimate manned mission by NASA (another mission would be added), the last for orbiter *Discovery*, was scheduled for launch on November 1. Doug and I chose to be there.

Anyone can go to the Space Coast and find a spot on the beach from which to view a rocket launch. My aunt had caught glimpses of Apollo launches when she lived in Florida in the 1960s. Journalists, though, can view a launch as close as any human beings can safely watch. A poet and a scientist weren't typical reporters following NASA's goings-on, but Doug and I—in tandem—applied for media credentials for the November 2010 launch. After some go-around with our university's magazine editor for validation, the NASA News Center's one-woman gatekeeper approved a credential, singular, as in, for only one of us: me! It didn't make sense to me that the poet instead of the scientist would be the insider, but the editor must have convinced the gatekeeper that I was reporter enough. And my mother had long told me that life wasn't fair. This time, it wasn't fair in my favor. I worried that this situation would strain my relationship with Doug, just as we were figuring out all over again our life together in a still-new place, so I tried to tamp down my giddy exuberance. He assured me that he was excited for me too. That's what I wanted to hear, but it was also something I wasn't sure I'd have convincingly conveyed had the situation been reversed. It can be difficult when one in a couple gets ahead in some way. I told myself we were happy that we were doing this crazy adventure together. Thankfully, Doug said the same thing. He is the better sport.

On October 29, the day before we left for the Cape—a month shy of the second anniversary of our desert jaunt to greet *Endeavour*—we woke to word that *Discovery*'s launch was delayed by a day, until November 2. This news seemed a good omen: the launch was now scheduled for Doug's birthday. Details changed. The story evolved. We'd planned to be in Florida for a week—with time before and after launch—so we adjusted to a new schedule.

The two of us spent the evening nestled together on the futon to watch a set of DVDs called *The Physics of Space Flight*. In part because we had half-botched seeing the shuttle land in the desert two years earlier, we did everything we could think to prepare for understanding the moment we were going to see. In my head, I applied the physical interactions in the video to the space shuttle. The shuttle, high above Earth—between 190 and 330 miles up, depending on the mission—is pulled toward the planet's center by gravity. The shuttle travels fast enough—roughly 17,500 miles per hour—to stay up in space. *When Discovery's orbit ends,* I thought, *it will end forever.*

The day before Halloween, Doug and I flew cross-country to Orlando, rented a car, and drove forty-five minutes to a rundown, 1960s-era motel in Titusville, which usually charged less than fifty dollars per night but could charge more than two hundred dollars the night before a launch. Titusville reminded me of another ramshackle Florida town after the end of Apollo that poet Jesse Lee Kercheval recalls in her memoir *Space.* She wrote of her then-boyfriend's home: "Inside, the house smelled of mold, damp, and mildew." I inhaled the dank decades.

At the front desk, a sheet of paper in a plastic sheath announced the shuttle's launch. November 1 was crossed out; launch had *slipped*—that's the insiders' term for it—until Wednesday, November 3. I welcomed the delay, the narrative drawn out like extra innings in a baseball game. I was happy for an extra day to get acclimated to the new environs of Kennedy Space Center, which we quickly referred to as KSC, one among a host of acronyms that are part of the language of this story.

With time to spare, Doug and I spent Halloween at the KSC Visitor Complex, a theme park of sorts that chronicles the Space Age. The bus tour stopped at an open structure several stories high so that we could see *Discovery.* To say that I could see *Discovery* is an exaggeration, another version of being at Edwards Air Force Base for *Endeavour's* landing two years earlier, when we saw the shuttle from afar on the tarmac. Now, with the shuttle several miles in the hazy distance, the orange peak of *Discovery's* external fuel tank poked above scaffolding that surrounded and almost completely obscured the orbiter. I played with my camera's zoom to get a still-hazy closer view than I could with my own eyes.

At the top level of the viewing tower, a woman in a sari approached to ask, "Is this as close as we get?" Doug explained that only NASA-approved personnel got beyond this point. "My father would really like to *touch* it," she said. The man had traveled from India; he expected to go right up to the launch pad, perhaps climb up like an astronaut to peek through the crew hatch opening. NASA had managed to inspire awe in a man halfway around the world and, at the same time, leave him unaware of the risks and serious work of getting a shuttle off the ground.

The next morning, November 1, at a small, isolated building, I picked up my media badge. We'd gone to the wrong badging place the day before, the one for foreign nationals that was closed on weekends. Though we knew a lot about the space shuttle, we'd kicked ourselves for our lack of experience and expertise as reporters. But now I felt back on track. I showed two government-issued IDs and filled out a form that included an emergency contact in case some catastrophic disaster occurred. *A hurricane?* I wondered. *An explosion?*

I left Doug at the Visitor Complex. I didn't let myself look back as I headed the short distance east to the KSC security gate. The guard peered into the rental car, checked my badge and driver's license, and pointed to the exit ramp, then gestured to indicate left at the light, then right at the Vehicle Assembly Building, the VAB. My heart beat firmly. I was excited, and I was on my own, longing for Doug's company and vast knowledge but feeling a thrill by myself.

The VAB looms two inches shy of 526 feet tall and covers eight acres. Inside, in preparation for each mission, the orbiter was *stacked*—NASA's term for assembling—with the external fuel tank and solid rocket boosters, or SRBs. When it was completed for Apollo in 1965, the year I was born, the VAB was the largest building in the world, and it still has the fourth largest volume of any building in existence. The VAB defies photography; with proximity, it doesn't fit into the frame, but distance doesn't capture its scale. It's a building so large that it skewed my perspective every time, seeming far away as I approached until it was suddenly right there, looming.

The NASA Press Site sits across the street. I turned right at a driveway and showed my badge to another guard. The parking lot wasn't huge and wasn't crowded. I'd expected hubbub. On a grassy area between the parking lot and the Banana River stood the countdown clock I'd seen on television. The News Center, a plain building covered in siding, was on a rise. I climbed the steps to become a space reporter.

Inside, long slabs-as-desks with chairs behind them beckoned journalists. Informational papers were available from the rack near the door and from the counter behind which public affairs officers sat and scurried. I milled about, eavesdropping like any good journalist, and heard of sign-up sheets for press activities, including interviews and the rollback of the RSS. I rifled through the press kit packet for STS-133—the 133rd mission of the Space Transportation System—that Doug had printed out and put in a binder as part of our preparation. I found "Acronyms and Abbreviations," a vocabulary list thirteen pages long. RSS—pronounced as three letters like VAB, not as a word like NASA—meant Rotating Service Structure. No one at KSC referred to the launch pad scaffolding by its full name.

The jargon might have grated upon my poet's ears or made me feel like an outsider. Instead, this vocabulary lilted in the air. The acronyms quickly began to slip from my lips as if I'd mouthed them since childhood. As with any culture, language was a way in. I like words.

I latched myself to the rest of the media and found myself not at whatever a rollback was, but at the now-defunct Launch Complex 39B, which was built in 1966 and refurbished for the shuttle after Skylab and Apollo-Soyuz. The first shuttle mission to use LC-39B was STS-51L. In the mid-1980s, NASA used a complicated mission numbering system: the first digit indicated the year, the second indicated the launch site (1 for Kennedy; 2 for Vandenberg, never used), and the letter indicated the spot in that year's sequence (L, the twelfth letter of the alphabet, meant the twelfth mission of 1985). But missions could be delayed, sometimes launching out of sequence, and their original designations were not updated as the schedule changed. Instead of launching in 1985, as its designation suggests, STS-51L was the second launch in 1986.

So LC-39B was first used to launch a shuttle on January 28, 1986. I took a deep breath when I understood that I was looking at where *Challenger* had last lifted off, only to disintegrate seventy-three seconds later. That day in 1986, I'd heard voices in the lounge outside the literary journal office, where I was working. Other students had gathered in front of what would now be considered a small television mounted high in the corner, like those in hospital rooms. Some students sat in the worn chairs and couches; others, like me, stood to watch the plume of white smoke burst, divide, and curl, knowing that seven astronauts were aboard. And then we watched it again and again, knowing that the families of the astronauts and the students of teacher-turned-astronaut Christa McAuliffe had watched the event in person, continuing to look at the sky even after hearing "major malfunction" from the speakers at KSC. Generation Space, whether in kindergarten or college, became shaped by that image: the burst, divide, curl of smoke. It may be burned more vividly in the memories of some; it also remains a collective memory. We brought more chairs in; we couldn't stop watching. Years later, Doug and I would meet Fred Gregory, one of the astronauts in flight control in Houston for *Challenger*'s last launch, but we couldn't bring ourselves to ask him about that day in 1986.

As I watched news coverage of the accident, I didn't yet understand that, because overnight ambient temperatures in Florida had been frigid, one of two rubber O-rings—roughly the diameter of my pinky finger—had become so stiff that it didn't quickly seal one of the joints in the right SRB as *Challenger* ascended into the sky. When the booster's joint didn't seal, a jet of hot gas wormed through the gap there. I can see that in the video now, in hindsight. Even if NASA had seen the flame in real time and determined its danger, a solid rocket motor cannot be turned off—that's why NASA used only liquid fuel for Mercury, Gemini, and Apollo, because solids can't be stopped. Had the problem been discovered almost immediately—though there was no quick enough way—might those boosters have been ditched so that the shuttle might perform a return to launch site?

One thing led to another: the escaping hot exhaust weakened a strut, the booster pivoted to break the orbiter's wing and also penetrate the external fuel tank, the highly flammable liquids poured from that tank, and the propellants in the SRB kept on burning. Within one second of the booster slamming into the external tank, Pilot Michael Smith said, "Uh oh." I hadn't known, as I watched the coverage as a college student, that the crew compartment fell to the ocean intact, with the astronauts harnessed firmly in their seats and three of the seven Personal Egress Air Packs—emergency oxygen—activated, as if egress were possible. In 2010, I looked into that Florida sky from *Challenger*'s launch pad and re-ran those images in my mind. My heart ached.

In 1986, the nation waited for a formal investigation. Whistleblowers like Roger Boisjoly and Bob Ebeling, two solid rocket booster engineers at Morton Thiokol who'd recommended launch be delayed, helped reveal what had happened. As Doug and I followed the end of the shuttle program, we met three whistleblowers who'd known the O-rings were a problem: Boisjoly, Allan McDonald, and Richard Cook. Boisjoly, whose papers are now archived at our university's library (and were followed by McDonald's), still wondered what else he might have done to prevent the accident. He'd gone home on the day before launch, after a conference call meeting in which he'd warned of the danger, and told his wife he feared they'd decided to kill the astronauts. He remembered watching the launch, feeling initial relief as the shuttle cleared the tower. He remembered the investigation, too, how hard people at Morton Thiokol had been on him and how Sally Ride, the nation's first woman in space, had been the only person to show public support. In 2012, after the Shuttle program ended, Boisjoly died at the age of seventy-three. Seventy-three, the number of seconds between launch and *Challenger*'s breaking apart.

As a result of the investigation, changes were made to the shuttle itself: an extra rubber O-ring in redesigned booster joints, a crew escape system involving sliding down a pole if the shuttle were miraculously both low enough and under control, and an extended list of parts—Criticality 1 and 1R parts—that absolutely had to be in tip-top shape for a "go" for launch. Changes were made to NASA too: key managers were moved out (Johnson, Marshall, and Kennedy space centers got new directors), and lead responsibility for the program shifted from Johnson Space Center to NASA headquarters in Washington, DC. The shuttle began flying again in 1988, the year I finished college.

I stood at the launch-pad-in-shambles and shuddered. *This is where it happened.* This was the place I'd seen on television, now quiet. NASA went on after *Challenger*. So did I; I went on after my father's death less than six months later. LC-39B was last used for STS-116 in 2006, which attached a truss to the International Space Station. LC-39B was revamped again for the test of the Ares 1-X prototype in 2009, but NASA's Constellation Program—designed to send astronauts back to the Moon, then to Mars—was underfunded and then canceled in 2010.

Looking at the defunct pad, I wondered whether the United States would send astronauts to space ever again after the Shuttle program ended.

Back in the News Center, flags from nations participating in the International Space Station—ISS, in NASA-speak—hung from the ceiling on permanent display. It was now Tuesday, November 2, Doug's birthday and the ten-year anniversary of human residency on ISS. The science laboratory that represents collaborative efforts of space agencies from the United States (NASA), Russia (RKA), Japan (JAXA), Europe (ESA), and Canada (CSA) had been occupied continuously since 2000. This big satellite represents global collaboration, evidence that nations can work together for the good of all. Space exploration is as much about politics and culture as it is about science and technology.

The first component of ISS, Zarya—electrical power, propulsion, and navigation systems—was shot into space, unmanned, by the Russians in 1998, the year I finished my PhD. Two weeks later, the second component, Unity, was delivered by *Endeavour* and assembly began. People moved in two years after that, riding up on a Soyuz capsule and establishing two official languages—English and Russian—on ISS. In 1999, *Discovery* was the first to dock with ISS and, over time, carried modules Harmony and Kibo into orbit. Kibo is the station's largest module; it hosts research in biology, materials, and communications. More than 150 components were added or attached to form a complex structure of modules, trusses, solar panels, laboratories, nodes, and bays. ISS is the most expensive object ever built.

The first time Doug and I turned our eager eyes to the nighttime sky to see ISS traverse a couple hundred miles overhead was in April 2001, when we were in Oregon. He was studying computer science as a PhD student, and, after three short-term positions, I had landed a tenure-track teaching job in Illinois. We were figuring out how to stay together while living apart. Then, as we looked up to see ISS, the second long-duration crew was in the midst of a five-month stint, separated from their loved ones. Later, in August of that year, *Discovery* brought the Expedition 2 crew home, leaving three new residents of Expedition 3 in their place. And so it goes with ISS, one expedition after another. And so it went for us for five years, traveling back and forth to live our individual lives and our together life in a carefully orchestrated sequence. Doug and I figured it out, out of necessity. That's what people do.

Circling Earth, making an orbit every ninety minutes or so, this science laboratory has been continuously occupied since November 2, 2000. Ten years later, the big screen in the KSC News Center showed the Expedition 25 crew waving to the world. Expeditions ran with six crew by then, three from the previous expedition who stayed and three who would stay for the next expedition, in a regular rhythm of overlaps and swap-outs by threes. NASA Administrator Charlie Bolden said, "It represents one of the most amazing engineering feats in history." Engineering was only part of what amazed me about ISS. Humanity was here all around me and there, up in space, too.

Pen and notebook in hand, the same day I saw the dilapidated launch pad, I attended a press briefing about Robonaut 2, the adaptable humanoid robot that uses tools designed for people in space and was set to go up to ISS on *Discovery*. NASA likes to show things off to reporters. NASA collaborated with General Motors and garnered input from Oceaneering Space Systems to build this machine. This shuttle mission meant something tangible: a mechanical version of the human upper body. The hope was that Robonaut 2—R2, like R2-D2 of *Star Wars*—could do some work that crew least like to do, like changing air filters. Seeing R2 made spacefaring more real to me. I could shake this mission's hand.

When the press briefing turned to questions, I, a natural introvert, decided to do something beyond my realm. I raised my hand, identified myself as from the university magazine, and asked, "I'm wondering how you decided how many tasks to start with and which tasks to start with and how you will decide to add tasks. You mentioned that you like to help the crew out—who makes the decision? How does that decision process happen to expand the tasks that the Robonaut will do?"

My question rambled a bit. I worried that my voice faltered from nerves but couldn't hear my voice over my pounding heart. But still, I wanted to tell Doug what I'd done. I wished he'd been there to see me. I knew he'd be proud of me.

My rambling paled in comparison to NASA's response:

That's an evolving process. The taskboard we sent up with the robot, which is also on the shuttle pad right now, has a variety of panels that can be replaced within its taskboard. It's a modular taskboard. We have a power panel with a variety of switches. We have a panel with a variety of IVA connectors, a panel with a variety of EVA connectors, a double-wide panel with soft goods and flexible materials on it. And we also have the ability to swap those panels out using materials on station. So we set up, we started with a certain set, we consider an indicative set of what's on station, and then working with crew over time, we will adjust that to go after what is going to be the most beneficial for helping crew.

I'd asked a relatively simple question. Surely, NASA knew exactly what was planned for R2, which task would be first and next and how many the robot could handle. In return for my question, they offered mumbo-jumbo for me to sort. They took me seriously; I was happy to parse what they said.

Looking at this Robonaut in the News Room, I could imagine it moving along a track in front of panels of knobs, switches, buttons, and handles like an old-fashioned telephone operator. Each switch or knob that R2 flipped or turned performed a specific task. To change the tasks for R2 to perform, an operator would have to replace one panel of switches with another.

Eventually, NASA wants an EVA—Extravehicular Activity—Robonaut at the ready to do repairs on the exterior of the space station. In the vacuum of space, a miniscule hole in a spacesuit can cost an astronaut's life. Inside ISS, one can wear shirtsleeves instead of spacesuits. So, if a robot could do some EVA work, astronauts could take fewer risks. A robot won't be able to replace an ammonia pump on a truss, which took two astronauts three spacewalks totaling more than twenty-two hours in August 2010, but replacing batteries and adding cables might be robot-level work.

Talk of R2 and plans for another made it seem as if the shuttle program were plugging right along into the future. But *Discovery* would also carry up items that signaled how close the end of the Shuttle program loomed: a sensor to be installed on ISS that the private company SpaceX would use in its resupply flights there and also a logistics module—a big container—to be left on ISS because the shuttle wouldn't need it anymore. Three of these modules—temporary storage pods—were built by the Italian Space Agency, each named after an important Italian artist (or Teenage Mutant Ninja Turtle). NASA's role is cultural as well as technological. Donatello never went to space, and Leonardo was the workhorse, eventually flying eight of the twelve missions that used these pressurized containers. Both Leonardo (which was on that shuttle we saw after it landed in the desert in 2008) and Rafaello are still circling overhead now, fixed inside the space station with no way to ferry cargo back and forth.

While I became entranced by the minutiae of my first press briefing, Doug spent his birthday scoping out the best possible viewing spot for launch. He completed a six-mile run—hotel to coast and back—and decided Space View Park offered a great vantage for the next day's launch as well as an outdoor exhibit of cast handprints and signatures of Mercury astronauts, this nation's first seven astronauts. We were ready for the next day. We were ready for launch.

CHAPTER 6
CHASING THE SUBLIME
ANNA

If only my rotation and orbit
were as synchronous as the Moon's, half-lit

with its dark side always slipping from us,
its uppermost point longing with light-lust.

O, to both stand on it and look at it.
If only a Googled Moon were the real

thing, if only listless chip under seal
said the whole of it, if only the few slides

chronicling all our imagined tides
eclipsed fear. O, to be Galileo,

to be Armstrong, to wholeheartedly know
that a picture of the Moon is not me,

nor is it the Moon's own deep, gibbous grief.

—Anna Leahy, from "Google Moon"

On Wednesday, November 3, the launch clock held at -11:00:00—eleven hours and *not* counting—in an extra twenty-four-hour delay for what NASA called a "little glitch" in a main engine controller, a problem they'd discovered during Tuesday's power checks. Doug, had he been awarded media credentials instead of me, would have understood exactly what NASA was telling me, but I began to comprehend for myself what was going on. This tale of delay convinced me how complicated the space shuttle really was. One of the three phases in a circuit inside the computer dedicated to the third of three main engines hadn't come up. But it was in the redundant—not the primary—system, and it did come on later. Then, the team power-cycled—turned on and off—the circuit breaker five times to clean whatever oil or carbon had built up there. In other words, no big deal. *Jiggle the switch—that works at home,* I thought, as they explained the situation at the press briefing. *Such a small thing in a big machine.*

Later in the process on Tuesday, however, NASA engineers had seen "a little blip in all three phases of the same circuit." They called the problem "dribbling." A shuttle launch was a vivid, evolving narrative. Some of the story was told through mathematical and physical explanations that connected and explained actions and events and also predicted a possible conclusion. Mike Moses, the Launch Integration Manager, was the person who best explained technical information to the press. He wanted to be careful "not to craft a solution based on what we think is the problem." Had all this happened after launch, these blips wouldn't have presented any problem. Still, Moses wanted his teams to take the extra day to "polish that story and bring some history" to bear on the explanation for the blips, glitches, and dribbles.

I tried not to fret about the increasing possibility the shuttle on the pad wouldn't launch in time for us to see it. Launch delays were common at NASA. Besides, there were launch windows for *Discovery* every day through November 7, and this glitch was merely a tiny problem in a backup system. I gathered more information. I stayed busy.

Though I'd honed my skills over decades in front of classrooms, Doug's definitely the more socially adept and also the more technologically proficient of us. *This should have been Doug's opportunity,* I thought. *The press credentials should be his.* But that thought made me all the more bent on proving myself by interviewing three-time Shuttle astronaut Mike Coats—if Doug had had a media badge for this first trip, I may never have done some of the things I did in the following months and years. I preferred being a fly in the wall. Doug's absence forced me, as he would say, to go all in.

Looking back on this decision to sign up for an astronaut interview, I think of television writer Shonda Rhimes and her *Year of Yes* and know that I, too, was a kid who lived in my head. She wrote, "I think a lot of people dream. And while they are busy dreaming, the really happy people, the really successful people, the really powerful, engaged people? Are busy doing." Doug and I had made our move to California as our way to *do* something more with our lives, and the space shuttle became something around which this doing began to revolve. This adventure was teaching us to be really, deeply happy with ourselves and each other. Interviewing an astronaut was hard for me; I felt queasy as I waited for it. But it was part of doing something about our dreams.

I talked with Mike Coats, who was then Director of Johnson Space Center (home of the astronauts, from which he retired in 2012), in a small conference room. I'd signed up on a sheet of paper, and here was an astronaut across the table from me. Just the two of us.

I set up my digital recorder on the table, still not quite sure what to ask or how. Apollo 11 astronaut Michael Collins wrote: "My eyes have been privileged to see extraordinary scenes; their recollections and meaning far outweigh the aggravation of answering the same old questions." Going to space affects a person, but that spacefarer returns to the same Earth. Human beings who travel to space—the astronauts—are natural protagonists in the evolving story of space exploration. Those of us who write about the Space Age are part of the narrative, too, providing context and interpreting events like a chorus in ancient Greek drama. But I didn't want to have the same old questions; I wanted to stand out and sound smart.

Coats was congenial but formal. He relaxed when I asked him about growing up in Riverside, near where Doug and I lived. "I thought Southern California was heaven," Coats recounted with a smile. "As a young person, being an hour from the beach, an hour from Dodger Stadium, an hour from the mountains, life was pretty good." Coats came across as a regular guy recalling his happy childhood. I was having a casual conversation with a real astronaut—my mind was reeling, and my hands were shaking. I didn't sound like myself, but he couldn't have known that. When Coats revealed that he "grew up at Disneyland," I blurted out that I'd never been. He teased, "Oh, Anna, shame on you."

I'd won him over. And my nerves calmed. I was in the moment and observing the moment; I was having fun. Coats must have been having fun enough too and began to recount memories that many astronauts of his generation share:

> When the first seven astronauts were selected in this country, I was [...] thirteen years old. And that made a huge impression on me. So I have kind of had the privilege of experiencing the whole space program. The first Mercury launch, Mercury, Gemini, Apollo, Apollo-Soyuz, Shuttle, and now [the International Space] Station. I've seen it all, and I've been very privileged to participate in it in one form or another.

He watched others, then jumped aboard when he had the chance. Witnessing space exploration shaped us all. *How*, I thought, *will thirteen-year-olds tomorrow imagine themselves going to Mars if we no longer launch ourselves even to orbit?*

Emboldened, I formed another question (stolen from Stephen Colbert, who made *great or greatest* his go-to, offbeat question): "*Discovery*, great shuttle or the greatest shuttle?" I felt bold and brilliant. As a college student, I never spoke in class, and now I was consciously conquering my great discomfort, in part because of my own resolve but also because this astronaut was more congenial than I'd expected. Coats smiled. He liked *Discovery* best; Coats had piloted *Discovery*'s first mission and twice commanded *Discovery*. "I think it has served us well because it has flown the most missions," he said. "It is kind of the work-horse of the fleet because it's the oldest. I'm kind of prejudiced that I think it's kind of special." *Discovery* was the orbiter on LC-39A, right then getting ready to return to space. It was why we were all here, and I felt as if an astronaut had revealed a little secret to me. "I'm going to be sad when *Discovery* rolls to a stop," he said. I was going to be sad too.

Before that could happen, though, *Discovery* had to launch.

The launch was now set for Thursday, November 4. During the delays, Doug wandered the visitor's center Rocket Garden to see the rockets planted there, dominated by a Saturn I-B. In fact, this Saturn rocket is so large that it's displayed on its side. The two of us have stood next to it, dwarfed by its girth, struggling to imagine what it had looked like towering on a launch pad. Saturn I-B rockets, with their eight engines, launched Apollo 7 in 1968, three Skylab missions in 1973, and the Apollo-Soyuz American-Soviet handshake in 1975.

I remember Skylab, NASA's first space station. The shuttle hadn't been completed in time to push Skylab—seventy-seven tons, nine stories tall—higher in orbit to extend its life for a few more years. Bets on the date of Skylab's demise were wagered; t-shirts were printed up. *Time* magazine allayed people's fear of being hit by debris by pointing out that most of Earth is water: "What all that means, contend NASA's statisticians, is that the chance of any remnant striking a human being is only 1 in 152; the probability of any specific person being struck is 1 in 600 billion—far less than the chance of being hit by a bolt of lightning or winning a lottery." My aunt has been struck by lightning—twice. The chance of Skylab debris hitting inside a decent-sized city was estimated at one in seven; those odds seemed, to me, pretty good for disaster.

When Skylab fell to Earth on July 11, 1979, a Wednesday, I didn't see it. NASA miscalculated the process slightly: the spacecraft didn't burn up as fast as predicted over the Pacific Ocean, and some debris landed in Australia. NASA, in an unusual move, let people keep stray parts they found. A piece of Skylab, weighing more than a ton, was displayed during the Miss Universe pageant in Australia on July 20. A teenager, I watched that pageant with my great-aunt Ro and my sister, placing bets on the winner. That day was the tenth anniversary of Apollo 11's first-ever Moon landing. NASA had included women in its astronaut class for the first time the year before, when I was thirteen years old. For me and other girls of my generation, it was easier to play beauty pageant than space mission. Despite my own mother's accomplishments and my deep curiosity about science, only after I saw women in the astronaut corps did I question notions of womanhood I'd absorbed as a youngster whose favorite show at four years old was *I Dream of Jeannie*. There's a subtle difference between saying that a girl *can* do anything she wants (a belief) and saying that a girl can *do* anything she wants (an actual example).

On the evening of November 3, reporters and photographers gathered in the parking lot, were put through a security screening—we were told not to reveal exactly what kind—and loaded themselves (myself! I was a reporter!) onto buses for the few-minutes drive to LC-39A for the RSS rollback. A litany of rules was issued: stay away from the two large alligators in the ditch, watch for vehicles on the road, leave lighters and other flammables on the bus, head to the crawlerway and stay there. *Alligators?* Was this why I'd had to list an emergency contact when I picked up my media badge? I quickly put dangers aside and scrambled out of the bus. If I were to die by alligator, at least I'd see the shuttle up close.

The crawlerway is a rock-covered pair of lanes each spanning forty feet, with a fifty-foot grass median. It runs more than three miles from the VAB to the pads. Weeks before launch, one of two flatbed crawlers—the largest tracked vehicles ever, each of which weighs six million pounds and burns 150 gallons of diesel fuel per mile—hauled the upright orbiter, stacked with external fuel tank and SRBs, to its last perch. *Discovery* had made its last rollout to the pad on September 20 for this November launch. The crawlerway was designed to give way under the great weight of the crawler and shuttle. The rocks crunched and slipped even under my human foot.

The mosquitoes were vicious around sunset, so press officers and volunteers passed around insect repellant. Before the repellant made its way to me, I had huge welts and specks of blood on my ankles, hands, and face. I was a mess, and I missed Doug. I was deeply happy too, as if I'd found my purpose. *Purpose*, from the Latin meaning *to put forth. To put yourself out there*, I thought, *to experience life anew and see what happens*.

Discovery remained enshrouded by the RSS, the scaffolding that allowed engineers access to all parts of the shuttle in preparation for launch. The RSS had five levels and was 130 feet tall, so the orange tip of the external fuel tank—153.8 feet tall—peeked out the top, just as it had when Doug and I viewed it from farther away during our bus tour of the space center. The press was allowed to stand roughly ten yards from the fence surrounding the pad, probably fifty yards from the pad—from *Discovery*—itself.

It was easy to lose perspective this close to the looming structure on the slight hill. Even if I stood four hundred feet away, the heat from launch would kill me; at eight hundred feet, the sound would kill me, as blast pressure ruptured my body's tissues. Everyone snapped photographs before the sun set, taking advantage of waning daylight for good exposures. Finally, word worked its way around that the RSS had started to roll back.

At first, the scaffolding didn't seem to move, then suddenly the edge of the orbiter's right wing glistened white in the twilight. Little by little, the rollback revealed the whole of *Discovery*. Its black nose pointed skyward, its wings stiff, displaying the NASA insignia on the bottom of the left wing and the American flag over the name *Discovery* on the right.

"There is something incredibly awesome to think that we staple human beings to a fuel tank and light it on fire, and it circles Earth and everybody comes back almost all of the time." I had said that in a newspaper story that ran at home before we left for Florida. "That is an amazing feat all by itself. You might call it sublime." *Sublime*, that's how this moment felt. The word *sublime*, as it's used in art, refers to something immense and awe inspiring—beautiful, whole, but also powerful, threatening.

My time at the launch pad felt large and wonderful, and I felt small, dwarfed by the orbiter, the vastness of outer space, and the past and future that spanned out in either direction. I was pulled into *Discovery*'s story, into history. Doug lived the moment vicariously, listening to the stumbling, tripping joy in my voice over the cell phone. I had to appreciate the moment enough for both of us, and he had to let me revel in it.

One by one, four spotlights—each from a different corner in the distance—illuminated the orbiter. This was the image I'd seen in books, only more vivid, sharp, and three-dimensional. "Standing before costly objects of technological beauty, we may be tempted to reject the possibility of awe, for fear that we could grow stupid through admiration," writes Alain de Botton in *A Week at the Airport*. "And yet to refuse to be awed at all might in the end be merely another kind of foolishness."

Standing close to the illuminated orbiter, I felt awed and like a fool, filled with inarticulate intelligence. *Sublime* also has a meaning in chemistry: to convert a solid substance directly into a gas, or vice versa, without going through the intermediate liquid phase. Indeed, I was instantly transformed, made more intense and larger than myself.

NASA press officers and volunteers had seen dozens of rollbacks, but they gasped and grinned. Reporters and photographers, whether or not they'd been here before, stared in wonder, relishing this intimate experience with technology. The moment was the pinch-me sort. My eyes stung from not blinking: the shuttle upright, spotlights illuminating it in the pitch dark, the orbiter's curves and scuffs visible, its windows and engine nozzles evident to the naked eye.

The press officers let everyone stay longer than usual, knowing that this was the last night before the last launch for *Discovery*. Eventually, everyone boarded the buses, spent from the experience and eager for the next day.

CHAPTER 7
YOU FLY WHEN YOU'RE READY
ANNA

Nothing exists in itself. If you flatter yourself that you are all over comfortable, and have been so a long time, then you cannot be said to be comfortable any more.

—Herman Melville, *Moby-Dick*

As it turned out, that wasn't the last night before the launch. Doug and I had moved to California because we had become uncomfortable being comfortable in our routine. Pursuing the end of the space shuttle program—packing up and leaving our lives for a week, forcing myself to ask questions of astronauts and at news conferences, tag teaming in unfamiliar environs—was teaching us to enjoy the unknown, the unexpected, and the uncomfortable. Delays, by their nature, are uncomfortable.

On Thursday, November 4, NASA decided not to fill the tank because of heavy cloud cover and rain. For liftoff, weather had to meet basic launch commit criteria, which were outlined in my media packet and seemed reasonable in order to reduce risk of near-catastrophe; Apollo 12 was struck by lightning twice as it rose from the launch pad and then headed toward the Moon safely, and the *Challenger* launch ended in catastrophe on the cold morning it launched. Temperature, wind, cloud cover, chance of lightning, precipitation—all of this mattered. These criteria ensured good viewing for launch, and a quick look out the motel window confirmed the dark clouds and rain about which Doug and I heard on NASA-TV when we woke up.

Woke up isn't quite accurate, since I wasn't sure I'd slept. I was so enamored with the process of launch preparation that I didn't sleep much, so I wasn't disappointed at the morning's dismal weather and NASA's decision not to proceed. We could climb back into bed and relax into each other's arms. We could go to a sit-down restaurant to eat pancakes instead of eating protein bars while we wrote. It occurred to me, of course, that these delays could continue to pile up. But we'd booked our trip for the whole week to accommodate the unexpected. And if the unexpected kept happening, in a strange comfort with the uncomfortable, maybe the shuttle program would never end.

The next day, November 5, NASA started filling the external fuel tank before sunrise. The orange tank was actually two tanks, an upper one into which liquid oxygen was filled, and a lower one for liquid hydrogen. Together, these super-cooled propellants powered the shuttle's three main engines for the first eight-and-a-half minutes of the flight, after which the almost empty tank was jettisoned to disintegrate in the atmosphere.

Doug and I listened to NASA-TV as we dressed. *This is it*, I thought. Delays had given me time to acclimate to this place and story. I was ready for a launch. I was ready to appreciate it fully.

I arrived at the News Center by 7:30 a.m. so I could go to the astronaut walkout that morning. The astronauts in their orange flight suits would wave to the press and KSC employees, as they had for decades. This crew was headed up by Commander Steve Lindsey, for whom this was his fifth shuttle flight, and Pilot Eric Boe. Boe was one of the astronauts Doug and I would have seen in the desert two years earlier, had we stayed to watch the STS-126 crew emerge after that *Endeavour* landing, and now we were—or *I* was—going to see him closer than I'd imagined possible.

The Mission Specialists were Tim Kopra, Michael Barratt, Nicole Stott, and Benjamin Drew, Jr. Because, as teenager, I'd wanted to become a surgeon, Michael Barratt especially intrigued me. He'd worked on the Shuttle-Mir program (a collaboration between the United States and Russia involving long-duration missions) as a flight surgeon and a CAPCOM—capsule communicator—for the American astronauts in

1994. In 2009, he'd flown up and back to the International Space Station aboard Soyuz for a 199-day stint on Station. (*On Station*, not *on the space station*, is the insider lingo.) When the Shuttle program ended, trips like Barratt's in a Russian capsule became the norm. I'd have liked to talk with Barratt, but, of course, he was preparing for flight.

That a woman and an African-American—Stott and Drew, respectively—were among the crew demonstrated that cultural attitudes had shifted since the all-white, all-male days of earlier space programs in the United States. Stott was three years older than I was, which made me wonder why I'd never taken astronaut seriously as a career for me. Even though I was raised as a feminist, even when I started college with notions of becoming a surgeon, I must have clung to the male and female roles in *I Dream of Jeannie*, the first adult television show I watched regularly. While I'd come into my own as a poet and a professor (instead of discovering I was a genie), Stott had been to space three times, including three months on Station in 2009. STS-133 was Drew's second mission, and he'd do a couple of spacewalks this time. He was the last-ever African-American to fly on a shuttle.

By 8:30 a.m., word trickled out that NASA had scrubbed the launch. *Scrubbed* (as opposed to *slipped*), the term for delay after the tank had been filled. Launch had been scrubbed at 8:11 a.m. I was dumbfounded.

The problem: a leaky ground umbilical carrier plate (GUCP, pronounced something like *gup*, said as a word like NASA not as individual letters like RSS and VAB). The devil is in the details, and technical details—in this case, the GUCP, a small part in a big machine—can be tiny flaws that become the great undoing of a tragic hero. The GUCP, which I saw in a photograph of the metal plate attached to the fuel tank, had caused problems twice before, on STS-119 and STS-127. Each time, it had taken four days to fix. I didn't have four more days here. In addition, the team couldn't look at the problem up close until the external tank was completely purged of hydrogen because it was too dangerous to muck about with any fuel still in the tank. Purging the tank took time, another day. The leak from this plate was significant, which was thought to be a good thing. The cause of a big leak was likely more obvious than that of a small leak. If that were the case, maybe the

GUCP could be fixed and tested more quickly than before, perhaps in three days. I recalculated in my mind. That pushed launch to November 8, the day after we were scheduled to head home.

But when engineers had perused the images of the external fuel tank earlier in the day, as was standard before launch, somebody also noticed a crack in the foam that covered the tank. Ever since the Columbia accident—when a piece of the foam insulation broke off during launch and nicked a wing—cracks in the external tank's covering were taken very seriously. Columbia launched on January 16, 2003, for a sixteen-day mission designated STS-107. Columbia was set to land on February 1, but never did.

Less than four minutes after entering Earth's atmosphere, after banking to reduce speed from the original 17,500 miles per hour, a sensor indicated that the leading edge of Columbia's left wing was hotter than on any previous flight. That data was recorded by a black box inside the shuttle but wasn't sent to the crew or to flight controllers on the ground. Instead, the astronauts looked out the windows at what seemed like any other reentry—we know this from an astronaut's home video recovered amidst the debris.

That day, as soon as I heard the news about Columbia, I called Doug. He was in Oregon, working on his PhD in computer science, and I was in Missouri, teaching in my first tenure-track job. We were figuring out how to live separately and stay together for the five years that it would take for him to finish graduate school. Never did we feel more uncomfortable being thousands of miles from each other than the day of the Columbia accident. We stayed on the phone a long time, watching television together in separate places. We called each other several times that day.

"This is amazing," Pilot William C. McCool remarked in that video found among the debris. "It's really getting fairly bright out there."

"Yeah," Commander Rick Husband replied, "you definitely don't want to be outside right now."

In the thirteen minutes of amateur filming, Mission Specialists Laurel Clark and Kalpana Chalwa were all smiles.

The orbiter crossed over the California coast just north of San Francisco. From the ground, the bright spot in the dark sky overhead became brighter, a sight some of our current colleagues remembered seeing, though it wasn't yet 6:00 a.m. in California. Controllers at Johnson Space Center noticed odd readings—*off-scale low,* or below the sensors' ability to record data—in the hydraulic sensors of the left wing, then lost communication with the shuttle.

The crew struggled to control the orbiter—we know this from instrument tracking viewed in hindsight. *Columbia* broke up, the cabin remaining intact temporarily. The crew was likely killed when, within seventeen seconds, the compartment depressurized and spun violently, tearing asunder. Streaking multiple trails behind, the shuttle's parts were strewn over Texas and Louisiana. What could survive such a horrific fall to Earth? People looking for wreckage found worms from a science experiment to see how well—and with how little care—the creatures could grow in space. Thirty-seven pages of Israeli astronaut Ilan Ramon's personal diary. On the sixth day of the mission, Ramon wrote, "I turned out to be a man who lives and works in space, just like in the movies."

This accident was traced to a piece of foam insulation that broke off during launch from the shuttle's external fuel tank and punched a hole of six, maybe ten, inches in the thermal tiles that protect the vehicle from heat when it glides through Earth's atmosphere to land. Engineers who reviewed the launch video during the mission requested that NASA get ground-based images of the orbiter from the Department of Defense to check for damage before reentry, but no visual inspection was done. Foam had broken off and hit orbiters during previous launches, so managers didn't think such light material could do much damage. Fast-moving things hit with greater force, however, even if they're light. NASA should've known better. *Atlantis,* which had been damaged by debris during launch almost fifteen years earlier, had completed STS-27 only because it was lucky; the damage to hundreds of tiles somehow had not landed in critical spots. According to reporter William Harwood, Hoot Gibson, the commander of STS-27, had told himself while orbiting Earth, "oh, holy smokes, we are going to die." And in 2003, an entire shuttle crew did.

All members of *Columbia*'s last crew were in their forties, a little older than I was then. Five of the seven were on their first shuttle flight. I watched television coverage of the accident all weekend. Doug and I talked on the phone again and again. Unlike *Challenger, Columbia* was not replaced. Before a year had passed, the end of the space shuttle program was announced.

Maybe this delay is a good thing, I thought at the press briefing about *Discovery's* scrub. *Better safe than sorry,* as if a cliché could simplify my feelings. *Columbia,* the first shuttle to fly, had been declared "fully operational"—no longer experimental—on Independence Day in 1982, at the end of its fourth flight, but the shuttle had remained, in many ways, one big, long experiment. The modified Grumman Gulfstream II that shuttle pilots used to train for shuttle-like landings remained an experimental aircraft for its thirty years of service, but the orbiters were thought of as operational. Over its three decades, the program continued to test new equipment and new maneuvers, modifying the orbiters time and again. It was possible for things to go awry.

History had shown that it's difficult to predict which glitch really matters in the end, that NASA shouldn't get comfortable with its past successes, that each mission is a different story. That's why shuttle workers had to fix the GUPC and the crack. Something small—that crack in the foam—could be catastrophic. So engineers tried to control every risk they noticed because risk can't be eliminated completely.

It was Friday, and Doug and I had to leave Florida on Sunday. I'd come to know Mike Moses's intonations well enough to sense that he thought a Monday launch iffy at best. Moses and Shuttle Launch Director Mike Leinbach had mixed feelings. They were going through this pre-launch process with this orbiter for the last time. As Leinbach put it, "You fly when you're ready, and if you're not, you don't go."

The press quieted and resorted to photographing each other. Doug, having sauntered down to the Space View Park for the launch, watched exotic birds, a manatee, and a small shark negotiate the choppy, brown water.

If *Discovery* didn't launch on Monday, everything got pushed to December. I'd learned a lot about launch windows—which day, what time of day, how much wiggle room at that time, how many days in a row. Because Earth, ISS, and the shuttle were all moving—and Earth is moving in two ways, orbiting the Sun as well as rotating on its own axis—the calculations were, though well understood, complex.

ISS orbits at 51.6 degrees relative—askew—to the equator. Earth rotates a smidge faster than ISS circles so that each orbit threads over the globe in a slightly new position relative to planet's surface and, therefore, offers the station crew a shifting view below. That's different than a geosynchronous orbit, in which an object—a telecommunications satellite, for instance—remains in the same spot over Earth. It's as if it were tethered by gravity like a balloon to a child's hand and moved in sync with the globe, at the same speed, one orbit every twenty-four hours. As ISS rounds the globe roughly every ninety minutes—Earth curving beneath—the station crosses over the equator heading south, then re-crosses north. For the shuttle to chase down the space station and also drop its external fuel tank while still over ocean, ISS had to be traveling north over Florida's side of the globe when the shuttle rose from the coast of Florida.

A launch window, then, was the time—about ten minutes—on a particular day during which the shuttle could lift off and catch up with ISS. Often, launch windows were available every day for several days in a row, as in the case of *Discovery* this time, because the change in relative position of ISS to Earth's surface is small each day. A slew of daily windows gave NASA flexibility, the ability to slip or scrub once or twice without weeks or months before another opportunity. Unless delays piled up. Like this time.

Discovery seemed in no mood to leave Earth. No one on the Space Coast seemed ready for *Discovery* to leave, to inch us all closer to the end of the space shuttle program. Everyone wanted to linger in this place, in this moment, a little longer. For a week, *Discovery* had been my center of gravity. My orbit had been simple and constant: motel, visitor center, press center, motel, visitor center, press center. I wanted to keep circling.

As Herman Melville wrote in *Moby-Dick*, more than a hundred years before sailors ventured to the Moon, "But oh! shipmates! on the starboard hand of every woe, there is a sure delight; and higher the top of that delight, than the bottom of the woe is deep." I tried to wallow in not-launch woe. *Surely*, I figured, *I'm disappointed.* But my melancholy felt flimsy. I had no regrets. And we didn't predict what delight would happen the next day.

CHAPTER 8
GENEALOGY
DOUG

Some days the magic works.

— Buck Rogers, *Buck Rogers in the 25th Century*

Saturday, November 6: a full week had passed since Anna and I arrived on the Space Coast. We'd come to appreciate the ways in which the space shuttle program was about Kennedy Space Center and about orbiters and rockets. Had *Discovery* launched on Wednesday or Thursday, I would have suggested we catch an early flight home. I had a job back in California, and I didn't have a media badge. But the way the week played out—one thing leading to another but not to the launch we'd come to see—left us time to indulge in a little more space-nerdiness at the KSC Visitor Complex before leaving.

A chill hung in the air that sunny afternoon, so, before touring the Rocket Garden as we'd discussed, Anna and I ducked into the Dr. Kurt H. Debus Conference Facility, named for the Director of KSC (from 1962 to 1974)—NASA's gilded years of Mercury, Gemini, Apollo, and Skylab. The building is filled with 1960s kitsch, like phonographs and hand-held View-Masters, which I remembered fondly. Impressive space exploration relics have found a home here, too. The spacecraft used in the Gemini 9 mission—*capsule* is common parlance, not technical terminology—sits in a corner, tilted so that visitors can peek inside at where Tom Stafford and Gene Cernan spent six days in orbit in June 1966, five months before I was born. The building is a museum filled with the *things* that make the Space Age tangible—objects are what we went to see that day.

The original Mercury program control center consoles in the museum harken back to the first US successes in manned spaceflight. When the last Mercury mission, in a spacecraft called *Faith 7* in 1963, was designed for full automation and little control by the astronaut aboard, the sound-barrier-breaking test pilot Chuck Yeager referred to the mission's astronaut, Gordon Cooper, as "SPAM in a can." Yeager's point was that, compared with a jet pilot, an astronaut was more cargo than commander, a mere lump of flesh in a metal container.

When a power failure occurred on that Mercury mission's nineteenth orbit, Cooper proved otherwise, however, as he took manual control and used his knowledge of the stars to maneuver his way home. Buck Rogers ingenuity. As a kid, I wanted to be that kind of Buck Rogers.

Gus Grissom, the Mercury and Gemini astronaut who later died in the fire during the Apollo 1 test, asserted: "No bucks, no Buck Rogers." Spacefarers are the stuff of comic books and television shows. Though it costs more to fly humans than to fly unmanned missions, astronauts, at the very least, have been good public relations in the federal funding game. Space exploration isn't just about things. People matter.

Standing in the entryway, beneath the sea-foam green Russian Soyuz spacecraft that hangs from the ceiling—similar to those that take astronauts to ISS now that the shuttle has stopped flying—Anna and I swapped out sunglasses for our ordinary spectacles and looked around. Suddenly, as if my prescription lenses had acquired magical properties, I thought I saw Edwin "Buzz" Aldrin emerge from the men's room.

I grew up on *Star Trek* and *Buck Rogers in the 25th Century*. As a kid, I built an imagined force field out of real rods and wire on the planet that was my backyard. Astronauts are cool. Some days, you don't see what you came to see, but the magic works anyway. I was sure I'd seen Buzz Aldrin in the flesh. I said nothing to Anna.

Aldrin is a member of perhaps the most exclusive group in the world. One of twelve men who walked on the Moon, he followed Armstrong down the ladder of the Lunar Module nineteen minutes later and became the second man to set foot on the lunar surface. Aldrin had also flown in the Gemini program. Though Aldrin was not the first spacewalker, his deft Extravehicular Activity during three spacewalks on Gemini 12 helped prove that astronauts could work outside their spacecraft, a proof of concept upon which the Moonwalks and the Shuttle program later depended. More recently, Aldrin and his famous feet were swiftly booted off *Dancing with the Stars* in its tenth season. Of all astronauts, Aldrin embraces celebrity most. Here was the stellar celebrity—a bona fide Buck Rogers—before my very eyes.

I gave chase and ended up in the Atlas conference room. When Anna caught up with me, we looked around to see models of spacecraft and rockets. *NASA's yard sale?* Then, my eyes refocused on the people in addition to the space trinkets for sale. I started an internal count: *two, five, ten—dozens* of astronauts in this room, positioned behind tables. Mercury, Gemini, Apollo, Skylab, and Shuttle—within a few steps, the real, live people who flew those spacecraft. Genealogy is the study of generations, and here they were, the multiple generations of American space exploration.

Next to each table was a placard with a name, an official NASA photo, and mission designations. I noted names of Apollo astronauts—Buzz Aldrin, Alan Bean, Gene Cernan, Walt Cunningham, Charlie Duke, Fred Haise, Jim Lovell, Edgar Mitchell, Dave Scott—six of whom had walked on the Moon. I noticed a large sign: *Astronaut Autograph and Memorabilia Show.* This event was a fundraiser to support college kids studying STEM subjects: science, technology, engineering, math. Looking around, I saw models of spacecraft and glossies of astronauts—memorabilia—in visitors' hands. Each autograph had a price. Gene Cernan, last man on the Moon: $300. At auction, autographs the Apollo 11 crew signed on envelopes while the men were in quarantine before launch, then mailed by a friend on launch or Moon landing day for a postmark, ran $30,000.

US manned spaceflight was about people: about all of us kids who grew up with the space program humming in the background, about the engineers who designed rockets and vehicles, and about the thousands who worked at KSC. The human beings who traveled to space—the astronauts—garnered the popular attention, from interviews in print and on television to the MTV logo and the recent television show focusing on their wives.

Anna and I grinned. I'm sure my eyes have never been wider. We spoke in half-sentences. We stood in a room full of astronauts, one Buck

Rogers after another. We hadn't purchased tickets, and we didn't want to ask for fear of being booted from a sold-out event. I looked around the room; I'd never happened upon astronauts from all eras of spaceflight. I couldn't leave. I had to talk with these people. Anna still had her media badge and didn't realize she wasn't supposed to wear it outside the gates of KSC proper; that badge became our cover. As interlopers that day, we agreed to contribute to the Astronaut Scholarship Foundation in recompense because we weren't supposed to be there in the midst of the astronaut corps I'd once dreamed of joining.

Dee O'Hara was the only featured person at the event who hadn't been an astronaut, and no one was at her table. I thought it might be easier for me to talk with her than with an astronaut, so we made our way over and introduced ourselves. Anna flashed her media badge confidently. I offered O'Hara a business card for our blog and, in a low voice, explained we were writers, hoping she'd take us seriously but not be put off. At first, the woman was suspicious of Anna and me, her large eyes looking for chinks in our journalistic armor. When we asked to interview her, she sneered at our video camera. But O'Hara agreed—magically?—to talk with us on camera anyway. She had a brassiness in her eyes and voice.

In November 1959, O'Hara was six months into her service as a nurse with the Air Force and was stationed at Patrick Air Force Base in Florida, where the space program hoped to get off the ground. The first seven astronauts for the Mercury program had been chosen that spring. As O'Hara told Anna and me, "[I] decided, well, we'll go see the world. Let's join the Air Force." One day, her commander offered a new assignment, something more unusual than the labor and delivery room where she was working nights. "At that time, I didn't know what an astronaut was. I didn't know what NASA was. I didn't know what Mercury was." When the commander said *Mercury*, O'Hara wondered whether that meant the planet or the substance in a thermometer.

NASA needed someone who'd get to know every astronaut well enough to tell the flight surgeon if one had a health problem, some ailment an astronaut wouldn't admit to the man who could ground him. For her part, O'Hara said, "Right place at the right time. I just lucked into it. And the timing—it was timing." *Serendipity*, I thought, *happy accident*. Over the course of twenty years, O'Hara witnessed every US manned rocket launch—Mercury, Gemini, Apollo—through to the first space shuttle launch. In interviews with others, she remembered utter relief when she saw Alan Shepard, the first American in space, for his post-flight physical. Even after that flight, she didn't think it got any easier or less tense for launch or return.

O'Hara's approach to her career—to her life—reminded me of what Stephen Colbert said in the commencement speech that Anna and I saw him give at Knox College, our alma mater, in 2006: "[T]here was really only one rule I was taught about improv. That was, 'yes-and.' In this case, 'yes-and' is a verb." *Yes* puts us in motion. Life is improvisation; we don't know exactly what's coming. *Yes*, O'Hara said, many years ago, *let's be a nurse to astronauts and see what happens*. When you say *yes*, things happen. *Yes* is a cause that generates sometimes unanticipated effects and paths. *Yes* gives rise to serendipity. It occurred to me that Anna and I had said *yes* to moving to California and *yes* to this Space Coast adventure of our own without knowing exactly what we were up to. We hadn't expected the launch to be delayed and scrubbed. We certainly hadn't expected a conversation with the first nurse to the first astronauts.

O'Hara was willing to jump in with confidence and still exuded that confidence, looking me squarely in the eyes as she spoke. "When you're young, you're really not sure all the time what you want to do. But you just go in what direction you think you want to go. And sometimes things fall in your lap, like they did mine." Some days, the magic really does happen.

At least in terms of general fitness and health, committees that selected astronauts knew their business. I saw the evidence in the room that day. The vitality and enthusiasm of Apollo 7's Walt Cunningham and Apollo 16's Charlie Duke seemed at odds with their age that day, seventy-eight and seventy-five, respectively. Dave Scott, Apollo 15 Moonwalker, was still matinee-idol handsome even in his late seventies.

Alan Bean entered through the door on the opposite side of the room from where Anna and I stood trying to eavesdrop on Cunningham and Duke. Bean flew on the Apollo 12 mission, during which he became the fourth Moonwalker. He also served as part of the third Skylab crew, spending fifty-eight days on the orbiting space laboratory, studying the effects of space on his own body and getting a microgravity haircut from a fellow crew member. Since 1981, when the shuttle first took flight, Bean has devoted himself to painting, specializing in lunar landscapes. He mixed particles of Moon dust from the patches from his spacesuit into his paint.

Bean gave a quick wave to Jim Lovell and Fred Haise, who were in the midst of signing and chatting, and an echo of "Hi, Al" followed in Bean's wake as he crossed the room toward us to see Charlie Duke. The two men shared a warm handshake and a pat on the back. Astronauts—and men from that generation, older than our parents—weren't men who hugged wholeheartedly, but these two showed great affection for each other. I could see they considered each other friends in addition to colleagues.

I've wanted to think that three men (in the case of Apollo) or as many as eight astronauts (in the case of Shuttle) on a given mission would be the closest of friends, training together for months, depending on each other for their lives, and understanding space exploration in a personal way that few humans do. Deep friendships, and even marriages, exist in the astronaut corps, and astronauts acknowledge the bond of their shared, rarified experience, but they're not always the inherently close-knit bunch one might expect. In 1974, Apollo 11 astronaut Michael Collins, in his book *Carrying the Fire*, wrote about the relationship among his generation of astronauts:

> I wonder whether all Apollo crews are satisfied to remain amiable strangers? It's certainly true that astronauts begin as competitors, but we three [Armstrong, Aldrin, and Collins] no longer have to worry about being picked over others for the *big flight*; it has happened, and we should be able to lower a few barriers now. [...] A closer relationship, while certainly not necessary for the safe or happy completion of a space flight, would seem more 'normal' to me. Even as a self-acknowledged loner, I feel a bit freakish about our tendency as a crew to transfer only essential information, rather than thoughts or feelings.

While still gripping Charl e Duke's hand, Alan Bean waved at Cunningham, who was sitting at the next table. "Hi'ya, Walt." Cordial, professional, not especially warm.

Three Apollo astronauts—American culture's leading men—chatting, about their lives, about the end of the Shuttle program. In the documentary film *In the Shadow of the Moon*, Bean said, "Not a day goes by that I don't think, this is great, this was wonderful, somebody had to go, and they happened to pick me." *Happened to pick him?* Does serendipity explain how Bean went to the Moon instead of someone else?

Certainly, there was a generational component to who became an astronaut. If you set aside Alan Shepard, who was born in 1923, all other astronauts to walk on the Moon were born between 1930 and 1935. Older than my father, these were also men of the Silent Generation born between the ends of world wars. Half were born in 1930 alone. An astronaut's average age at the time of selection is thirty-four. So if you want to be an astronaut, it helps to be in your thirties when NASA is hiring.

I turned thirty years old in 1996, the year Mark Kelly, Mike Fincke, Sandy Magnus, Rex Walheim—among those who flew the last Shuttle missions—became astronauts. Two years later, Chris Ferguson, Greg Johnson, Greg Chamitoff—more who flew the last Shuttle missions—became astronauts. I find this difficult to think about. I was seemingly the ideal age and deciding what to do next, and I didn't apply to be an astronaut then. I closed that door years earlier when my plans to become a military pilot were thwarted. Most of my thirties were spent earning a PhD in computer science, and, while that qualified me to become an astronaut, at least minimally, serendipity intervened. A PhD in computer science also qualified me to work at Fermi National Accelerator Laboratory, at that time home to Nobel prize winners and to one of the two most powerful atom-smashers in the world, the Tevatron. So, I said *yes-and* to that opportunity.

Alan Bean earned a degree in aeronautical engineering, became a Navy test pilot, and then was selected at age thirty-one in Astronaut Group 3 in 1963—in hindsight, a model path to space. Bean's Navy flight instructor had been Pete Conrad, who was in the second group of astronauts ever chosen, a year before Bean was selected. These guys attracted serendipity. These guys made the future into which I had been born, in which I, too, might have become an astronaut. I attracted what seemed to me a bumpier serendipity that knocked me from one path to another before I could find my way to my current life.

Within this museum of Space Age kitsch and technological wonders, Bean leaned over Cunningham's shoulder, and Duke started talking to someone else. Before long, Bean found his own place in the room, and the long line of people waiting to meet the astronaut-turned-artist soon extended out the door.

Like two eighth graders at a dance with backs to the wall, too frightened to make the first move, Anna and I stood in front of an unoccupied table and tried to summon up our shared courage to speak with our heroes. Charlie Duke exuded the kind of warmth and charm that disarms and suggests an ordinary Joe, even if you're standing in front of one of the handful of humans who set foot on another world, so we decided to speak with him first. As endearing as I think Duke would have found it and as much as I wanted a connection or an anchor, I decided, at the last second, not to hold Anna's hand in front of someone who possessed *the right stuff*. I wanted to appear as a serious journalist.

The first thing we noticed about Duke when we spoke with him was what the world heard when he served as CAPCOM—capsule communications, the voice of Mission Control in the astronauts' ears—during the most-famous Apollo 11 mission: that warm, Southern drawl. His voice spun tales, connected his memory with mine.

On July 20, 1969, Duke was the person representing Earth to the Apollo 11 crew, a role he described to us as one of his greatest experiences. He exchanged information with Armstrong, Aldrin, and Collins and said "Roger" a lot. As Armstrong flew the lunar module over boulders and craters to find a spot to land, alarms warned that the computer wasn't keeping up with all its tasks. The fuel was running low, too, leaving them in danger of crashing into the surface of the Moon. Duke said, "Sixty seconds." One minute of fuel, then he'd have to call an abort. Then, "Thirty seconds." Before Duke could make the dreaded abort call, Armstrong confirmed contact with the Moon's surface.

Duke's other great experience, as he told us, came in 1972. Less than three years after that first Moon landing, Duke got his own chance to serve as the lunar module pilot. The commander of Apollo 16 was John Young, who'd already flown two Gemini missions and one Apollo mission and who'd go on to command the first space shuttle flight. Of the Apollo 16 launch, Duke recalled, in the film *In the Shadow of the Moon*, "I found out from the Flight Surgeon later on that my heartbeat was 144 at liftoff. John's was seventy." As Anna and I talked with Duke in 2010, that first time we met him, he still conveyed that exuberance.

My own heartbeat that day undoubtedly exceeded Duke's at liftoff. I'm amazed that my heart didn't burst. That Anna and I were there together in that moment mattered, and I realized that any jealousy I'd felt over her media badge was unwarranted. Magic takes work, and magic works in strange ways.

Of his Moon landing, Duke told us in 2012, "I was tenth man on the Moon, on Apollo 16. [...] We were six hours late landing so we went from massive disappointment that we weren't going to land to exuberant exhilaration when we did get to land. And it was a great three days." Duke and Young ate breakfast in the lunar module, gathered more than two hundred pounds of rocks and soil during EVAs, and drove the rover from crater to, in Duke's word, "spectacular" crater. There they were, up on the Moon, when I was five years old; there they were, two people on that bright orb in my night sky. And now here was one of them right in front of my eyes, talking with me as if we'd actually known each other all that time.

Duke, the youngest man to stand on the Moon, left a military medal and a signed photograph of his family on the lunar surface. When Anna asked Duke, two years after we first met him at that Astronaut Scholarship Foundation event, whether he'd like to go to the Moon again, he smiled and replied, "I was ready to go when I got back."

During that first interview with him, Duke was very supportive of NASA in general and, in particular, of NASA's efforts to encourage the study of STEM fields. That made sense to Anna and me because we're educators. "Every time I speak to young kids, I try to get them motivated to study the hard courses and do their best," he told us. "We're trying to do our part to help these kids stay in school and to develop into some of the leading scientists that we're going to need in the next generation." As someone who'd left Earth and looked back from the Moon to see our planet in its place in the universe, Duke couldn't help but believe we must use the knowledge and skills we've accumulated or, as a culture, lose them.

NASA must like guys like Duke; he was an especially upbeat spokesperson for the space agency. Even as the Shuttle program was folding around us, he looked to the future. If there's too long a lag between manned programs, we'll need to re-learn and re-invent to get people off the ground. Duke knew this, and so did I.

In his book *Space Chronicles*, physicist Neil deGrasse Tyson pushes this idea about the relationship between spaceflight, education, and our nation's future further:

> If you double NASA's budget, whole legions of students will fill the pipeline. Even if they don't become aerospace engineers, we will have scientifically literate people coming up through the ranks—people who might invent stuff and create the foundations of tomorrow's economy. [...] We want the best biologists in the world. If there's chemical warfare, we want the best chemists. And we would have them, because they'd be working on problems relating to Mars, problems relating to Europa. We would have attracted those people because the vision was in place.

Kids follow Buck Rogers; astronauts are cool. Spaceflight is shiny; the glow of Mars attracts attention. The bucks follow Buck Rogers, too. If we want kids of today to be scientists, engineers, and astronauts of tomorrow, working on all variety of complex problems we face, we need manned spaceflight. Not every kid who wants to go to Mars will become an astronaut. I know that from my own experience, planning to become an astronaut and ending up a scientist, a librarian, and a writer. The idea—the saying *yes-and*—of going to Mars will excite kids to study science and engineering, just as Apollo excited me and Mike Coats, the shuttle astronaut Anna interviewed. Then, serendipity—which seems like magic in the moment and luck or fate in hindsight—will inevitably lead to new possibilities.

At the end of our interview with Charlie—I didn't call him that, but I wanted to—I asked him which had been his favorite aircraft.

He said, "It depended on what we were doing." He talked about the F-102 as a "great, stable" plane that "would go supersonic barely." At the very thought of speed, of breaking the sound barrier—once the sole privilege of test pilots like Duke—his eyes twinkled. Duke reverted to habits understood by test and fighter pilots the world over, demonstrating with his hands an airborne climb to highlight how much fun the F-104 Starfighters out at Edwards Air Force Base had been to fly in zoom maneuvers. When he spoke about his thirty-minute flights in the F-104, his excitement, like that of a gleeful child, overwhelmed his ability to form sentences: "It was really fantastic. That was probably the most fun missions I flew as a pilot." The way he said *zoom* still echoes in my ears

As we wrapped up our first conversation with Charlie Duke and thanked him, he shook my hand and wished me, "All the best." *All the best,* from the best. He was Buck Rogers, if Buck Rogers were your favorite uncle, remembering the good old days and encouraging you to make a great future for yourself.

Walt Cunningham, on the other hand, didn't couch his opinions in pleasantries. He liked to have his say and had plenty to say to me. No wonder they stuck him in the corner of this autograph show.

Cunningham's mission in 1968 was an orbital flight to test systems for the planned lunar landing; it didn't get more than a couple hundred miles away from the surface of Earth. That Apollo 7 crew—Walter Schirra, Donn Eisele, and Cunningham—were the first to use the space pen, a version of which I used to jot notes, having purchased it at the gift shop at the Visitor Complex when Anna left me there to traipse off in her journalist role. On their eleven-day mission, the first mission since the Apollo 1 accident that killed all three crew in a capsule fire on the ground, the Apollo 7 astronauts endured Schirra's head cold, which he passed on to Eisele, and testy relations with Mission Control that included complaints about the food. None of the three men went to space again, and they didn't receive the Distinguished Service Medal from NASA until 2008, years after Shuttle astronauts had started receiving it and when Cunningham was the only one of the Apollo 7 crew still alive. When we wrote about Apollo 7 on our blog, we sent Cunningham a quick email about the post. Much to our surprise, a few days later we received a response: we'd gotten all the facts in our post right.

Cunningham wanted to talk to us; he had a message. Seventy-eight years old when we interviewed him, Cunningham exuded passion for the sort of space travel that accomplished something meaningful. He was very convincing. Cunningham, harkening to the past to point to the future, wanted "people out doing things that have never been done before, not even dreamed of" instead of falling into a "risk-averse" malaise that had subdued the country. "I currently do not see NASA doing much that's inspiring." *Ouch!*

Cunningham told us that there was no reason to return to the Moon, dismissed it with a been-there-done-that wave of hand. As far as he was concerned, his generation solved those problems and answered those questions—how to subdue gravity, how to live off-planet for a couple of weeks—with Mercury, Gemini, and Apollo. I had to agree; he emboldened my thinking. He expected more from those after him; he didn't think my generation was doing enough with what his generation had accomplished. With piercing, clear eyes and a forceful voice, Cunningham said that he wanted the country to say *yes* to a Mars mission. "It ought to have timelines," he said, "very aggressive but not impossible timelines. And we need to have some kind of commitment to spend the money to do it." *Yes-and,* I thought.

Definitely Buck Rogers, if Buck Rogers were a bit gruff and worried that time and money were running short. He talked as if he was ready to go to Mars himself. Right then, just strap him to a rocket. *Me, too,* I thought. *Let's go.*

CHAPTER 9
CAST OF CHARACTERS
DOUG

> [Y]ou can't connect the dots looking forward; you can only
> connect them looking backwards. So you have to trust that
> the dots will somehow connect in your future. You have to
> trust in something.

> —Steve Jobs, commencement address at Stanford University

Shuttle, the idea, is a product of people as much as it is a machine:
the people who designed it, flew it, cared for it, and even those of us
who admired it from Earth's surface. The astronauts of Apollo, like
Charlie Duke, filled the daydreams of my childhood with an imagined
life in space, but it was the next generation, the astronauts of the
space shuttle program, coming as it did during my teenage years, that
influenced the decisions I made, the planning for college and life as an
astronaut.

As Anna and I looked around the many tables of Astronaut
Autograph and Memorabilia Show in 2010, it was obvious that even
the scaled-back actual launch schedule for Shuttle (NASA's initial
program called for six hundred flights over twelve years) meant a lot
of astronauts: 355 astronauts in 852 crew spots, according to NASA, for
more than twenty-one thousand orbits over three decades. The nation
knew the names of the Mercury Seven, and the media could focus on
individual men, even though, or perhaps because, they collectively spent
less than fifty-four hours in space over two years. The Apollo program
employed thirty-one astronauts, a dozen of whom were the only
humans to have ever walked on the Moon. Several Apollo astronauts

became household names. But NASA didn't want Shuttle to be the story of individual characters or rarified accomplishments.

Anna and I debated quietly which of the Shuttle astronauts to interview first, and we admitted to each other that we didn't know many of their names. We glanced from table to table, eyeing astronauts in conversation with enthusiasts and eyeing photographs on large placards in an attempt to recognize any of them. These people—many of them PhDs or MDs from America's finest universities, others nervy military test pilots like astronauts of yore—could have been mistaken for our university colleagues or the pilots who'd flown us across the country. Hoot Gibson had indeed flown for Southwest after flying Shuttle five times.

Shuttle astronauts seemed the character actors to Apollo's leading men.

Eleven shuttle missions occurred while I was in high school and three more during my first semester of college (1981-1984). With each mission, Shuttle opened space travel to more kinds of people. That didn't start right away. The STS-1 crew consisted of two white men who had been born in the 1930s and had served in the Navy: John Young and Bob Crippen. By STS-5 in November 1982, though, the crew included two mission specialists—Joseph Allen and William Lenoir—and the program was overtly thinking more broadly about who was best suited to do what in this long-term effort.

On June 18, 1983, Sally Ride became the first American woman in space and, at thirty-two years old for STS-7, remains the youngest American to have flown to space. She was born in California (a typical place for astronauts to grow up) in 1951 and earned her PhD in physics from Stanford University. She joined NASA in 1978, after responding to their ad for astronauts in a new program; that was the first time NASA accepted applications from women. She was one of six women chosen for the astronaut corps that year.

Thirteen women had participated in an unofficial First Lady Astronaut Training program, a privately funded test project alongside Mercury in the early 1960s. Right round the time Alan Shepard took his and America's first spaceflight, thirteen-year-old Hillary Rodham (who would become Clinton) wrote to NASA to ask about becoming an astronaut. NASA replied that women couldn't be astronauts, and young Hillary was "crestfallen" but picked herself up and pursued other challenges. NASA put a stop to the testing of women as possible astronauts after the project's early phases.

Though two Soviet women beat her to space, Ride paved the way for many more women in the Shuttle program. Dozens of women have since traveled to space, including the first Chinese woman in 2012, in the long-emerging Shenzhou program. Anna never really considered becoming an astronaut, as I had, even though she has always been interested in science and medicine. I often think about how different the obvious choices and well-worn career paths can look for elementary schoolchildren, in the 1970s but also now. I easily imagined myself flipping switches in a space capsule on my way to Mars, and seeing Ride aboard a shuttle made it easier for girls like Anna to see themselves that way too. Women make up half of NASA's latest astronaut class. May some of the young girls in pink princess dresses today don blue flight suits in a couple of decades.

Also in 1983, on STS-8, Guion Bluford became the first African-American to fly in space. He earned his PhD in aerospace engineering from the Air Force Institute of Technology and flew on four missions. Bluford paved the way for thirteen more African-Americans to fly on the shuttle. The Civil Rights and Women's Rights movements of my childhood had tangible results that I sometimes take for granted now.

In August 1984, on STS-41D, Shuttle opened its flights to NASA outsiders connected to the mission's payload, in this case a McDonnell Douglas employee named Charles Walker. He and the company shared the patent for a method of protein separation, so he accompanied the equipment into space. Payload specialists remained regulars on crews until after the *Columbia* accident in 2003, when NASA stopped risking civilian lives in this way.

There existed many more varieties of Shuttle astronaut: natives of Belgium, Italy, and Japan; members of Congress; married couples, including Mark Lee and N. Jan Davis, who flew together on STS-47; twin brothers, though the Kelly boys missed meeting up in orbit; and so on. Some quibbled with this widening of what it meant to be an astronaut. Did Representative Bill Nelson get a seat merely because the Space Coast was in his district and he planned to run for Senate at the next opportunity? Was it a carnivalesque publicity stunt to send John Glenn back to space at an age when most of us hope to be sitting in our easy chair in the living room, tussling the hair of a grandchild?

I am awed by the whole of these firsts—the kinds of people these firsts represent—and the range of people in the astronaut corps. This inclusivity makes important statements about Shuttle in particular and about Generation Space in general; both are reflective of the demographically diverse reality in which Anna and I grew up. Still lacking is the first openly gay astronaut, though Ride's longtime partnership with Tam O'Shaughnessy is now acknowledged even in her official NASA biography, an indication of changes in NASA's military-influenced culture. Anna and I grew up during a time when notions of the limitations of gender, race, and nationality changed. It would be naïve to assume that prejudice has disappeared from this world, but collaboration, inclusion, and shared achievements are powerful tools against ignorance.

In addition, the program drew resources and talent from across the nation: orbiters came from California, SRBs came from Utah, external tanks were made in Louisiana, launches occurred in Florida, and missions were run from Texas. Those are only the big pieces, with contractors spread even more widely for its two-and-a-half million parts. The shuttle belonged everywhere and to everyone and, therefore, because of the way public relations and perceptions work, also belonged nowhere and to no one in particular.

For nearly twenty years, Anna and I had been working everywhere, but not really living anywhere. Then, we moved to California, saw the shuttle in the desert, got married, and focused on Shuttle. In my mind, these events are interdependent.

This temporarily inchoate existence, this relative scatterdness—for both us as a couple and for NASA—makes for great gains and an odd cost. As Shuttle developed and evolved without a Buck Rogers, NASA struggled to maintain public interest and Congressional support. Shuttle astronauts aren't exactly a dime a dozen, but NASA's efficiency model for the space shuttle downplayed their importance, especially as individuals. As a result, I recognized and followed Buzz Aldrin when he emerged from the restroom at KSC that day, but not these others who'd flown what NASA had once promoted as a space truck. How did they, these run-of-the-mill-looking people at the autograph show, become astronauts? What did this slew of astronauts actually accomplish? Here I stood among them in 2010. I was going to find out.

Eventually, we decided to speak with shuttle astronaut Hank Hartsfield because of his involvement with one of the more peculiar manned space programs in American history, the Manned Orbiting Laboratory. Hartsfield was an old-timer, born in 1933, which should have made him an Apollo astronaut. Instead, he'd chosen a slightly different path, and it had almost cost him his chance to become an astronaut.

When I mentioned my interest in the Manned Orbiting Laboratory program, the astronaut's eyes lit up, but he didn't want to say much about the super-secret, space-based spy program called MOL. Hartsfield was soft spoken and, even if he seemed a bit leery of our video camera, his round face looked like that of an elf ready for mischief more than an almost-astronaut-spy sworn to secrecy.

MOL was a spy-in-the-sky program run by the US Air Force in 1966, at the time NASA was flying the Gemini program and revving up for Apollo and I was making my way into this world. MOL planned for forty-day reconnaissance missions using Gemini spacecraft, but it never got off the ground, canceled in 1969. By then, unmanned spy satellites were effective and cheaper than astronaut spies. Hartsfield had chosen his career path, and then that path disappeared. NASA extended an offer to those MOL astronauts under the age of thirty-five to transfer to its corps. Only seven of the fourteen MOL astronauts met the requirement. Hartsfield one was of them. Hartsfield sat around in support roles during the end of Apollo and Skylab. Not that such roles aren't crucial, but Hartsfield, for many years, was an astronaut who stayed on the ground. Had the shuttle not come along, he would never have gone to space. Lucky accident. The dots connected.

Hartsfield's first mission was on *Columbia* in 1982. STS-4 was the last Shuttle flight with a crew of just two and the last with a designated back-up crew, as if, after that, it had been tested enough and deemed ready for regular service. *Columbia*, in Shuttle's signature combination of military and science goals, carried science experiments from college students and top-secret Air Force missile detection sensors that ended up not working. Hartsfield also flew STS-41D on *Discovery* with Mike Coats, who was Anna's first astronaut interview a few days before we met Hartsfield. During that mission, Hartsfield used the shuttle's robotic arm to remove an icicle of urine that had formed on the outside of the orbiter when the waste system became obstructed. Buck Rogers, the space plumber? Hartsfield ended his Shuttle career with STS-61A, using Spacelab—a reusable science laboratory loaded into the cargo bay—aboard *Challenger* in 1985, the year before that orbiter's fatal accident.

When I asked about the relationship between NASA and educating the next generation, Hartsfield replied that NASA should play "a big role." He explained, "We need to get the right kind of science people into orbit to solve the kind of problems that are better solved in microgravity." But then he paused. Without much expression, he added, "I'm worried now where we are as a nation." NASA's diminished role in national policy and the current state of funding for NASA concerned him, just as it did Walt Cunningham. What astronaut wouldn't be worried by the end of US manned spaceflight, with no replacement spacecraft or clear future goal established? I was worried too.

Next, Anna and I walked up to Kathy Thornton, crew member for the first and crucial Hubble telescope repair mission. The mission corrected Hubble's optics—specifically, the flawed mirror—by giving the telescope corrective lenses. The sharpness of the images improved dramatically and turned Hubble from a failure to one of the most amazing scientific instruments in history, one that showed us parts of the universe we'd never before seen.

In 1993, when Thornton was aboard *Endeavor* on STS-61, I was working as an abstractor-indexer—I read and interpreted scientific articles and reports—at NASA, and Anna would joke that I helped save Hubble. Thornton also performed an EVA to replace bent and wobbly solar arrays that made it difficult for Hubble to point precisely. I wish I'd had a hand in Hubble. She'd had her hands on Hubble.

The official NASA photo on the placard above Thornton's head showed what looked to be a schoolgirl in a white EVA spacesuit, sporting the feathered, shoulder-length haircut that Anna claimed to have had in seventh grade. Now, Thornton looked like any other suburban resident.

Thornton told us, "I kind of did it all backwards. I had no idea I would go into the space program." She earned a PhD in physics without knowing where that would take her. I heard what she was saying, but a PhD in physics set a direction that wasn't at all backwards for being an astronaut. Two-stepping Aldrin, after all, earned a PhD from MIT; his was in astronautical engineering, but physics is a STEM field too. Maybe Thornton didn't plan ahead, but her path, which included millions of miles in orbit, didn't look backwards to me. No, the path looked like dots lining up with a clear trajectory.

Fred Gregory sits on the gregarious end of my astronaut personality spectrum. A three-time shuttle veteran, he'd also served as an Air Force and NASA test pilot. But he called becoming an astronaut "a quirk" and "a nice thing to do." Gregory was jovial and talked with us as if he were making new pals. His hair was thin on top, but not much thinner than during his years as a shuttle crew member from 1985 to 1991. Some other astronauts showed aging, mostly because some looked like teenagers in their photos, but Gregory still looked like the NASA photograph on his placard.

Still a kid at heart, Gregory, who was one of two African-Americans in the 1978 astronaut class (Guion Bluford beat Gregory as the first African-American into space), had a model of the shuttle on his table and liked to explain how it worked. His bachelors and masters degrees were in science and information systems respectively, and he talked like an engineer, jazzed about forces and functions. But he was an advocate of the liberal arts, with an undergraduate minor in English: "I wondered why I had taken those liberal arts courses, until I entered the world, and the world was not loaded with engineers. I had to talk to people, and I had to understand economics, I had to understand history, and so I found that a mixed education was really a benefit that prepared me for what I was to encounter in the future." I glanced at Anna; her smile made it clear that's what she wanted to hear, that she was warming up to Shuttle astronauts and picking favorites.

Months later, STS-133 astronaut Michael Barratt (Anna's favorite of that crew) reiterated Gregory's stance, telling us, "You could characterize astronauts as people who have very broad interests." Being a military pilot like Hartsfield or Gregory or having a science PhD like Thornton did not, in and of itself, set a person on the path to astronaut. There was something more to astronauts. Look online at the *Life* magazine spread "Up Close with Apollo 11," and you'll see Michael Collins, the man who orbited the Moon by himself while Armstrong and Aldrin walked on it, painting in one photo and reading on the beach in another, with a stack of books propping up his head. "[E]ncouragement does not necessarily lead to creativity," Steven Johnson writes in *Where Good Ideas Come From*. "Collisions do—the collisions that happen when different fields of expertise converge in some shared physical or intellectual space." Many of the astronauts we met were full of quirks, and their lives were full of varied interests and intellectual collisions.

These astronauts were bookworms, puzzle solvers, quick learners. A curious lot, in both senses of *curious:* interested in many things and a bunch of oddballs. That went a long way to explain why I liked them. I couldn't help but think I could have fit in among them.

Gregory was so engaging that we talked for a while after the formal interview. He asked where our university was located and revealed that he'd visited Orange, California, as a Boy Scout, taking the train all the way from his hometown of Washington, D.C., to attend an enormous yearly jamboree. He'd ridden horseback through the hills overlooking our neighborhood, probably around the time the house we were in the midst of purchasing was built. He added, with a touch of sadness-tinged laughter, that he imagined the area had changed a bit in intervening years. "Yes," I said; everyone knew of recent decades of urban sprawl in Southern California. All three of Gregory's missions ended at Edwards Air Force Base in California, and I imagined he'd head from the runway to Domingo's for good Mexican food and hearty laughs with his crewmates.

Hoot Gibson, a tall man in a sports jacket, was another enthusiastic astronaut. As Gibson talked, the downslope of his mustache and ever-so-slight smile made him look sad and happy at the same time, which seemed appropriate with *Discovery* waiting on the launch pad for its last mission.

He claimed, "I had a little different story than many of the astronauts." But his story of how he ended up going to space was what I could have guessed. When astronauts look around at each other, they obviously see differences and distinctions. When I compared their paths to becoming an astronaut, I saw many versions of the same story. And I wondered whether a version of that story had ever really been possible for me.

Perhaps his story had a small twist. "I wanted to be an aeronautical engineer and a test pilot from the time I was ten years old or so because that's what my dad was," he said. "Part of it was I was crazy about airplanes. And the other part of it was I was pretty good at math. But the other part was hero worship of Dad." Instead of worshipping the first astronauts as a youngster, as Mike Coats did, Gibson wanted to follow in his own father's footsteps. These men looked to the generation who'd come before—examples of lives they thought worth living—to create their own destinies and to create the future in which we now lived. I'd done the same thing with my engineer father, a dot at the beginning of my past.

Gibson explained that, in about 1974, when he was in his late twenties, "I saw an artist's concept in *Aviation Week* magazine of a space shuttle. And I looked at that, and I said, *Oh man, I have got to get me one of those.*" Gibson rolled his eyes and swung his head for emphasis. I recalled scouring magazines for cool spacecraft myself. "Luck of the draw, just all kinds of great luck every step of the way—I got selected in the very first space shuttle class and got to fly as copilot on the tenth launch." Gibson credited the right-time-right-place, saying, "I've been a very lucky boy in my life." *Luck,* that's what Dee O'Hara had claimed, too. *Serendipity,* I thought. Connecting the dots, wherever they might be positioned next and in the future.

An artist's concept of a space shuttle caught Gibson's imagination and stuck there. His interests primed him to see meaning: an image of a spaceship with wings suddenly became his goal, and the arc of his career began. Gibson looked backward, saw causes and effects, and connected the dots of his life. But there was a lot going on that created momentum, that made the next dot—the next note in the melody of his life—shine as a goal in the future

I, too, began to see my own life in similar terms: I've long described myself in job interviews as an *opportunistic learner*, someone willing to take on unfamiliar challenges to add new skills. I also began to see the adventure on which Anna and I had embarked as an investigation of the connections between our individual lives and a larger cultural history. Seeing a shuttle launch had become a shiny goal for me, a dot that created hindsight and momentum.

Gibson might well have flown me across the country on Southwest Airlines during the five long-distance years of my romance with Anna, and he'd also flown on four of the five operational orbiters, missing out only on *Discovery*, the one that still sat on the launch pad as I spoke with him.

STS-41B was the first mission for Gibson and also for Ronald McNair. McNair was assigned to fly on *Challenger* again for his second flight and died when that orbiter exploded seventy-three seconds after launch in 1986. Gibson participated in the investigation, along with the likes of Moon walker Neil Armstrong, physicist Richard Feynman, and first American woman in space Sally Ride. We learned, months after our interview with Gibson, during a serendipitous dinner party with Allan McDonald, the Director of the Solid Rocket Motor Program at the time of the *Challenger* accident, that Gibson was bent on redesigning the SRBs and was dedicated to making the shuttle better at a time when many others shied away.

On his third mission, STS-27 in 1988, Gibson saw damage to the thermal tiles after foam insulation had broken off one of the two SRBs and hit the outside of *Atlantis*'s right side. During the mission, Gibson worried that the orbiter would burn up on re-entry, that he and his crew would die. This scenario, of course, is what happened to *Columbia* in 2003, fifteen years later. Gibson helped with that investigation, too.

Gibson was a hub in the network of dots and astronauts that comprise the Shuttle program, with ties to both fatal accidents and to the expanding network of astronauts. He is six-degrees-of-Kevin-Bacon for Shuttle. He flew with Charlie Bolden, who's now NASA Administrator, and with the first African-American woman in space, Mae Jemison, on his fourth mission. Though we didn't know it yet, we would see both of them and talk with another of Gibson's crewmates, Mark Lee, during future visits to the Space Coast. Gibson's last mission, on *Atlantis* in 1995, marked the first time the shuttle docked with a Russian space station. The shuttle carried two Russians and American Norm Thagard to Mir, and someday we'd meet Thagard, too. As large as the astronaut corps had become during the Shuttle era, it was still a tightly connected community, each individual with his or her own perspective, in the larger, shared story.

Growing up, even though I was too young to be one of Hoot Gibson's crewmates, I'd wanted to be part of that network of astronauts. Instead, I became someone else.

CHAPTER 10
TRUST
DOUG

Destitutus ventis, remos adhibe.

If the wind will not serve, take to the oars.

—Latin proverb

In 1983, when I was in high school, my history teacher revealed at the beginning of that school year that he had taught one of the astronauts who'd launched aboard *Challenger*. Dale Gardner had gone to space for the first time on his thirty-fifth birthday for a six-day mission, the first to launch and land at night. Gardner had gone to college at the University of Illinois at Urbana–Champaign on a Navy R.O.T.C. scholarship, then onto a career as a Naval Flight Officer and an astronaut. I planned to follow that same path, all the way to astronaut.

In the fall of 1984, I started what I thought would be the same journey. I'd secured a Navy R.O.T.C. scholarship and been admitted to the University of Illinois to study Aerospace Engineering. But in the spring of 1985, while on a Navy R.O.T.C. spring break trip to Pensacola Naval Air Station, a US Navy physician informed me that I'd never become a jet pilot. I couldn't properly perform the Vasalva maneuver, a technique of forced exhalation with closed mouth and nose that most people can use to pop their ears. The physician never mentioned that such inability might be caused by a head cold, only that it would jeopardize my chance of flying jets.

The spring break trip was meant to be a mini-introduction, perhaps indoctrination, to the rigors of Naval flight training. Other midshipmen—the traditional name for student officer cadets in R.O.T.C. or attending the Naval Academy—on the trip suffered their own setbacks: a broken ankle on the obstacle course, failure to complete the swim test, and even the humiliation of vomiting from airsickness (or possibly a hangover) during one of the acclimation flights in a T-34C training aircraft. I'd been prevented from taking the T-34C joyride because of my inability to pop my ears.

All midshipmen interested in becoming pilots knew that the competition for coveted flight slots was intense, brutal even. Those of us who'd suffered some sort of calamity left Pensacola convinced that a permanent black mark marred our military service files. Whether that was true or not, such shared narratives have a powerful effect on the way we see ourselves as we grow up.

Less than a year after that spring break trip, during the first week of the spring semester, I started to see more warning signs that the dots were not connecting to the future I'd planned. I was having little success staying engaged with my classes. I'd been part of a minor R.O.T.C. disciplinary action in the previous semester for wearing an earing to a campus Halloween party. I was coming to terms with what that Navy physician had told me, making sense of the unexpected, replacing the next step I'd sought.

I quit Navy R.O.T.C. Did that mean an end to my dream of becoming an astronaut? Of course not. But I'd definitely made the project more difficult, and it wouldn't be attainable by following the only path I had mapped out.

Days later, on a Tuesday, a friend approached as I walked to the cafeteria. "Can you believe it about the space shuttle?" he said, as if I already knew. *Challenger* had broken apart. I made my way to a television. The shuttle had failed catastrophically, and the space program itself was in jeopardy. In that moment, I thought grimly that perhaps it wasn't just me who wouldn't become an astronaut. Maybe there wouldn't be any space program for astronauts to fly.

Within weeks, my high school girlfriend dumped me for my high school best friend. The life I had mapped for myself burst open when I was nineteen years old, coming apart over the course of a few weeks. Disoriented, I felt as if everything were up for grabs and the terrain had become unfamiliar. It would take me a while to process what had happened. In the fall of 1988, I left the University of Illinois and transferred to Knox College, where my brother was in school. I needed a new beginning.

At a Valentine's Day party later that school year, from across a crowded room, the floor sticky under my feet, dance music swirling in the smoky air, I saw a woman and asked who she was. The sister of a friend, Anna was visiting, having graduated from Knox the year before. She was holding court with three of the guys I most admired. My friends seemed to hang on her every word. Their body language suggested that she was one of the guys, someone they felt comfortable around, someone they respected.

To say that I was intrigued doesn't capture the moment. I was still making my way into Knox and it's various subcultures, and I'd landed in a much artier, more Bohemian existence than the engineering entourage that had previously surrounded me. Anna didn't notice me that night at the party, but we met by happenstance the next day. By that time, I'd already found out that she was a poet and a graduate student at Iowa State. Before she left, we walked across campus together. She tells me that she fell in love with me at first sight then. I don't remember the specifics of what we talked about, but I remember clearly her long wet hair, the jean jacket covered in hand-painted art, and her effortless smile and easy laugh whenever I tried to be funny.

While Anna and I conversed with Hoot Gibson, he half-heartedly remarked that he and his wife brought their whole family to the Cape for what Anna and I had come to call the not-launch. His wife sat at the next table. So we took a couple of steps and introduced ourselves to three-time shuttle astronaut and physician Rhea Seddon, whose given first name is actually Margaret. Anna mispronounced her name, said "Ree-ah" instead of "Ray." Astronauts expected only cursory knowledge of space exploration from reporters, and this marked the first time we'd lived *down* to their expectations. Though Anna hated to make even such a small mistake—we had worked hard to become experts—Seddon didn't roll her eyes when she corrected us. Despite our lifelong interest and how much we'd prepared for this adventure, we were not insiders or experts; thousands of Shuttle workers knew hundreds of times what we'd learned about orbiters, and we didn't hang out with astronauts day to day. Our perspective was that of Generation Space, of inching closer to something that mattered to us but that we might never fully understand.

Seddon sported the same bright smile and blonde haircut that's in her placard photo, but, in that photograph, she floated weightless, hand poised on hip. The image echoed a *Seventeen* magazine cover. In that transitional cultural moment of the 1970s, when I was in high school, pin-up girl had somehow melded with astronaut. Culture had some work to do, and Shuttle was doing some cultural work.

Seddon told us about her path to the space program. "I had gotten interested in spaceflight when I was young and watched all the space missions go and thought it would be interesting to do that. But they didn't take women. And they didn't take non-pilots." By the time she was wrapping up her medical residency, though, NASA was ready to accept women and science-educated non-pilots into the astronaut corps. Seddon and Hillary Clinton are the same age, born within a couple of weeks of each other; Seddon held out for astronaut, and Clinton moved on.

"I had the right credentials," she said. "I just happened to apply." *Really? Just happened to apply?* Her path didn't sound like sheer luck as much as the product of connecting dots relatively conscientiously, mapping points into a particular life—though perhaps we all do that in hindsight, make sense of what got us to where we are. Maybe we can *only* do that in hindsight. In the years since, talking with Anna about her choices has convinced me that, just as many astronauts with whom I spoke said they *happened* to apply, Anna *happened* not to apply to the astronaut corps. Though she might have made a good astronaut if she'd stuck with chemistry instead of creative writing, Anna hadn't mapped out a course as I had, so, while she may have sometimes felt disoriented, she hadn't struggled with the sense of being off-course.

All three of Seddon's missions involved extensive study of the crew's physical responses during and after the flights. STS-58 in 1993 was devoted to life sciences research and involved looking at sensory perception changes in space, including the vestibular (inner ear) fluctuations associated with motion sickness, as well as cardiovascular (heart), musculoskeletal (muscle and bone), and metabolic (food and energy) function. The crew collected their own saliva, blood, and urine and also studied the forty-eight rats on board. So both NASA and Seddon got what they wanted out of the seeming happenstance of her astronaut service.

Had Gibson and Seddon fallen in love at first sight, as Anna and I had? They married three years later.

Seddon went on, revealing her pragmatic outlook. "I was very interested in what happened to the human body and living things when they went into space." She was a curious person, generally, and found NASA to be the specific way to tap that curiosity. Anna and I have found other ways to tap our voracious curiosity. And those choices led us to each other as well.

In Anna's interview with Mike Coats, she'd asked her Colbert-esque question: *Discovery*, great shuttle or the greatest shuttle? Anna wanted to ask that question of all the Shuttle astronauts, but I didn't want to seem glib. I wanted the astronauts to consider me smart and take me seriously. We compromised—as all couples must, from time to time—on a new version: Which is your favorite orbiter, and why? Anna wanted to get them to admit they had favorites, as she did—that inexplicable emotion is only human.

Kathy Thornton flew on three different orbiters, including *Endeavour*'s first mission. She scoffed. "There's no favorites. It's like, *which is your favorite child?*" Thornton elaborated on her analogy between orbiters and one's own children, indicating that picking favorites was bad form: "[O]rbiters are much more identical than children are. It's hard to know which one you're in when you're in it." That's the sort of thing Mike Coats said, too, *after* he admitted that *Discovery* was his favorite. Several astronauts pointed out the similarity among orbiters and, like good parents, hesitated to admit they liked one more than the others. Just as no Shuttle astronaut announced him- or herself as Buck Rogers, no orbiter was supposed to stand out as the greatest.

But not all astronauts resisted their hearts' leanings. When we asked Hank Hartsfield whether he had a favorite shuttle, he responded straightforwardly, "Yes, I did. It was *Discovery*. That was my first command, the first flight of *Discovery*. I thought it was a great vehicle." He smiled a sweet, wry smile—the first evidence of his warming up to us—and added, "I was hoping to see it fly again today, but it didn't."

Fred Gregory didn't miss a beat either, replying matter-of-factly and with a broad smile even before we finished asking the question, "*Discovery.*" His second shuttle mission, STS-33 on *Discovery,* was his first command and Gregory was the first-ever African-American commander. "Because it was my favorite crew," he burst forth and laughed, clearly remembering particular interactions. But he didn't elaborate on hijinks in the heavens among his crew, which included the more serious Thornton, on their classified Department of Defense mission. Sometimes crewmembers clicked, and when that happened, the orbiter on which they had flown together would naturally become their favorite. We're all nostalgic about the places where we had good times. Anna and I reminisce regularly, even though we are glad to be where we are.

It was tempting for *Discovery* to be our favorite, too, if only because we'd seen it in person and spent time with it here. But *Endeavour* in the desert two years ago set us on this sojourn. Did we ask this question of astronauts because Anna and I wanted permission for *Endeavour* to be our favorite, the object of our greatest affection? Anna especially is prone to wanting favorites, choosing affections or loyalties. Maybe that's why she stuck with me.

Hoot Gibson capitulated in response to our question, rolling his eyes back as if rifling through memories before coming up with what he called "a mixed answer." Eventually, after rattling off the names of the four orbiters he flew and lamenting that he'd flown *Atlantis* a second time instead of flying *Discovery,* he admitted, "I guess I want to say *Columbia* was my favorite for several reasons. One of them [is that it] was the first orbiter that I commanded, on my second mission. It was the flagship, first one to go to space." When reflecting on *Columbia,* Gibson added, as others did, in one way or another, "It's sad that she is not still around. What a magnificent vehicle she was."

Not having heard her husband's answer, Seddon responded quickly, "I think *Columbia* was my favorite. I was fortunate enough to see *Columbia's* first launch, *Columbia's* last launch, and ride on *Columbia* twice to space."

No one orbiter was better than another in a technological or aesthetic sense, but *Columbia* was heavier (engineers redesigned the others to lighten the load), and some astronauts said you could feel that extra heft during launch. Gibson and the rest didn't avoid talking about the 2003 tragedy but remembered *Columbia* at its height, what it accomplished, that it started it all for Shuttle. That it had been lost left a longing.

Favorites were not about objective engineering qualities, not about how smoothly one orbiter flew or how flawlessly another functioned. Our attachments to objects—our sense of their worth, their value— grow out of our experiences with them. First command, last launch, favorite crew, a month inside the thing, an object or friend lost forever.

We ended that night as we had every other night that week, with a ritual dinner and discussion at the mom-and-pop Italian restaurant adjacent to the motel. The locals shared stories about not-launch attendees, a group whose membership rolls now listed our names. One waitress teared up talking about a German man from a couple of summers earlier who saved for years and planned his American vacation around seeing a launch. He returned home after staying as long as he could, and the shuttle launched the next day. I offered my story about the Indian family we'd met earlier in the week, the father who wanted my permission to go touch the shuttle, the daughter who tried to explain the viewing tower was as close as tourists could get. They didn't see *Discovery* launch either.

Looking around the restaurant, Anna and I resembled the other couples, two lovers sharing salad, bread, and wine on a date. Were the others, with the night stars in their eyes, discussing the shuttle, reliving a day spent with astronauts? Had they talked with men who had stood on the Moon or orbited Earth? Had they ever had a conversation with someone who'd contributed to the continuously inhabited, endlessly orbiting home in space? It dawned on me that, in that few thousand feet of conference room, I had been in the midst of what may have been the highest-ever density of human beings to have visited space, dozens of them. Since that day, several of those astronauts—Scott Carpenter, Edgar Mitchell, Hank Hartsfield—have died. Godspeed to them.

The waitress suggested that, because *Discovery* knew that this was its last visit to space, its last opportunity to circle the planet from a vantage of two hundred miles above, "she was not going anywhere until she was good and ready."

Discovery launched on the afternoon of February 24, 2011. Anna watched it remotely on her laptop in California, but I didn't. As the clock ticked down, I knew it would launch without delay this time because we weren't there. I didn't want to see this launch if I couldn't see it in person. I began to wonder whether, at some point in time after the end of Shuttle, I'd be able to look back on the path of connected dots of my own life and see the one that was witnessing a launch.

CHAPTER 11
STAR SAILOR
ANNA

> The moon is backing away from us
> an inch and a half each year. That means
> if you're like me and were born
> around fifty years ago the moon
> was a full six feet closer to the earth.

—Dorianne Laux, from "Facts about the Moon"

When I look up at the Moon, I don't think about it inching away, as poet Dorianne Laux does, yet the Moon is slowly taking leave. I don't think about Norman Mailer's mistaken perception of the Moon, not so mistaken in its own time: "Lines of mountain had been pulled up and the moon's rotation had slowed. The moon staggered away into space, went out nearer to Mars, then caromed back and was captured again. [...W]hat spirit of earth and lunar forces must have been released, exchanged, and conceivably not lost forever?" Instead, I think of the Moon's two sides; the same light side always faces Earth. The Moon's phases offer a predictable reflection of the Sun's light, as Earth and Moon shift in relation to that light's path.

Laux's understanding is accurate. The Moon's gravity causes ocean tides on Earth, and the tidal bulge on Earth exerts energy that pushes the Moon into an increasingly higher orbit at a rate of about 1.5 inches per year. This gravitational relationship also slows the spin of Earth. Our days grow longer by smidges; in less than two hundred years, we've gained .002 seconds. So, fifty years ago, the Moon was indeed a bit closer, the days were shorter, and the United States was gearing up to send astronauts to its surface. When Doug and I look up at the Moon, that's what we think about: human beings having been there. At some level, *Generation Space* is our way to understand what that's meant.

One way we grappled with such meaning was through objects, the space shuttle itself and also its parts. A month before the scheduled launch date for *Endeavour* in April 2011, an artifact from NASA arrived at Doug's office. Last time—before *Discovery*'s not-launch—the boxes contained beat-up models. Now we held part of an orbiter in our hands.

When Doug first began requesting items by filling out a form on the GSAXess website late in 2009, there was a lot from which to choose, including clothing items from the days of Gemini and Apollo. Chapman University and other educational institutions didn't have much chance of getting coveted items because government-affiliated institutions, including the National Air & Space Museum, got first dibs. We were happy enough with leftovers. Doug pulled the bubble-wrapped packaging out of the shipping box to reveal a black-and-white block roughly five inches by five inches, two inches thick: a tile.

This shuttle tile was shrink-wrapped. The documentation in the box attested to the tile's authenticity and cautioned, "silica material in Shuttle tiles is *not* classified as hazardous. However, material from the silica fiber layer can cause temporary irritation of the throat and/or itching of the eyes and skin. Touching a bare tile should be avoided." The emphasis on *not* is NASA's two-step: this isn't dangerous when it's doing what it's designed for (i.e., protecting the space shuttle from the scorching heat of reentry), but if you touch it yourself, you will regret it. We left the square encased in its wrapping.

The tile was ridiculously light. The white underside was easily mistaken for polystyrene, like that of old coffee cups or childhood holiday ornaments. In reality, the silica material is lighter than polystyrene, 94 percent air by volume. The tile's black-and-white coloration made it seem as if the block had two halves. In fact, though, it was all one piece of silica, and the black part was a glass coating added to the tile to both waterproof it and enhance its heat-sink properties.

Doug noticed the sequence of numbers that had been painted onto the tile: V070-396050-020-008043. This number represented information such as: 1) the kind of tile type, out of several different surfaces that covered the shuttle; 2) the specific orbiter for which the tile was designed; and 3) the installation location on the orbiter. Doug used this number and a Boeing engineer he knew to track down its history. Ours was of the nine-pound-per-cubic-foot High Temperature Reusable Surface Insulation type. This particular tile was designed for the left Orbital Maneuvering System (OMS) pod, one of the two lumps at the base of an orbiter's horizontal stabilizer. The two OMS pods formed the shuttle's rear end and gave thrust when the crew needed that little extra boost into a safe orbit, to rendezvous, to de-orbit, and so on. Our tile was originally attached to pod #021 but never flew to space. For some reason, it was removed and replaced on July 14, 1982. This particular pod—OMS021—was initially attached to either *Challenger*, which was delivered to KSC that month, or *Columbia*, which would have been between STS-4 and STS-5 at the time, but the insider Doug had met was unable to verify which.

As we considered our impending trip to Florida to see *Endeavour* launch, holding the tile in our hands reminded us that each shuttle was made of myriad upon myriad little pieces, all fit together in a particular way. The machine's pieces symbolized the work of many individuals, each in sync to make a space shuttle mission go smoothly. The reason we were holding this tile, though, was that NASA didn't need it anymore.

The STS-134 astronauts themselves must have pondered similar thoughts, that the shuttles they'd flown would stop flying, the parts tossed into archives after they held them one last time. In fact, though STS-134—the next launch, *Endeavour's* last—was the penultimate shuttle mission, it originally had been scheduled as the grand finale. NASA had wanted to launch STS-135 on *Atlantis* all along and had been directed in October to plan for it, but specific funding for the mission from Congress —about $450 million—remained up in the air. In February, NASA said they'd fly STS-135 whether or not Congress allocated money specifically for that purpose, which Congress did in April.

That NASA announcement was so late that, in January 2011, eighty-year-old John Young, the program's first shuttle commander, was featured on the cover of *Air & Space Magazine* with Mark Kelly, the STS-134 commander, who was, at the time the issue hit the newsstands, set to be the last person to command a space shuttle mission. Because STS-135 had been in the works all along, Kelly must have known he would probably be knocked out of that last-ever spot, but I wondered how that must have felt, to be on the cover of *Air & Space* and then not last-ever after all. As we were readying ourselves to fly to Florida for *Endeavour's* launch, Kelly was part of the media frenzy, even though he was no longer the last-ever shuttle commander.

The Congress that passed the federal budget funding for NASA's last shuttle flight was one in which Kelly's wife, Gabriele Giffords, served. Their story became part of the STS-134 story because Representative Giffords was shot in the head during a public gathering with constituents at a Safeway grocery store on January 8, 2011, in her home state of Arizona. Several others died, and the shooter's motives remain unclear. It was awful. Giffords's friend and our colleague, author Tom Zoellner, in his book *A Safeway in Arizona*, writes heart-wrenchingly of the shooting and its larger cultural context. Of the media attention after the shooting, he wrote, "I knew that she would have absolutely hated the media carnival that had erupted around her, the obsessive attention to her health would have embarrassed her, and she would have tried to talk of the national interest instead." The story of Giffords's recovery was heightened by the pressing question, *Would Mark Kelly fly the penultimate shuttle mission?*

I knew astronauts took risks. It's a dangerous job. Catastrophes happen, and even when everything goes great, astronauts are exposed to more radiation than the rest of us get on Earth. Kelly discussed the dangers in his STS-121 preflight interview: "My family deals with those risks. The best I can do is talk to them about some of those risks. I'm not incredibly specific with them, especially with my kids. I want them not to be afraid that there's going to be another accident." Kelly said that in 2005, when he and Giffords were courting. The *Washington Post* quoted Representative Debbie Wasserman Shultz as saying the following about Giffords's attitude in 2008, after Kelly launched into space roughly eight months after they married: "There was definitely angst, there was obvious worry [...]. There have been two shuttles that have not come back." Everyone knew to worry about the astronaut on the launch pad, the astronaut on an untethered spacewalk, the astronaut reentering Earth's atmosphere.

But I'd rarely considered the reverse scenario: something awful might happen to an astronaut's family while he or she is unable to be there in person. In response to the shooting and to his sister-in-law's condition, Scott Kelly, Mark's twin, who was on ISS at the time, tweeted, "As I look out the window, I see a very beautiful planet that seems very inviting and peaceful. Unfortunately, it is not." That January, Scott Kelly was in the middle of a six-month stint in space. From ISS, he looked down on Earth and could not come home.

In fact, had *Discovery*'s long delays not pushed *Endeavour*'s launch date later, the twin brothers would have met up in space. Looking forward to that experience, Scott Kelly explained, "It's actually the first time that two blood relatives have ever been in space together. It's exciting." That didn't happen; delays did. Scott Kelly was on orbit, and Mark Kelly had a decision to make: would he fly in April?

For the most part, Doug and I have never been too far to get home if something terrible were to happen, though we've each experienced the exception. In college, as part of his plan to become an astronaut, Doug spent several weeks at Air Force R.O.T.C. training. The Air Force allowed no contact from home, not even when a friend of Doug's was murdered, another good friend's father was diagnosed with terminal cancer, and Doug's own grandmother was hospitalized. When I was on a study-abroad trip to the Soviet Union, my grandmother had a stroke. Without knowing this, I woke one night at the Hotel Cosmos, heart beating fast, wondering whether my family would get word to me if something terrible happened. I didn't know something had. They waited until I returned.

One astronaut to experience this sort of unexpected crisis was Dan Tani (a longtime Illinoisan like us), when he was a flight engineer on ISS in 2007 and 2008, as I was landing the job that sent Doug and me to California. Astronauts were asked before launch whether they wanted to be told while they were on a mission if something terrible happens to family. Did any astronauts opt to wait until they return to Earth for bad news, instead of knowing in real time? Did their pre-launch decisions depend on the length of the mission, their immediate circumstances, or their personalities? Doug and I have discussed this; we've said we want to know. But I'm not sure that's the right decision.

Tani's mother, a Japanese-American woman who'd been interned in Utah during World War II before Dan was born, was killed in a car-train collision. From space, he offered this statement: "Living on the space station means that I experience all aspects of life—be they joyous or tragic—while circling the Earth without a convenient way to return. Of course, I was aware of this situation before my mission and I fully accept that I will proudly complete my mission on the International Space Station and join my family when I return." That's the pact he made, and he had no choice in the moment. But he seemed deeply affected. "My mother was a complete joy. Those who knew her will know that words cannot describe her vitality, generosity, and warmth. She was my hero." After returning to Earth, Tani discussed how hard he'd worked to put other ISS crew at ease while he dealt with his grief. Grief alters a person. I knew this from my father's death less than six months after the *Challenger* accident.

Given this possibility of being "stuck at work" in space during a family crisis, as Tani put it—and the public gaze this situation draws—I seriously questioned, for the first time in my life, why a person becomes an astronaut. Though I'd finished degrees in creative writing instead of science by the time it occurred to me that I could have tried to become an astronaut, I realized what it might have meant if Doug had become an astronaut instead of a scientist-turned-librarian. When Doug was pursuing his PhD, we'd done the long-distance thing; we were in charge of our own ritual visits and could adapt as needed, and it was still hard. Work on ISS requires long stretches far from home with no way to change your mind halfway through your obligation. Had Doug been an astronaut, the distance between us would have been the vacuum of space, a nothingness through which there was no immediate way back.

So why did Mark Kelly stick with his STS-134 crew after his wife was shot, running between astronaut training and Giffords's hospital bed? NASA left his status up in the air briefly after the shooting, allowing Mark to make the decision himself. How did he know he could see the penultimate shuttle mission through, despite his own life's circumstances? And why did NASA trust that he could?

In a preflight interview in 2008, Kelly explained why he became an astronaut: "I watched the Apollo astronauts in the late 1960s, early 1970s.

I kind of remember Apollo 11 a little bit and then remember the last Apollo missions, remember seeing footage about what astronauts did in their careers before they were astronauts and then became interested at that point." The Moon landing at the beginning of Generation Space shaped what we thought the future might look like, individually and collectively. "It's not something I planned on doing my entire life growing up, but later on in my career I had the opportunity and that's the path I decided to go on." That's what we heard again and again from astronauts: the right place at the right time.

This and launch delays had me thinking about timing and about Doug. The last Shuttle astronauts were our age. Doug was thirty years old in 1996. We were in graduate school then, and his STEM degrees would have qualified him to apply. We didn't discuss the possibility, but now we've stared it in the face, stared in the face of astronauts whom he might have been. It took Mike Massimino, one of NASA's most public astronauts, four applications before he was selected to the corps. But in those same years, Doug hadn't applied at all. Doug shares certain qualities with astronauts: perseverance, attention to detail, a belief in serendipity. He chose something else; perhaps he chose me.

Mark Kelly told reporters that his wife was making quicker progress than initially expected and that she was busy, her days filled with speech therapy and physical therapy. "I started to think about STS-134, about the mission, my crew, the fact that I've been training for it for nearly a year and a half," Kelly said. "And considering a bunch of other factors, including what Gabrielle would want me to do and what her parents and her family and my family would like, I ultimately made the decision that I would like to return and command STS-134." The words "would want me to do" rung in my ears; no one had been specific about the extent of injury, and I wondered whether his wife was able at all to express her wants or fears. Would he have made a different decision if that mission were not his only opportunity, if he could have been reassigned to fly a shuttle a year later? NASA had picked Frederick Sturckow as a backup if Kelly didn't come through, and I wonder how Sturckow felt about the decision—Kelly's to go through with it, but also NASA's to leave it to Kelly. Peggy Whitson, spokesperson from the Astronaut Office at Johnson Space Center, said of Kelly, "He is a veteran shuttle commander and knows well the demands of the job. We are confident in his ability to successfully lead this mission, and I know I speak for all of NASA in saying 'welcome back'."

Doug is sure that he, too, would have followed through, as Kelly did. If Doug were recovering from illness or injury, I'm not convinced I'd risk being away. His life precarious, I'm not sure I would risk my own life in that way. I was in the hospital room when my father died; I'd almost not returned in time, and I'd have regretted it if I could have been there and wasn't there to hold his hand in his last moments. We can't be two places at once. Yet following the end of Shuttle had awakened in me both the desire and the ability to attempt things merely to prove to myself that I could accomplish those things. I might have gone to space, regardless, if it were my last opportunity. Doing the hard things. That's the attitude the Space Age has been encouraging in people all along and the one Doug and I encourage in each other.

The day after Giffords was shot, Scott Simon of NPR said, "Gabby Giffords has true grit." In early February, shortly after Kelly decided to stick with his NASA assignment, Giffords had spoken her first words since being shot; she asked for toast. Spokesperson C. J. Karamargin said of Giffords's aggressive, six-hour-per-day rehabilitation and her progress, "Don't discount the grit and determination of this particular patient." *Grit*, I kept hearing. Grit, this stick-to-it quality, was something Doug and I were learning in our own lives—something any long-term couple probably must learn—in smaller and less tragic but deeply meaningful ways.

In recent years, as part of my research into teaching creative writing, I'd read about the work of psychology professor Angela Duckworth. Drawing from William James's "The Energies of Men," she argues that there are qualities that unlock talent. In other words, talent in itself is not a harbinger of success. Talent needs to be present in combination with other characteristics to reveal itself fully. Duckworth asked, what is it that enables a person to become a world-class teacher or performer—or, I now thought, a Congressional representative or a space shuttle astronaut? Duckworth called this quality she studies *grit*, after the film *True Grit*, starring John Wayne (and remade in 2010).

In her TED Talk, Duckworth quipped that Francis Galton, meteorologist, inventor, and (unforgivably, to my mind) eugenicist, asserted that achievement depends upon talent, passion, and hard work. His half-cousin Charles Darwin, father of the theory of evolution and natural selection, replied that it was good to hear talent might play any role at all. Like Darwin, I've come to value stick-to-itiveness. While a certain amount of talent is important, and while talent and interest fuel each other, I know from experience that a sustained writing life requires spending years on a project, going back to it daily or after weeks or months. It requires grit. Doug and I each have different strengths, and twenty-seven years together has been sometimes gritty as well. Even our many months following the end of Shuttle depended on grit. Perseverance is the ongoing action that turns interest and talent into accomplishment or—I realized during my adventure with Doug—into the deepest kind of love.

Grit is why Mike Fincke immediately became my favorite among STS-134 crew. He attributed his ultimate success as an astronaut, in part, to five years of studying Latin—five years studying a dead language because the study itself was rewarding. I'd studied Latin every year in high school and for every degree language requirement since, which meant first-year Latin three more times. I liked Latin, in part because it's very organized and not subject to change; I found its patterns comforting. Fincke had achieved knowledge and skill because he wanted to do it, not for any grand purpose or specific, long-term goal at the time. Yet he posed, in hindsight, a cause-and-effect that hinged on Latin: it made learning Russian easier, and learning Russian allowed him to become qualified to fly as a left-seat flight engineer on Soyuz spacecraft and serve as commander on ISS. Though I'd traveled to the Soviet Union on a winter break study-abroad trip in 1986, I'd lasted only three days in Russian class, overwhelmed by its alphabet. Fincke speaks Japanese fluently too and was working in Japan when NASA first expressed interest in him. He'd been open to learning and possibility all his life. His decisions had accumulated over decades, as had mine, and there we were at our inevitable and surprising juncture: astronaut and poet waiting for a spaceship's last launch.

His grit runs deep. Fincke said, in a preflight interview in 2008: "I had a lot of challenges along the way but because I knew how to work hard and not give up, I was able to reach my goals." He held part-time jobs to help pay for private high school, where he earned a couple of Ds but stuck with it, then held an Air Force R.O.T.C. scholarship to pay for MIT. The oldest of nine children, he needed money and welcomed "high-tech opportunities," including the chance to pilot jets, which, later, led him to NASA. In his 2011 preflight interview, Fincke admitted that, after college and months of pilot training, "The Air Force and I agreed that I wasn't going to be God's gift to aviation [...], so I washed out of flight school [...] on my birthday." In other words, he failed. I cannot help but think of that fateful couple of weeks in Doug's college career: leaving Navy R.O.T.C., being dumped by his girlfriend, watching *Challenger* break apart on the television screen.

Someone suggested Fincke consider engineering; soon, the Air Force and he agreed he was very good at that. Had he not been a mediocre pilot, had he not studied Russian and Japanese even though it had little to do with rockets, he wouldn't have been exactly the sort of astronaut NASA wanted in 1996. Fincke summed up what I've learned myself, "You learn from your mistakes and learn how to rise above it. That gives you some really good lessons in life because nobody has the perfect, smooth life." Indeed, I've come to terms these last few years with the fact that I am a sum of my mistakes and losses as well as my achievements, that life's messiness is part of its pleasure and beauty.

Fincke admitted that he didn't think of his work as dangerous until he had children. Then, he understood why his mother had worried about him, and he considered why he accepted the risk. While he credits Apollo as initial inspiration, Skylab solidified his "calling." Fincke is the epitome of the Generation Space astronaut. Reasons he gives for being an astronaut, for accepting the inherent risk, reveal his exuberance: "We're expanding our scope as human beings, we're doing something constructive instead of destructive, and we're paving the way for future exploration, and I can't think of anything else I'd rather do." It struck me that Doug had thought of other things he could do, wanted to do. One thing leads to another, and, once he didn't see the dots ahead leading to astronaut, Doug allowed himself to see other dots, to look askew to see other connections and an unexpected future. As much as I like my job, my life could have gone other ways. But it didn't. At times in my life, I have felt stuck or as if I'm not in the best place for what I want to be and do. But I haven't felt this way since we followed the end of Shuttle.

Upon completion of STS-134, Mike Fincke, nicknamed Spanky (that must have taken grit to endure), would hold the American record for time spent in space, mostly a result of two earlier stints of six months each on ISS. (Scott Kelly would surpass the record in 2015.) Fincke shrugged when asked about that milestone before the mission. He emphasized that Russians have well exceeded the days in space he'd log. Still, Fincke considered ISS the place he "was supposed to be." That's what Doug and I had been learning all along: exactly who and where we wanted to be as adults.

Doug and I thought about why we'd reorganized our jobs and lives and were preparing to fly across the country again to try to see a shuttle launch. Though our insights were certainly not on the same scale, I thought of Darwin and the fun he had sailing on the *Beagle*, noting this and that about various species, the devoted naturalist's version of a leisure cruise. Darwin claimed that he came upon a theory by which he could understand evolution on September 28, 1838, while reading an essay, but the man's notebooks revealed he'd been working toward what became the theory of evolution for months without fully knowing it. Darwin was seemingly exactly where he was supposed to be all along, wherever he went and whatever he was doing, to get where he ended up, even if the ending was a surprise or a beginning.

Doug and I had been together a long time, and eventually my mother had run out of room on the page for me in her address book. Doug and I had never stayed put. In the summer of 2010, we decided to follow Shuttle's end, an adventure that was a lifetime—a generation—in the making. We had moved to California to jump into an unknown future, and we'd begun to accept that we were also where we were supposed to be, that we could stay put in California, that we could work together on large, shared projects. For twenty years, we'd moved jobs or apartments or states every couple of years. After we moved to California, our lives revolved around Shuttle, a past we couldn't pack into boxes and carry with us. When Shuttle ended, we were left revolving around each other in our new home. For the first time, we had no plans or even expectations to pack up and move on.

Decades earlier, Doug had dreamt about being an astronaut, but I didn't want a life any different than the life we were building together. He was coming to terms with this adulthood too, and our Space Coast adventure was part of our growing up.

CHAPTER 12
THE WHITE WHALE
ANNA

> Methinks that what they call my shadow here on earth is my
> true substance. Methinks that in looking at things spiritual, we
> are too much like oysters observing the sun through the water,
> and thinking that thick water the thinnest of air.

—Herman Melville, *Moby-Dick*

Endeavour was scheduled to launch on the afternoon of Friday, April 29. Doug and I planned to fly from California to Florida on Thursday. We'd miss some events at Kennedy Space Center, but I wouldn't miss teaching a class. I was responsible to a job I enjoyed.

I applied for media credentials using *Chapman Magazine* again as my news organization. Our article there about the not-launch of *Discovery*, illustrated with our photos, was published as we prepared to return to the Space Coast. Approval from KSC came quickly. I seemed to be in the NASA media club.

But I stewed that Doug and I might spend launch day apart. He called our undergraduate alma mater, Knox College, and used that institution's alumni magazine as his news organization. He asked the editor to let him know if NASA called to confirm. We heard nothing. I wondered whether demand for media badges was so much higher than usual that the Accreditation Manager would never get to Doug's request, even to reject it. A little more than a week before the scheduled launch, Doug got approval.

We reread the accreditation approval messages to make sure we hadn't imagined our success. Maybe NASA didn't want to turn anyone away, with only two launches left in the Shuttle program. Layoffs had already begun, with twelve hundred workers let go in October 2010, even before *Discovery*'s original launch date, and NASA didn't quite know what was next for itself. The Constellation program, a combo-follow-on to Apollo and Shuttle for both Earth and lunar orbit, had been cut from the federal budget early in 2010 after one test flight of its rocket. Whether or not NASA was reasoning through its uncertain future while deciding on our press credentials, we were amazed and delighted to get the thumbs-up for STS-134 media badges.

This time, we would be together as close as almost anyone could be to a shuttle launch—and we were confident that *Endeavour* would launch on time, if only because *Discovery* hadn't. *Elation*, from the Latin meaning *to bring out of*, as in Doug and I were brought out of a funk. *Elation*, meaning *joyfulness or exaltation of spirit as a result of success or relief.* In this case, success and relief. As much as he'd looked forward to walking the four miles from the motel to the coast, then holding his viewing spot for hours among throngs of people for *Discovery*'s launch the previous November, Doug was now looking forward to being right there with the rest of the press corps—with me, now more expert at this part of our adventure—for *Endeavour*'s launch.

Endeavour, under Mark Kelly's command, was scheduled for a fourteen-day mission to deliver parts to ISS. As soon as we arrived in Florida, late on April 28, my mother's birthday, this trip felt different than our visit last November for the not-launch. Last fall, the Space Coast had been chillier than our Southern California home, but now warm waves of Florida humidity welcomed us. Last fall, the drive to the coast was dark and solitary. This time, the car rental agent quipped that he'd checked in a party of thirty Brazilians the day before, all here to see the launch. We faced a vibrant display of lightning illuminating hundreds of cars sharing the road with us. We looked for differences and piled them up toward an actual launch this time, though lightning wasn't a good sign.

As we pulled into our familiar Titusville motel, we were stunned to find that the mom-and-pop Italian restaurant, Jimmy and Cora's II, where we had eaten every dinner during our last trip, had been replaced by the Garden Club. Another difference. While I checked in, Doug grabbed a table at the restaurant. It still served an old favorite on tap. After Shuttle ended, the motel closed (we once stayed at the slightly more upscale hotel with chain breakfast restaurant attached). Our motel later became the Garden Palms, and, by March 2015, was a bank-owned property available for sale.

After dinner, we flipped on NASA-TV to check what was what. After a relatively short delay and under rolling clouds and occasional rain and a setting sun, we learned that the Rotating Service Structure had been rolled back from the orbiter without us. With this news, we went to bed. Some things—the weather concerns, the moldy smell of the motel room—felt familiar now, but we hoped for a different outcome.

On launch day, we rose before the sun at 5:00 a.m., 2:00 a.m. in our California-based bodies. Writer Norman Mailer's words about Apollo 11's launch day wafted through our minds: "an awakening in the dark of the sort one will always remember, for such nights live only on a few mornings of one's life. Somewhere not so far from here, the astronauts were getting up as well." And, like he—Mailer's character Aquarius—had, we headed to get our media badges. We passed pockets along the coast filled with RVs, cars, and tents or, in Mailer's words, "families and tourists who were waiting for morning on the banks of the causeway." Newscasts recommended that people coming from Orlando, doing the drive that took us a half-hour the previous night, leave by 8:00 a.m. to catch the 3:47 p.m. launch, but we had US 1 largely to ourselves. We envisioned a twelve-hour day at the News Center.

The Badging Office was a plain white building, like a small-town DMV without a town. It had two front doors, each marked for its own group: press on the left, Tweetup attendees to the right. Journalists were already three deep at the counter. Doug and I showed two forms of identification and were given our badges, which looked like driver's licenses sans photo and had STS-134 emblazoned on the front. At the security gate to KSC, we showed our badges and our licenses and were waved on through. Doug and I were on our way to a launch together. I felt unreasonably excited. No, my great excitement was absolutely reasonable.

We passed the blue days-to-launch sign and, for the first time, saw it read "0." Zero: suddenly my new favorite number, an emptiness that was full of potential. When we reached Saturn Way, I thought this was the turn, but I wasn't quite sure because the size of the Vehicle Assembly Building momentarily threw off my sense of direction. I pointed to the right and said, "Follow that car—and all those ahead."

The whole place was buzzing, much more than for *Discovery's* planned launch last fall, with rental cars from the press and meandering KSC employees. The half of the parking lot closer to the News Center brimmed with vans donning satellite dishes. We were directed to an auxiliary lot, an empty field. The cloud cover overhead increased my sense of intensity. Despite how gloomy it looked this morning, the clouds were expected to break in the afternoon, and we heard 70 percent as the chance for launch. Good odds.

The Press Site was especially full, in large part because Mark Kelly and Gabrielle Giffords had become a compelling, national human-interest story and also because President Barack Obama was coming to see the launch. This launch wasn't just for the space geeks like Rob Pearlman from CollectSpace and Ken Kremer, who wrote for *Universe Today* and spent his spare time piecing together panoramic views from the Mars rovers. This launch was for all of us. At the two buildings with rooftop viewing (for specific media outlets), extra reporters were climbing up and down the stairs. The vending machine near the room for press briefings was already sold out of soft drinks. Thankfully, the food truck showed up behind the News Center at 8:00 a.m.

Doug headed there for caffeine. The truck was of the silver, Grumman panel variety similar to thousands of US Mail trucks across the nation. Several journalists thought that the food truck was from the Apollo era. Perhaps, it was the selfsame vehicle that Mailer describes in *Of a Fire on the Moon*: "The trailer interior consisted of a set of vending machines for chiliburgers, hamburgers, pastries—all people wanted were cold drinks. [...] Nobody was about to have machine-vended chiliburgers at half-past eight in the morning." If it was the same vehicle that Mailer described, it was a link in the chain of literature, events, and people that connected our childhoods with our adult adventure. Now it had heated and cooled stainless steel drawers instead of coin-operated vending machines. Doug, too, passed on the pastries and silver-wrapped burgers that early in the morning and brought me a welcome cold can of diet soda.

Reporters and photographers crowded around the News Center, camera equipment piled in corners. We requested a desk. Volunteers in the press office looked skeptical. All the desks in the main office were taken. We offered to share. We were assigned a desk in the Press Annex, a trailer made permanent, off to the side of the main news building and in the shadow of the semi-permanent structures belonging to CBS, NBC, and two Florida newspapers, along with the permanent trailers for Reuters and the Associated Press. Almost all of us were transients. Looking around, Doug and I felt lucky because almost all the Annex desks were assigned too. We knew that first-timers would not know to ask, and many reporters were only now trickling in for the first time. We plopped ourselves down next to someone from the *Miami Herald* who'd never been to KSC before.

I got antsy, so I made us hustle back and jostle our way into the News Center itself, listening for tidbits of information. We signed up for astronaut interviews in the afternoon, but the sheet for the crew walkout wasn't out. I asked a public affairs officer where to sign up for the walkout, proud I knew to ask, grateful I'd had some practice here. I was told the list was full. The sign-up sheet had been put out the morning before, and 150 spots had filled quickly. We got on a standby list, with about a dozen names ahead of ours and more names quickly added behind. A press officer said that, in his memory, they'd never taken 150 members of the media to the crew's short walk from the suit-up room to the Astrovan. We didn't know whether that indicated lack of interest or lack of room. Another reporter said he was on the list to go but couldn't imagine they'd be able to fit 150 people in the space there. He added that it was a lot of effort for a few seconds of waving. Mailer had described the walkout for Apollo 11 as "several hundred people standing on tiptoe at every bad angle and hopeless vantage point for a good look—would remain more than an hour on this chance of the briefest glimpse hardly more than a wave of an arm." Doug and I hadn't yet seen astronauts in spacesuits up close, so the brief waving was incredibly appealing to us and, sadly, unlikely.

We kept busy, picking up informational sheets about the mission and official photographs of the crew and orbiter and generally eavesdropping. A lot of information was in the air, part of journalist-to-journalist conversation. We watched the progress of countdown on NASA-TV. The three-hour mark in the countdown signaled a built-in hold, one of seven in this launch countdown. Really, much happened even in the downtime on these days we spent at KSC. Every minute seemed to matter that day.

Doug and I headed to the parking lot. The public affairs officers and volunteers asked stand-bys for the crew walkout to loiter in a clump at the back of the line, beyond where the buses lined up. This period was one of many hurry-up-and-wait situations journalists face all the time. For the first time, I found it excruciating. More buses arrived, enough to fit all of us milling about, hoping to glimpse the STS-134 crew decked out in space-age finery and ready to go. We put our belongings down and stepped toward the bus the for the security search. After everything checked out, the doors of the buses opened, and we boarded, bumping to find seats. The photographers manhandled tripods and stepladders, the tools necessary for the best shots over the crowd of heads, objects not conducive to the comfort of the rest of us.

The ride took about ten minutes. What must have been two hundred of us disembarked, the driver reminding us to return to the same bus. We shuffled behind a barricade in an area between two buildings. The photographers took the spots they wanted, elbowing the rest of us out of their way and knocking us with dangling cameras for good measure. Since Doug and I weren't on the early buses, we settled into a spot not too far in. I stared at the Airstream motorhome, its retro, curving shape, its silver skin, its bold NASA logo.

We waited. The waiting seemed to go on for an hour, but I was having fun. Many of us snapped photos of the helicopter making large circles overhead. With my camera's zoom, I saw that the side door of the helicopter was open, and a sniper in sunglasses and fatigues perched there, legs dangling out, rifle at the ready. Doug tweeted to the helicopter, and it tweeted back. Doug also noticed men on rooftops who held binoculars up to scan. Security, or workers securing the best view for launch? Finally, KSC employees traipsed in behind the press in the room remaining. We all waited some more. Every time someone—a soldier, a man in a suit—walked out the doors through which the astronauts would emerge, the crowd tensed.

Finally, real word got out, and photographers readied their cameras. First out were five men, one of whom opened the door of the Astrovan. The next three each carried two zippered, olive-drab, helmet-shaped duffel bags, and the last carried rectangular satchels, what I assumed to be the survival backpacks each astronaut would strap on before climbing into the crew cabin of *Endeavour*. At last, the six astronauts, led by Commander Mark Kelly, then Pilot Greg Johnson, walked out into the sunshine.

The astronauts lined up alongside the glistening Astrovan and waved. This crew looked happy, confident but not as excited as I felt. The press exuded exuberance. As a result, most of my photographs had heads and arms of other journalists in the way, skewing the auto-focus and blurring the astronauts' faces. The crew didn't linger long. Doug brushed my shoulder with his; I stuck out an elbow to keep track of his body in the crowd. But we didn't look at each other during the fleeting moments devoted to seeing astronauts just before they left Earth. Each astronaut ducked his head as he entered the Astrovan, his dark black zipper like a stripe down the back of an endangered species scampering way. The van's door shut, and the short convoy left, heading for LC-39A—a place Mailer called "a shrine"—to get settled inside *Endeavour* for its last liftoff.

It took some time for the press to squeeze through the way we came in. Once onboard the buses, volunteers did a headcount. None of the buses left until all buses had the right headcount. Doug and I found seats. We were still jittery from seeing astronauts in their last public moments before taking flight. As the buses start to move, I imagined the crew arriving at the launch pad and ascending to the access arm, donning their helmets and life support packs, getting everything cinched together, squeezing through the orbiter's hatch to be strapped into their seats. Their own version of hurry-up-and-wait.

Halfway back to the News Center, someone pointed out a left-side window. Someone else said, "I've never seen that before." Though Doug and I were seated on the opposite side of the bus, I glimpsed what the buzz was about. The Astrovan passed us, going the other way on the other side of the road. Within another minute, reporters saw Twitter chirping with news that today's launch had been scrubbed. I didn't want to believe it, but Doug and fellow journalists followed reliable KSC insiders on Twitter, and I'd seen with my own eyes the Astrovan heading away from the pad. I hadn't calmed down yet from the walkout— my heart remained fluttery from seeing six readied astronauts in person—but events asked me to gear up for letdown. Though my cheeks ached from smiling, our second chance to see a launch seemed another blown chance.

Back at the News Center, there was confusion about when the press briefing about the scrub would be held. More waiting, but I didn't mind because, without a launch, I wanted more of something. It became clear that the briefing for the scrub wouldn't occur until after the president had come and gone, sandwiching this visit in between touring Alabama, which had been hit with deadly tornadoes, and a speech at Miami Dade College's graduation ceremony. Doug and I had a couple of hours to catch up and prep. Two o'clock came and went. Finally, press and KSC staff mingled outside on various raised surfaces to get a good look at Saturn Way, where we assumed the presidential motorcade would appear. I shifted from foot to foot. Other journalists talked about whether the weather would have been good enough to launch, and everyone agreed it would've been. Without launch as the goal, I lost track of time.

As a group, we glimpsed the motorcade heading from the direction of the launch pad. The shiny black vehicles, one odd silver van among them, turned before they passed us. They disappeared quickly behind a set of buildings. That was that, so Doug and I headed to the briefing room to grab seats, for there was no way all the press could fit in for the news conference. We waited there, too. NASA-TV covered the president's visit, so that footage was up on the two large screens in the briefing room. The screen's resolution was so good that some of us snapped photos as if we, instead of the White House press corps, were at the VAB with the Obama family.

Jay Barbree, an NBC reporter who'd covered every US manned launch of the space program from Mercury through Shuttle, walked into the briefing room. Clearly, he'd seen his share of not-launches too. The First Lady and girls went one way, and the president climbed aboard Air Force One, the presidential seal on the door he entered. We waited some more. I began to feel exhaustion seep in.

When George Diller, the public affairs officer, led KSC Director Bob Cabana, Launch Integration Manager Mike Moses, and Launch Director Mike Leinbach into the room, my adrenaline surged. Diller announced that the briefing would cover two topics: President Obama's visit and the status of STS-134. All I really wanted to know was why I wasn't going to see a launch today.

In a safety-always-comes-first-at-NASA plug, Cabana began, "I'd much rather be on the ground wishing I was flying than in the air wishing I was on the ground." But he didn't talk about the not-launch. He recounted that Obama and his family toured the Orbiter Processing Facility and *Atlantis*, which would fly the program's final mission, and Obama met with the crew in the Launch Control Center and then with crew families, including Gabrielle Giffords, whom we didn't know was at KSC—didn't know was well enough to be here—until he mentioned it, and now she, of course, was already gone.

Thinking back the following week, I realized the best question came from Ken Kremer, who asked whether Obama would return for the launch, an unusually benign question from an uber-space-geek like Ken. I figured he was making sure Cabana knew who he was, maybe giving the director a chance to say something before the guys who knew nitty-gritty Shuttle goings-on took the mic. Cabana replied, "He did say that if it was Monday, he wouldn't be able to make it back." Clearly, the president already knew when he visited KSC on Saturday—though those of us in the briefing didn't—that, on Monday, May 1, Osama Bin Laden would be killed by US Navy SEALs.

Finally, the two Mikes explained what went wrong with launch plans, and I soaked it up like a good story. The problem was either a faulty thermostat, relatively easily to switch out, or a line of heaters on a string that wraps around a hydrazine fuel line. I tried to imagine a string of heaters, like holiday lights. Had they discovered this problem once in orbit, the crew would have burned off that system completely and gone on their happy way. As a known problem before launch, the possibility existed that the line was frozen, and, if so, would thaw at some point after pressure had built up, in which case the line could rupture and leaked hydrazine could catch fire during reentry at the end of the mission. This problem put the shuttle in violation of launch criteria. The decision to scrub was, both Mikes agreed, "straightforward."

Everyone hoped that a faulty thermostat—measurement of temperature, not temperature itself—was the problem. Leinbach said that changing out the larger system, the box that houses various parts involved, would take an additional two days of retesting even after the fix itself was completed. That would make a Monday or Tuesday launch impossible, after which NASA would run into a conflict with the Air Force next door, which planned to launch an Atlas rocket. Then, managers had to look at the whole mission schedule so that undocking from ISS in preparation to return to Earth didn't fall on the same day as the already-scheduled Soyuz undocking. It was a really complicated re-syncing up they'd have to do if they couldn't launch soon.

So we drove back to our hotel unsure of whether we'd see a launch on this trip. It took NASA a full day to get into the shuttle to take a look because, once the external tank is full of fuel, it takes twenty-four hours to drain it and let the remaining hydrogen evaporate. In addition, they had to roll the RSS back into position to provide access to the shuttle. The next day, back at our KSC desk, we heard the inside scoop that workers had entered the aft section of the shuttle, where the heater was located.

On Monday, May 1, we went to a briefing—briefings run on NASA-TV and sometimes others pick up the feed—on the status of *Endeavour's* launch with the two Mikes and hosted by Allard Beutel, one of the helpful public affairs officers. The pattern of briefings was always the same: the press officer introduced himself and introduced the people to his left in order, then each person on the briefing team spoke in that order, and finally the floor opened for questions. Doug and I made a pact to each ask a question. I listened intently—above the sound of my beating heart at the thought of speaking aloud here—so that I had a chance to ask a question that made sense.

Mike Moses announced that the heaters of concern on launch day weren't the problem after all. Was I relieved for split-second? The failure was a problem in "a box of switches that we use to control power feeds," so power wasn't going to the heaters. *Switches, power feeds*—I knew this guy was setting us up for a not-launch. Moses said that the box needed to be swapped out, which at first sounded like a quick and simple task, but he added, "That work's going to take us a while. So unfortunately we're not going to be able to make a launch attempt in the next few days." Our second trip, our second not-launch. I couldn't stop listening to the details of failure.

Even after they swapped the boxes, they would have to test the bad box to make sure it was really broken and that the problem wasn't somewhere else. And Leinbach made it clear that, after the new box was in place, they'd have to do all sorts of retesting in the whole aft compartment. Moses went so far as to say, "I'm here to disappoint everybody by saying I'm not going to tell you what the new launch date is because I have no idea." No launch, no new launch date. They'd already sent the crew home to Houston.

But my adrenaline was pumping, and now I had a question. It seemed a bad sign that the crew wasn't kept at KSC, but at least they weren't allowed to resume life with their families yet. Could information about crew goings-on reveal something about when the Mikes thought *Endeavour* would launch? It was clear they did have some idea of the new launch date, probably the middle of May, not before May 8. And I needed to plan my life around that date.

Knowing about quarantine and other pre-launch crew scheduling, I asked, "How long do you have to *know* the delay is going to be before you send the crew home? Does it have to be at least five days because that's what they would normally spend here?" I could not have asked such a question last November, but I knew a lot more detail about the shuttle and launches now, partly from listening to the two Mikes. Moses's answer revealed little practical information, but I was fascinated to find out that, if a delay would mean they'd get to Houston only to turn around the next day to return, the crew would probably be given the choice. Clearly, this time, they were in Houston for what was a long wait, not a short turnaround. As disappointing as the news was, I couldn't help but be proud of myself for being a person who could ask a question at a NASA news conference. I'd not always been that person.

Because he understood electrical systems, Doug asked the tough question about the fusing system and where the real problem might be: "Doesn't that allow for the possibility that something upstream of that

fuse is malfunctioning, and if so, what would concern you the most?"
Moses was especially forthcoming. "Yes, definitely." In other words,
they were fixing a perceived problem, but it was possible they hadn't yet
located an underlying problem. He mentioned debris, blown wiring,
a re-opened solder connection, things they'd have to seek out. Doug's
question was so good and the answer so disheartening to everyone that
it wrapped up the briefing.

We were done. My head was spinning, but there was nothing left to
discuss or do.

CHAPTER 13
2011: A SPACE ODYSSEY
DOUG

If anyone understands it on the first viewing, we've failed in our intention.

—Arthur C. Clarke on the film *2001: A Space Odyssey* (quoted from the biography by Neil McAleer)

While watching Shuttle come to a conclusion, there were things that Anna and I hadn't been able to articulate, either in writing or in speaking to each other. Some of this was reticence, an acknowledgement of gentle but substantial dread associated with saying things out loud for fear of unleashing an unwanted possibility in the world: the very real possibility that we wouldn't see a shuttle launch. *Seeing is believing.* This most human sensory desire—a physical and emotional need—underpinned one of the unspoken questions between us: *How would we complete our understanding of Generation Space if we did not witness human beings launched into space?*

The STS-134 launch was eventually rescheduled for May 16, 2011. We rearranged our lives. Just hours before boarding our flight, we cleaned up the plates and wineglasses from our end-of-school-year party, the first Anna and I held in our newly purchased home. I was a good sport on the coast-to-coast flight despite being jammed shoulder-to-shoulder like a concert-goer on the floor of a general admission rock show. Despite the grubby reality of sticky tray tables and who-knows-what stuffed into seat backs, I loved the concept of flying, moving vast distances across the surface of Earth in manageable, more-or-less precisely allotted slices of time, and I thrilled at the chance to return to the Space Coast. At the same time, like most denizens of the twenty-first century, I found different levels of joy in the reality of travel via commercial aviation.

According to an Associated Press study in 2007, the shuttle lifted off on schedule only 40 percent of the time. Two different missions on *Columbia* had scrubbed six times each. After two not-launches under our belts and this low on-time record, our optimism should have been dashed. Instead, Anna and I thought we'd paid our dues. The more often we showed up, the more likely we'd see a launch in person. We noted concerns about the weather on the Space Coast even before we departed California, but weather hadn't been the final problem last time.

On that previous STS-134 trip, Anna and I had encountered a journalist from *Physics Today* who'd made nine separate pilgrimages to witness a shuttle launch. He'd convinced his editor to send him each time by finding some physics tie-in with the mission. That last time, he'd also had to convince his wife, home in England with a young child. That was his last chance, and he'd returned home with another tick in the loss column. Anna and I were 0–2 with no desire to see our losing percentage get any worse. The journalist's name was among those things we didn't allow ourselves to voice for fear of a jinx, a hex.

After arriving on the Space Coast, we fell into a version of the routine that we'd established: car rental, short drive to Titusville, quick showering away of cross-country flight funk, dinner and planning session at the restaurant in the parking lot of the motel, and a fitful night of sleep. The time-change, adrenaline, and anxiety conspired against needed rest.

On Sunday, May 15, 2011—the day before STS-134 was scheduled to launch—we wanted to be sure to get to the sign-up sheets early this time, both for the rollback of the RSS later in the day and the crew walk-out the following morning. Each of us had had our shakedown cruise— a nautical term I'd learned in Navy R.O.T.C. for the process of testing a ship's crew and systems—as a member of the media. Anna's was during the not-launch of STS-133 back in November and mine was for the not-launch of STS-134 two weeks ago. After two NASA press corps stints, Anna was starting to feel comfortable with the rhythm, the hurry-up-and-wait of NASA. It was a pace not unlike that of teaching—which Anna did as a professor and I did on a regular basis as a librarian—with hours of prep time for a brief session with students, followed by reading through their work, looking for gems.

Each seat at the News Center was reserved with a printed sheet listing the occupant's name and news organization. Some names were familiar, names that made us pause to wonder what we were thinking, being in this mix. It was thrilling. We were good observers, and we learned quickly by doing. We'd convinced ourselves we belonged, and a few regulars and several newbies treated us as if we might have information to swap. For the first time, we were able to arrange for two assigned seats in the Annex building: *Chapman Magazine* and *Knox Magazine* had seats at the table. We unpacked, reiterated our ideas for blog posts, and started in on the day's writing.

Two weeks earlier, the celebrity press had been here *en masse* for the story of Representative Gabrielle Giffords and Shuttle Commander Mark Kelly. Like the cool kids in your high school—with the main press site and the Annex standing in for the lunchroom and study hall—they owned the place. A surprising number of the celebrity press had given up and not returned, moving on to the next hot story. Some of those journalists were back, though, and, as with the previous time, they weren't the least bit interested in the RSS rollback or pre-launch mission updates.

The high school study hall analogy wasn't quite right because the members of the regular NASA press corps trend older, at least our age but mostly even older. They were high-school-age teens when Apollo got to the Moon. Yet much like high school, the dress of space-geek reporters marked them as separate from the mainstream and television cool kids: t-shirts from previous shuttle launches, baseball caps with logos of universities they attended, khakis and jeans, comfort over fashion. Anna and I fit neither clique exactly. The NASA press corps was collaborative in ways that I remembered from pop-culture portrayals of journalists like *WKRP in Cincinnati*'s Les Nesman and the staff reporters on *Lou Grant*.

Anna and I soon grew used to random voices in the room calling out questions to no one in particular. *How do you spell such-and-such?* Spelling and grammar are Anna's forte so that was the sort of question she answered. Details stick with me, and I've read a lot of space and engineering books, so I cleared up some technical confusion for a *Miami Herald* reporter. I knew she'd have our backs if there were breaking news.

Also common was the quick circulation of information about onsite events: news conferences, bus trips to photo-ops at the launch pad, and sign-up sheets for added astronaut interviews. Like an *ad hoc* version of the children's game *telephone*, information circulated through the room: a journalist with a new piece of information entered through the Annex door, made a beeline for her people, and shared an update; ears around her pricked up, and, after a polite pause, the curious leaned toward the journalist's group. *When's the new rollback time?* If asked, a journalist shared the information at hand. But you had to know to ask. Nobody seemed leery of asking a question, and so it went. Hearing others, we scooted to sign up for the RSS rollback and the crew walkout (scheduled for the wee hours of the next morning).

During one long shift in the Annex, a Canadian journalist, an older man from a large newspaper, leaned over to me and pointed at the Twitter client that was open on my laptop. Unsure of the correct terms, the veteran journalist paused before asking, "Are you twittering?"

"Tweeting," I replied.

Relieved, the journalist relayed that his editor had asked him for a short piece on the STS-134 Tweetup, and he needed to turn it around quickly. "What's a tweetup?"

I wanted to reply with mild bitterness, *Something I didn't get invited to.* I'd applied to the social media extravaganza and not made the cut. The STS-134 Tweetup had become something of a sore spot with some old-guard journalists, who'd nicknamed that crowd "tweety-pies." I treaded carefully while I explained the concept of a tweetup—an organized gathering of Twitter users, in NASA's case for a specific launch. To my surprise, the journalist started typing away. I was a member of the NASA press corps, treated as an authoritative expert, acting as a colleague. It was a heady feeling, one that Anna and I experienced on several occasions. People listened to us. Journalism was practiced as a form of open inquiry here, a tool for gathering facts and sharing that information with the public.

My growing feeling of confidence came to a sputtering halt later that day as Anna and I waited for the buses to whisk us away to the impending RSS rollback. I'd taken the principle of comfort in the dress code to heart. Shorts and a t-shirt seemed the obvious way to dress in the radiant warmth of Florida's sunshine. As Anna and I prepared to board the bus, along with a hoard of other reporters, a press handler stopped me and pointed to the canvas bag slung over my shoulder: "You got long pants in there?" I shook my head, *No*. I could see from the crestfallen look on Anna's face that she knew what was coming, that she'd forgotten the rule she'd heard months ago.

"The rollback takes place on an active industrial site," the man went on. "Long pants and closed-toe shoes only." It was as if he were reciting the requirements from a manual, as if he were pelting me with the rocks I wouldn't stand upon on the crawlerway. I wouldn't be going to see the rollback, a moment that Anna had described rapturously to me over the phone back in November for STS-133 when she was the holder of press credentials and I was not. This time, I had press credentials, but I'd failed.

"You can't get on the bus. You'll have to get out of line," the man said.

Even as the man spoke, Anna was saying, "This is my fault. I knew this. I'm so tired, I forgot." Anna rarely sounded frantic.

I stopped listening. Ten seconds earlier, I was at the top of my game. Now, I wanted to slink away.

I put my hand on Anna's shoulder and gave her a gentle squeeze. "No biggie. I've got plenty to work on. Go."

I moved away from the bus. I avoided eye contact with the real reporters, the ones still in line, the one's who knew you didn't wear shorts today, the ones headed out to watch *Endeavour* emerge in a moment of technological glory from the cocooning RSS.

I trudged back to the Annex. Along the way, I imagined word spreading through the press corps that some rookie had tried to wear shorts to the rollback. The reality, of course, was that only Anna and I noticed. If a few others knew, they wouldn't mention it; they'd imagine how it felt and cringe.

Years later, as I looked through photographs of our adventure on our blog, I noticed something in Anna's photos from the STS-134 rollback: a reporter wearing cargo shorts. Had the NASA handler for another bus forgotten or not known the long-pants rule, had no one noticed the rule breaker, or had a veteran space-geek been given a pass when I hadn't? I was crushed all over again.

Back in the Annex I struggled to concentrate, and, instead of working on what I was there to work on, jotted notes for a novel. Eventually, Anna returned from the rollback. She wore a smile from ear-to-ear, and I was glad she'd embraced the moment on her own. Trying to pretend for my benefit that she hadn't witnessed something amazing would have cheapened it for both of us. Had she not allowed herself amazement, I'd have been disappointed in her. There's a lovely contradiction built into our relationship: a dependence and a respect for independence, a need and a lack of neediness.

On Monday, May 16, 2011, we left the motel for KSC a little before 3:00 a.m. The night was pitch black. Driving south on Route 1, we caught a glimpse of the shuttle on the pad in the distance across the water. Banks of powerful flood lamps bathed the spacecraft in white light, drawing a sharp outline of *Endeavour* against the black Florida night.

The shuttle's form, its overall shape, was very different than the sleek, needle-nosed cylinders that took flight during the Mercury, Gemini, Apollo, and Skylab programs. Even after thirty years, the Space Transportation System's design, with the dull orange external fuel tank attached to the orbiter's black underside and straddled by two white, solid rocket boosters, evoked the possibility that it was put together by a child in a 1960s bedroom: *What if I start here with a brick? Add some wings. How about a oatmeal can at the back to hold the whole thing up? Sure there's room here on the sides, enough for two candles, flipped so the lit wicks will be rocket engine flames. Zoom.*

Except, of course, the designer's dictum of *form follows function* ruled the shuttle's development, played off against an extraordinary mix of constraints: reusability, airplane-like landings, a cargo bay to accommodate enormous spy satellites. In designing the shuttle, NASA had to accommodate its own goals and also those of the Department of Defense (big payload bay) and the Air Force (maneuverability). That a balance of functionality was struck and that the shuttle's eclectic mix of sharp angles, easy curves, and Platonic shapes flew at all was a testament to human will, engineering acumen, and money from the federal government.

Anna and I drove to the security gate and, after showing our badges and driver's licenses, passed through. The Press Site parking lot was almost empty—no auxiliary parking lot for us this time. Some tech folks were already setting up the satellite trucks for the television news crews. Rows of trucks and generators exhausted warm air into the cool Florida predawn and thick, black cables ran in neat rows. Sometimes I'd confuse all the technology with the local wildlife: poisonous snakes, gators, scavenging birds, and insects of the Space Coast. The vacant spaces and others' steady but subdued efforts made me feel as if Anna and I might have slept later without missing any action.

Our satchels slung over our shoulders, we stopped for a moment and turned toward Launch Complex 39A, *Endeavour's* cradle for about five more hours. We hoped *Endeavour* wouldn't sit on the pad much longer than that for fear our seeing a launch would slither once again into the uncertain, swampy terrain of the future. We didn't say it aloud, but we both thought it: how many more times could we rearrange our schedules, drop everything, and return to the Space Coast for a shuttle launch that might not happen? We certainly wouldn't be able to come back six more times like the empty-handed physics journalist.

Even as we walked into the News Center, we heard word circulating that buses would soon be loading for the drive over to the crew walkout. We dropped off some of our gear in the Annex, headed back to the parking lot to wait for a bus, and, after the security check, boarded the first one that arrived. The day was going smoothly for us.

When dealing with NASA, everything proceeded according to a timeline. On the bus to the walkout, held outside the Operations and Checkout Building where crew quarters are located, our press handler announced the walkout would take place at 5:11 a.m., wonderfully specific information.

We'd learned at the previous STS-134 walkout that a *de riguer* piece of the photojournalist's toolkit was the stepladder, some of which were a full six feet. In order to avoid cluttering the press buses, the ladders and the odd kitchen stepstool were transported separately to this walkout. Of all of the ways that a member of the press might meet an untimely end (including the local gators), being trampled by photojournalists seemed the least dignified, like a form of cannibalism. The mad dash for

the most advantageous perches from which to photograph the walkout—
while carrying a ladder—made heart attack seem the most likely means
of demise for our fellow photogs. Anna and I held back from the rush to
the front of the fencing that separated the press from astronauts and
Astrovan. As we made our way to the second wave of positions, it became
clear that our photographs would have to be obtained by shooting
around the human bodies perched above and beside us.

Having arrived at our positions a little after 4:00 a.m., Anna and I
faced more than hour of standing around before the astronauts would
emerge. From pre-launch briefings and previous experience, we knew
some of what the crew would be doing while we were waiting: getting
suited up. I wondered what the crew was thinking in those last few
moments before heading to *Endeavour*. Though insights on their last-
minute thoughts weren't available, NASA has long provided copious
amounts of information about its astronauts, including an astronaut-
by-astronaut menu for the pre-launch breakfast. They ate lobster, pasta,
and whatever else each desired, like a celebration, or a last meal.

By that point, we'd read a lot about Commander Mark Kelly, and we'd
done our research on Mission Specialist Mike Fincke, but there were four
other astronauts preparing to head to space that morning. Greg Johnson,
who was born in the United Kingdom, was the pilot for STS-134 and had
been the pilot on STS-123 in 2008. Mission Specialist Andrew Feustel, a
geophysicist, took part in the last servicing mission to the Hubble telescope and was scheduled to do several spacewalks on this mission. We'd
later overhear his parents talking as they wandered the KSC Visitor Complex, making the small-world interconnectedness of the space program all
the more obvious to us; we felt connected to its edges. Mission Specialist
Greg Chamitoff had served on ISS in 2008 (and is now a professor, living
life like Anna and me). Finally, Roberto Vittori, an Italian astronaut with
the European Space Agency, had visited ISS twice prior to STS-134 and
was set to be the last non-American to fly on a shuttle.

More or less on schedule, the walkout started. First, a group of help-
ers carrying the astronauts' helmets appeared and loaded them onto
the waiting Astrovan. Murmurs of *There they are!* and sounds of a few
cameras taking photos rippled through the crowd. Shortly after, the
astronauts appeared in the doorway of the building opposite where we

stood. As a group, they smiled at the assembled crowd and began waving as they walked out and took positions alongside the Astrovan. Calls to individual astronauts—*Look this way!*—sang out. Staccato bursts of clicking camera shutters crescendoed into an eerie buzz, like a swarm of insects winging their way through the Florida dawn.

Anna's a much better photographer than I, so she wheedled her way as close to the fence as she could. The outstretched arms and cameras of our fellow press corps members were like a human canopy. Anna found a gap between bodies and shot photos until her battery ran down, sometimes holding her camera above her head and hoping for the best. Looking at them later, I was impressed with our walkout photos. In one, Mike Fincke—Anna's favorite among this crew—looked directly into Anna's lens with his radiant smile.

The science that was present at a launch extended far beyond the technological accomplishment represented by the shuttle itself. There was also the work, the science to be done on orbit, and this mission would deliver a science experiment to ISS that fascinated me: the Alpha Magnetic Spectrometer (AMS).

At the Department of Energy's Fermi National Accelerator Laboratory, called Fermilab, I worked on simulation software for particle accelerators. Accelerators are machines physicists use to create beams of charged particles—either the fundamental constituents of atoms like electrons, protons, and neutrons or sometimes entire atoms, such as gold or uranium. The beams of charged particles are directed into a target or into each other, which produces particle collisions, and can then be manipulated in such a way as to reveal even more fundamental constituents of matter. The machine that analyzes the results of those ensuing collisions is called a detector, and that's what AMS was: a sixteen-ton, three-meter square, space-going particle detector.

As Anna and I made our way on our designated bus back to the Press Site, AMS was tucked away safely in *Endeavour's* payload bay, situated at the rear, near the shuttle's OMS pods, waiting to be carried up and attached to ISS. AMS-02 is looking for dark matter, antimatter, and cosmic rays. In addition, AMS-02 will help NASA characterize the radiation environment facing future human travelers to Mars.

In many ways, outer space was the natural choice for a hosting a particle detector. The universe itself produces charged particles and cosmic rays of higher energies than would ever be possible on or detectable from Earth itself. On the other hand, the space environment is an extremely daunting one in which to run a particle physics experiment. AMS-02 required the collaboration of more than five hundred scientists from sixty institutes in sixteen countries to design, build, test, and run the project (not to mention approximately $2 billion).

Nobel prize winner Sam Ting, the man in charge of AMS, celebrated his eightieth birthday while I was revising this chapter. As of fall 2016, there hadn't been any dramatic, headline-grabbing announcements about the nature of dark matter—not yet. Instead, there has been the steady accumulation of data and a dedicated group of scientists producing academic papers—creating knowledge—in a manner that echoes what astronaut Michael Barratt once told us: "Basic science [happens...] where progress is won in steps." In 2013, the first scientific article produced by the AMS collaboration included more than two hundred scientists as co-authors and had been cited more than 350 times by the fall of 2015. People matter to science. Dark matter matters to people, even if they don't know it. And I was going to see this machine for detecting this mystery of the universe carried from Earth to the heavens by the space shuttle.

Back at the News Center, without putting her gear down, Anna walked directly to a table toward the far side of the main press room, near where we normally signed up for interviews, and asked to try on the glove of the spacesuit there. The glove belonged to an Extravehicular Mobility Unit (EMU). The EMU was used by Shuttle and ISS astronauts for spacewalks. An enhanced EMU spacesuit is still in use on ISS (and a Russian suit, the Orlan, is used by Russian astronauts—and some Americans—for spacewalks).

The most obvious difference between the EMU and the shuttle-only ACES (Advanced Crew Escape Suit) type of spacesuit—the one the six *Endeavour* crew members were wearing at the walkout—is the color. EMU suits are white to reflect the Sun while on orbit and reduce the risk of astronauts overheating, whereas ACES suits are orange because of that color's high visibility in case of rescue. In fact, a US Navy study in the

1960s found that orange was the most visible color under water, so orange was used as the dial color of some 1970s wristwatches used by skin divers. Logically, the Navy wanted astronauts, in case of emergency, to be wearing orange as they bobbed on the water after ditching a mission. The ACES suits, adapted from the high-altitude suits of the SR-71 and U-2 spy planes, existed primarily to provide a stable, Earth-like atmosphere for the wearer during launch but are not constructed to be used outside a spacecraft. The sturdier, more rugged EMU suits provide much greater protection from the unforgiving environment of space. Form follows function.

In this case, form followed fashion as Anna struck a pose for a photograph while wearing the multi-layered, surprisingly flexible glove. She liked the glove, amazed by its pliancy, imagining an astronaut making finely tuned repairs during an EVA. The countdown continued, and I didn't have time to try on the glove myself. Time to launch was running out.

As Anna and I walked out of the News Center, hundreds of reporters and photographers were already milling about near the countdown clock. Big cameras occupied positions with the unobstructed views, those closest to the edge of the water. The rest of us, the have-nots, seemed gripped by a nervous energy. As if we were random particles under the influence of Brownian motion, complete with occasional bumping into one another, we wandered about the grassy plain. Gradually, in unconscious synchrony with the countdown clock and a version of the space-maximizing algorithm with which people fill elevators, everyone slowed down, settled into a spot, and began waiting.

I forced myself to pass the final minutes of the countdown without watching the clock, since a nearby loudspeaker uttered updates. I allowed myself a glance or two at Anna. The look on her face suggested that we were sharing at some level the same disbelief that our lives had brought us—together no less—to this place, in this moment. When the assembled press corps took up the final ten seconds of countdown in a single voice, I was caught by surprise, as if I'd forgotten they were there, that Anna and I were part of the larger group.

At T-7 seconds, I experienced an unbidden instant of elation: *This is really going to happen—*

I'd read through the shuttle's countdown sequence dozens of times in my youth and dozens more after I took up this project. I knew by heart that, at T-6.6s, the magic began. *Endeavour's* main engines ignited. Once launch started, there was no stopping. Ignition fired up across the water from where I stood.

Things happened quickly at this point: white clouds erupted from around the base of the shuttle and the launch pad, an almost imperceptible spot of light emerged beneath *Endeavour*, and, in half an eye-blink, the light came to resemble a small glowing sun.

Later, in the thinking about the shuttle's ungainly shape and enormous bulk, a quote attributed (disputably) to Galileo came to mind: *Eppur si muove.* In the moment, I did think something akin to, *And yet, it moves.* And move it did!

The Space Shuttle Main Engines and Solid Rocket Boosters unrelentingly traded chemistry for overcoming gravity. All told, the SSMEs and SRBs generated almost seven million pounds of thrust at liftoff, working against the four-and-a-half million pounds of the shuttle stack. *Endeavour* inexorably cleared the launch tower.

A deep, human experience of awe merged with technology in a single moment. A placard somewhere at the KSC Visitor Complex points out that, if the shuttle were to explode all at once on liftoff, the energy released would be roughly equivalent to one-eighth the force of the Hiroshima atomic bomb blast, about 2.5 kilotons of energy.

In short order, a wave of radiant heat took me out of my childlike reverie of watching. The warmth made the physics of launching a space shuttle tangible to me, embodied in a way that hadn't been obvious only moments before. It occurred to me that the three miles separating me from the launch pad might not be enough distance. The heat had dissipated over three miles and, yet it still washed over me. I was right there.

From the direction of the launch pad and the quickening shuttle, I heard a wavering sound. My sensory perceptions were distinct, yet interwoven in a way I'd never before experienced. The sound grew to a shredding, like tearing canvas, ripping the air apart. Then, all at once, it was a thunder, crackling. Sound waves—produced by the mechanical vibration of the molecules of our atmosphere—hammered *inside* my chest. The spectacle of my youthful dreams of space travel and the Space

Age met the spectacular sensory reality of witnessing the most power-ful, human-created event that I was likely to ever experience.

Endeavour rose and disappeared into the clouds. It lit the top of the clouds from above. The cloud cover obscured my view too quickly. The next day, an extraordinary photo of *Endeavour* streaking above the cloud deck at that moment, taken from a passing plane, would appear in newspapers around the world. I stood quietly, not really paying atten-tion to the commotion, the hugging and crying around me. All I wanted was more. More time. More fire. More thunder.

Later, during the post-launch press conference, there were stark moments of contrast between the mainstream NASA press and the few hangers-on from the national media. A question about the color of the flowers that Mark Kelly's twin-brother Scott had given to Gabby Giffords before the launch drew audible scoffs and visible eye-rolls from the KSC regulars.

Ultimately, in that moment, I didn't care too much about either group. I was still coming to terms with the fact that I had lived up to my child-hood yearnings. This moment was more connected to my childhood notions of spacefaring than when I'd worked for a NASA contractor just outside the DC beltway. I had snuck closer. I wasn't on the shuttle itself, but I was there in that moment. I stood proximate to the fundament-shaking roar. I saw, with my own eyes, the space shuttle out-muscle grav-ity and work its way to a velocity of 17,500 miles per hour. I knew some-thing of what it meant for a human being to rise from this Earth and stay suspended, circling far above our heads for ten or so weightless days. I'd been able to witness these things. I'd been able to experience these things, to learn to experience these things. I was there.

When I first came across the Arthur C. Clarke quote that opens this chapter, I had an abstract sense of its meaning. Now, I knew it in my launch-rattled bones. First viewing wasn't enough, if more could be had. When Anna and I left KSC, I knew that I would be coming back for at least one more viewing. I had to return. I had to be there again.

Anna with the Mercury 7 mural at KSC

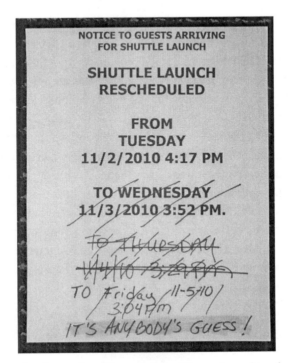

Delay sheet at hotel front desk for *Discovery*'s not-launch

Three astronauts at the STS-134 walkout: Andy Feustel, Roberto Vittori, Mike Fincke

Endeavour at launch pad LC-39A, (almost) ready for last launch

Doug and reporters on crawlerway at LC-39A before last launch of *Atlantis*

STS-135 crew boards Astrovan to head to the pad

Atlantis, last-ever space shuttle launch, July 8, 2011 (NASA photo)

Final takeoff of *Endeavour*, aboard SCA heading to California

CHAPTER 14
THE COMPANY TOWN
DOUG

The question is not so much where we are as when we are.

—*Planet of the Apes*

Before the summer of 2010, Anna and I had never heard of Titusville, Florida. I knew much about nearby KSC; I'd followed the goings-on there on and off since 1969, when, as a toddler, I watched Walter Cronkite broadcast the first Moon landing on television. I knew of nearby Cocoa Beach, the town where astronaut Anthony Nelson and his un-bottled genie lived in the television series *I Dream of Jeannie.* That 1960s-era, Hollywood version of Cocoa Beach—with its officers' homes and perfectly manicured lawns—remained my image of the Space Coast. I knew nothing of other towns there, nor about the places where real people who lived launch to launch resided.

Scouring the Internet as we planned to see the final Shuttle launches, I found numerous references to Titusville's Space View Park, not only an ideal place to watch a launch, but home to memorials, including cast handprints for the Mercury, Gemini, and Apollo programs. One night, Anna and I were having dinner and a couple of beers at a watering hole near where we teach in California. At the next table, three college-age guys, likely students at our university, were making loud, happy plans to go see a shuttle launch. One student was trying to convince the others that Titusville was *the* place to be, though his only knowledge was also via online research.

I wasn't sure what to expect. On the edge of Titusville sat the Indian River, full of birds, fish, and one-third of the nation's manatee population. A few miles of fresh water—always brownish and on windy days choppy in a way that pleased sailboarders—separated hopeful launch viewers from KSC and the spectacle of a shuttle launch.

Across the water, two launch pads make up Launch Complex 39: LC-39A and LC-39B. Decades ago, during Apollo, the parking lot of Miracle City Mall drew thousands, young and old, to watch as Saturn V rockets thundered away from the two pads. Last time Anna and I visited, the mall maintained a J. C. Penney and only a few other shops. It has since been demolished. LC-39B shut down on October 28, 2009, roughly a year before our first visit. LC-39A was last used by NASA on July 11, 2011.

The 2008 economic downturn, of course, affected the whole country, not just the Space Coast. In January of 2011, between our first trip to Florida and the end of the program, Anna and I bought a house close to the university where we worked in Orange, California. A few years earlier, as the nation's overheated housing market reached its zenith, we couldn't have afforded a house in Southern California. But the national economy had tanked, and mortgage rates had dropped to levels some people called *free money*. With some job stability, Anna and I had benefited from the economic mess by buying a home we couldn't afford three years earlier when we first moved to California.

As I looked around Titusville during our trips to Florida to see launches over two years, no one there seemed to be benefiting from the slow, steady upturn. Florida had been hit especially hard by the economic crisis, and Titusville faced the additional blow of the Shuttle program ramping down. People in Titusville looked as if they were positioned like dominoes waiting to tip.

We drove around town over the course of our visits. *For Sale* and *For Lease* signs dotted the landscape of houses and small businesses. An enormous, water's-edge condo project sat empty. Once, Anna and I pulled into the parking lot there. Two men leaned against a pickup. A quick *hello* and hurried conversation revealed they were removing snakes from the building. We snapped a few photos and bid hasty retreat when we felt too much discomfort. We could fly back to a recovering Southern California.

The day after the last space shuttle launch in July 2011, fifteen hundred workers at KSC—employees of Shuttle operations contractor United Space Alliance, or USA—went home from work with no plans to return the following Monday. That forced exodus came on the heels of nine hundred jobs lost at KSC the previous October, even before *Discovery's* last launch was supposed to occur, and another 550 in early 2011 at USA. While I waited for the last launch of *Atlantis*, it occurred to me that pink slips would be doled out in dribs and drabs for the next few years. Workers waited for word every few months as the program wrapped up. Some were able to stay, always waiting for the next round of layoffs. Others joined the country's growing unemployed and underemployed as the Shuttle program waned and no longer needed workers.

Titusville Mayor Jim Tully told me in July 2011, "I've not seen any number higher than eight thousand people, and a lot of those layoffs have already happened." Even after Shuttle ended, everyone was still guessing what effect layoffs would have. Tully emphasized that job losses were spread throughout Brevard County, not solely in Titusville, as if this dispersal made the blow less devastating to Titusville. But even by Tully's conservative estimates, 15 percent of the town's residents lost jobs within a year or two.

The sense of loss, not just of jobs but of an identity as a Space Age town, was palpable on every visit that Anna and I made to Titusville. In 2011, the *St. Petersburg Times* reported that the Moon-Light Drive-In, a family-owned restaurant for three generations, had a customer base that looked increasingly elderly. Owner Susan Hamed was concerned that the middle class wouldn't stay in the area. The pharmacy chain store where Anna and I ducked in on each trip to buy forgotten items— batteries, bug spray, an umbrella—no longer stocked Shuttle memorabilia as impulse purchases at the checkout counters.

Still, each morning while in Titusville, I made my way down Route 1. The usual line of cars trailed into the fast food drive-through. Evening boded well for a crowd at El Leoncito's restaurant down the road, where I raised my mug of beer over an oversized plate of burritos, rice, and beans and peered out the window at the launch pad across the water. The town wasn't exactly becoming a ghost town. In the long wake of the end of Shuttle, however, Titusville's absences and the melancholy went beyond the nation's nostalgia for space exploration and seeped into daily life—and livelihood.

Sitting in Space View Park on a balmy Florida afternoon, Mayor Jim Tully bluntly told me, "We were essentially a company town." The company—NASA—cut its biggest, most visible program in 2011.

What exactly is a company town? Certainly, people there were not living in NASA-owned homes, not like Ford Motor Company employees living in Ford-owned houses in the yesteryear hamlet of Alberta, Michigan. Companies no longer commonly provided education and other public services to their employees. Instead, a broader understanding of the concept was suggested by Oliver Dinius and Angela Vergara in their book *Company Towns in the Americas*: "Key is the combination of a single dominant industry with extensive company control over the daily life of the town."

That definition was brought home when Omar Izquierdo, a NASA contract employee whom I met through fellow space writer Margaret Lazarus Dean, remarked, "It'll be quite an adjustment for people in my generation who have never known the idea of no future Shuttle launches. For me, there's always been a sense that the definition of life in this community is simply prep time between Shuttle launches. What do we do now?" Izquierdo pointed out that the area code on the Space Coast is 3-2-1, like a countdown. Everything reminded residents that life was about launches.

When Anna and I were there in 2010 and 2011, all manner of goings-on in Titusville were tied to the launch schedule at KSC. The Salvation Army boasted a "shuttle sale." Grocery store cashiers bandied about NASA acronyms like VAB (Vehicle Assembly Building), OPF (Orbiter Processing Facility), and RTLS (Return To Launch Site) as they scanned and bagged food items. Business signs all over town wished "Godspeed" to whichever orbiter waited on the launch pad, just as business signs have done for decades of launches, ever since CAPCOM (Capsule Communicator) Scott Carpenter said to the first American to orbit Earth, on February 20, 1962, "Godspeed, John Glenn." After even the not-launches I'd witnessed, discarded signs for launch parking lay piled outside empty buildings with empty lots.

The idea of the company town permeates the American imagination: Detroit is Motor City; Seattle is Jet City; Las Vegas is Sin City. Often, it isn't just a city but an entire region that a specific industry dominates. The federal government is said to be *inside the beltway*, and we launch spaceships from the Space Coast.

Anna's grandfather grew up in the region that would become the Rust Belt. He was born in the mining region of Michigan's Upper Peninsula in 1902, the last of thirteen children. In the late nineteenth century, the economy in the Rust-Belt-to-be had been anything but decaying: it was soaring. Ishpeming was a company town in the classic sense, where young Henry's parents lived in a house owned by the mine into which his father descended every day. Rail lines between Ishpeming and Negaunee and the big city of Marquette on the shore of Lake Superior shipped millions of tons of iron ore pellets each year to cities like Pittsburgh. Eighty-five percent of the iron the United States consumed during World War II came from the Lake Superior region.

But by the Vietnam War, the high-grade ore was almost gone and underground mining had become prohibitively costly. Even by the time Anna's grandfather reached adulthood in the 1920s, the prosperity in the Upper Peninsula was already diminishing, and he left for Chicago. Of those children who survived to adulthood, only one remained in Marquette County. As their company town waned, the sons and daughters of immigrants left to become part of the rising middle class elsewhere.

Growing up in the depths of the farm crisis on the edge of the Rust Belt near a railroad town, I recognized Titusville's beleaguered look from my childhood. But the story of Titusville differs from others in history. Titusville's boom came late and fast.

In 1962, four years before I was born, NASA purchased 131 square miles that has become KSC. Its central VAB and the two pads of Launch Complex 39, used for Apollo and Shuttle, were completed in 1965, the year Anna was born. Titusville's population in 1950 was just 2,604. Over the following twenty years, as the Apollo space program emerged, the population multiplied by almost twelve times to more than thirty thousand. Down the road, the much smaller Cocoa Beach saw its population of 246 explode by 1000 percent in the 1950s. The Space Coast was born with rapid influx and little time to plan.

The end of Apollo in 1972 devastated the region. When we visited, people in Titusville, whether or not they were there to experience those layoffs, talked about the ghost-town years. Resident John Litchfield recalled, "I got here January 1, 1971. Between 1969 and 1971, they laid ten thousand people off. It was 16 percent unemployment, and that's when two hundred thousand lived in the whole county. Life was dependent on the Cape. People were leaving town right and left. It's never going to be that bad again."

Mayor Tully reiterated to us, "First of all, after Apollo, the numbers were entirely different. The county was half the size, and the [NASA] workforce was probably double the size, and so [NASA employees] made up a much larger portion of the population, so layoffs then were just devastating. Here, now with a larger population and a smaller work-force, there will be some people who will suffer and be stressed out. But it's not going to be anything like it was." The mayor's words seemed a relief to anyone worried about Titusville, reason not to fret much over the dip they were experiencing. But these constant references to post-Apollo years also signaled that Titusville couldn't stop seeing itself as a company town.

Tully, a former employee of a contractor at KSC himself, acknowledged the risk the company town takes. "For far too long, we were far too dependent on those buildings across the river there. We didn't have to fight for our jobs like most communities do around the country. They were kind of plopped in our lap."

Liz Wirth, a local restaurant manager, backed up that point. "NASA's not going away. [People] have the misconception that there are going to be tumbleweeds rolling out there," she told me. KSC and the adjacent military base remained major employers and now play important roles in commercial spaceflight. Wirth even joked about the possibility of a new company for the town: "Put the word in: We need Mr. Branson. If Branson [and his Virgin Group of companies] comes in and takes over the VAB, we're good. *Okay, door's open now. Bring your stuff down here.* If he comes, I'm sure others will follow suit."

Maybe that wasn't far fetched. Virgin Cruise Lines, another of Richard Branson's holdings, operated down the road from Titusville in

Port Canaveral. Once Shuttle ended, Virgin Galactic, Branson's space tourism company, hired Shuttle Launch Integration Manager Mike Moses. Underlying the jokes was the sense that life would be easier if Titusville could continue to depend on a space program—the government's, a company's, any would do—and continue to take company jobs for granted.

It's not that everyone in Titusville was a NASA employee. Many were employed by contractors, including USA. But the company town was a mindset. "As contractors come and go out there," Tully said, "the people don't think of themselves as being first and foremost contractor employees. They think of themselves first and foremost as being Shuttle employees. It's hard to imagine a better job."

Given the role that NASA played in shaping Generation Space, the conflation between NASA and contractors was understandable. It rested upon the subtle difference between two prepositions: *for* and *at*. Since my three-year stint as a NASA Center for AeroSpace Information (CASI) abstractor/indexer came to an end in 1994, I've told anyone who'd listen that I worked *at* NASA CASI. The listener, though, tends to hear that I worked *for* NASA. But like Mayor Tully, I, too, had been a contract employee.

Shuttle employees, contractors or otherwise, believed in what they did for a living. It was their livelihood, not merely a job, and, no matter who signed their paystubs, I knew that they, like me, were proud to have worked at NASA.

Kimberly Guodace, a vehicle engineer, got laid off nine weeks short of fifteen years in the space program. She remembered seeing a news story about the first shuttle mission in 1981, when she was eight years old, and thinking that's what she wanted to do when she grew up. In 1986, when the *Challenger* accident occurred, Guodace reaffirmed her desire to work on the shuttle to prevent such an accident from happening again. In 2003, after *Columbia* disintegrated on re-entry, she spent more than five weeks on a debris recovery team in Texas. Over the years, she'd worked on the shuttle's electrical, potable water, fuel cell, and wireless video systems. When I met her in 2011, she couldn't let go. She was volunteering at KSC, giving NASA Tweetup participants a tour and waxing nostalgic about *Endeavour*, to which she referred as "105" or "my baby."

It was a common sentiment. Omar Izquierdo worked meticulously to keep the shuttle secure, checking what went into the orbiter and that nothing was left inside that didn't belong there for the mission. "The number of good times I've had working closely around the shuttles is simply ridiculous," he said. "I've sat in the commander's seat of *Discovery*, on the launch pad, lying on my back pointing up! It'd be criminal for me to complain." In the months after Shuttle ended, Izquierdo transitioned to new work at KSC and returned to school. Instead of living from launch to launch, he lived from one layoff round to the next. When he considered the possibility of being let go from KSC, he talked of becoming a docent there. No one had found a new way to talk about their lives and their town. That attachment was understandable, venerable; I respected his awe and loyalty.

Whether you were a writer there for a week at a time like me or a longtime resident, it was difficult to imagine this place as anything but a company town organized according to a launch schedule. For thirty years, Titusville was a space shuttle town. It had to envision another identity or, along with the rest of the country, shift to new ways of defining the space program.

Company town or otherwise, Titusville seemed a pretty good place to live. Titusville held its own in terms of education levels, exceeding or nearing national rates through the bachelor's degree. Over half of workers commuted more than fifteen minutes because, from Titusville, it was a beautiful twenty-five-minute drive across the river to KSC. Three-quarters of the jobs were white collar, home prices were far below national and state averages, and Florida had no personal income tax.

Titusville's toughest challenge was the beach town model established by its most immediate neighbors and the favoritism seemingly paid to those communities in the south end of Brevard County. Before Shuttle ended, Titusville resident John Litchfield remarked to us, "The rest of the county always looked down on the north end of the county. People stick their noses up." But he recognized that other beach towns made important shifts in those dark post-Apollo days: "All that stuff in Melbourne [and other beach towns] were all started by people laid off at the Cape in the sixties. Now Melbourne's not even affected by the Cape anymore." Liz Wirth agreed and pointed also to Melbourne's shift from depending on space contracts to cultivating defense contracts, in addition to the beach tourism industry.

Pointing to the non-NASA success of towns to the south, Litchfield talked of Titusville's haphazard effort to mimic its south-county neighbors. Cocoa developed a quaint, historic downtown. "That's why we wanted the condos downtown: because Cocoa had condos. We're never going to be Cocoa Village. The only way you can stop people to shop downtown is to put stop sticks in the middle of the road." Though it initially flourished because of the space program, Cocoa Beach redefined itself as a family-friendly beach escape to the tune of more than half the tourist tax dollars in the county. Titusville can't compete on the terms other towns set years ago.

Perhaps each company town faced with the possibility of a post-company future must ask, *What's ours and only ours?* For Titusville, the untapped resources were not unconnected to the concepts undergirding the old company town mentality. Titusville could become a city of flight—from birds to airplanes to rockets, with the Merritt Island National Wildlife Refuge, the Valiant Air Command Warbird Museum, and the KSC Visitor Complex. It's not as if KSC closed its doors, after all. And there's more in the area than KSC.

On its eastern side, across the new expanse of bridge, lies the Merritt Island National Wildlife Refuge. I visited Titusville four times before Anna and I investigated those acres of natural habitat, not because we didn't have time or interest but because nobody mentioned it to us earlier. When we finally made our way there, we watched birds swooping to catch fish and manatees rolling on the surface of the water. Another time, we drove out to the beach, the longest stretch of sand unobstructed by condos or billboards that I've seen anywhere on Florida's coast. It was post-card-home-to-make-co-workers-jealous gorgeous. It was also almost empty, as if nobody else had been told it was there either.

Later, while talking with residents, I discovered one possible reason that no one in town had casually mentioned the spectacular beach of Canaveral National Seashore, run by the National Park Service. At one end, clearly marked by signs, was a section that was clothing optional. A nude beach!

The nude beach might well have been a part of Titusville's puzzle in the hoped-for recovery, but the town must have thought it untoward. Drawing a European crowd to the clothing-optional beach—or even a homegrown crowd, judging by reviews of the beach on Yelp—could be good for the economy, but decades-old stories about arrests of nudists by the sheriff lingered. Technically, the sheriff can't do much about naked people on federal land, but technicalities don't prevent scandal.

The attractions that don't get mentioned indicate the underlying problem in a company town: a singular identity precludes variety and makes it difficult for insiders to see what might be most attractive to visitors or investors unlike themselves. So, while the mayor talked a good talk about drawing new businesses into the area, there remained soft resistance to different ways of thinking about this place and its people, both from insiders and outsiders.

Some maps of the Rust Belt portray the Southwestern edge as an arc through the geography that defined my childhood; it ran through Decatur, Bloomington-Normal, Peoria, Galesburg, the Quad Cities. That fuzzy arc took in my hometown of Abingdon, Illinois, just nine miles south of the larger Galesburg, a railroad town.

A number of the counties included in this swath lost more than 50 percent of their manufacturing jobs from 1958 to 2002. Even that staggering number fails to capture the true impact. My hometown lost all its manufacturing jobs in 2000 when the Abingdon Pottery closed. The announcement of the factory closing came in December, days before Christmas, and, just like that, 150 jobs—in a town of three thousand people—were gone. Though many families of my friends were sustained by jobs in Galesburg, most of those factories were gone too. Even my high school no longer exists, forced by dwindling demographics into consolidation with neighboring Avon, Illinois. I grew up an Abingdon Commando; thirty years later, my brother's sons are A-Town Tornadoes.

Some of these factory closings made national headlines. While President Obama was a member of the Illinois legislature, he made five trips to Galesburg, and the flight of the local Maytag factory to Mexico became a part of the speech that he made to the Democratic National Convention in 2004, where he introduced himself to the world beyond Illinois.

My father spent most of his working life as one of the engineers at a small factory in Galesburg. Originally family-owned, the company manufactured stainless steel industrial screens. It changed hands several times over its final decades; each sale was to a progressively larger, more remote, less interested parent company. The last owners shut them down in 2003; my father locked the factory's doors for the last time.

My father, certain he had something left in the tank, formed a new partnership with fellow employees in 2004. They manufacture the same stainless steel industrial screens and have kept the doors open for more than a decade. They rose from the ashes.

Titusville, too, has risen from the ashes we saw five years ago. The town is cultivating its identity based on its location and resources, and, like my father opening a company that does the same thing as one that was shuttered, Titusville has not given up on the Space Coast to which it clings. There are, after all, reasons spacecraft launch from Florida: physics and safety. It isn't obvious when standing still, but anything attached to the surface of Earth is moving quickly eastward (that rotation is why the Sun rises in the east and sets in the west). At the equator, Earth's rotating surface moves at 1,037 miles per hour. Rockets launched from KSC, because of the geographic location close to the equator, start out moving at about 915 miles per hour eastward, a head start that saves fuel. In addition, by launching over the Atlantic Ocean, the rocket, if something goes wrong, can safely be destroyed over unpopulated waves.

Titusville has slowly emerged from the double whammy of the economic crisis and the end of Shuttle. By the fall of 2015, housing sales were up. Unemployment for the years 2010-2015 went from 12.1 percent to 6.1 percent. In addition, Sperling's Best Places predicted that the region's job growth rate for next ten years would be slightly ahead of national growth. A new developer was planning a sixty-million-dollar, open-air entertainment complex where the mall had stood. *Florida Today* reported a "comeback" for the region.

Certainly, these encouraging signs were a result, in part, of Titusville maintaining its identity as a space town. Shortly after the end of Shuttle, SpaceX—a private space company founded by Elon Musk, who also co-founded PayPal and Tesla Motors—leased LC-39A. They'll launch Falcon 9 and Falcon Heavy rockets there. In 2015, commercial space company Blue Origin announced their plan to build a $200 million factory south of KSC. The factory will bring 330 jobs to the area, with an average annual salary of $89,000. Even NASA has big plans and is revamping LC-39B, preparing for the Space Launch System, the underfunded program to support a Mars mission.

Like the waters of the Banana River in Florida, like the cornfields of my Illinois childhood, the rapport between NASA and Titusville ebbs and flows. Titusville became a part of the way I understood Generation Space, of the way I understood our dreams and resilience.

CHAPTER 15
BIRDS OF A DIFFERENT COLOR
ANNA

> There is one reason for caring, and I believe no other is
> necessary. [...] And it's simply this: the world would be a
> poorer, darker, lonelier place without them.

—Douglas Adams and Mark Carwardine, *Last Chance to See*

In 2011, when *Endeavour* rose from the launch pad that May, Doug and I were three miles away. Even that far away, we saw the fire under the orbiter; we heard the roar of rocket boosters and main engines. A wave of heat rolled over us, warmth on our faces even at that distance.

The space shuttle was among the rarest of machines. To see one of the shuttles in person was exceptional. Only six orbiters were built in total, and only five traveled beyond Earth's atmosphere. The shuttle was a technological species of only a few individuals. When we saw it launch, the fleet was scheduled for extinction. I believed that the world would be a poorer, darker, lonelier place without shuttle orbiters.

In their book about endangered species, science-fiction writer Douglas Adams and zoologist Mark Carwardine write, "Extinctions, of course, have been happening for millions of years: animals and plants were disappearing long before people arrived on the scene." I don't want to create false equivalencies between a host of endangered animals and a thirty-year space program, nor do I want to ignore the problem of animal species extinction. Yet, what Adams and Carwardine wrote about animals struck me as similar to what shuttle worker Omar Izquierdo told us: "Good things start and good things end, and the shuttle isn't an exception."

When we traveled to Florida, our intention was to examine technology. Doug and I weren't looking for nature; we didn't expect to notice it.

The birds caught our attention first. The variety of birds on the Space Coast fascinated me: songbirds and waders, shorebirds and seabirds, migratory birds and year-round fowl, more than 330 species, though I had no way of cataloguing or counting myself.

In the Midwest, we grew up with what I consider run-of-the-mill birds: robins, cardinals, blue jays. I recognize these species without thinking. The robin, it turns out, is the cognitive prototype for the concept *bird* for the majority of Americans. It's the default image of a bird in my head; it's the bird often pictured in children's books. My grandfather taught me how to identify male and female cardinals by pointing out the pair that lived in his backyard; the male was bright red, whereas the female might be mistaken for any of many brown birds. I'm not a bird watcher; I'm no expert.

What first caught my attention, as we drove the road that traversed the Indian River between Titusville and KSC, were birds' legs. Long, thin legs that anchored creatures as they sunned and fished near the edge of the water. Spindly legs that, when folded up, allowed birds to be perfectly at home in the air but also, when extended, to function elegantly on the ground, sometimes perched on one foot and grabbing lunch with the other. Over several trips, I never got used to seeing water birds, roseate spoonbills that look like flamingoes, rare reddish egrets, tri-colored herons. Their grace stood in sharp contrast to the clunky bird-machine I'd come to see take flight.

Nature photographer Stephen Dalton calls flight a miracle. In his book, he writes of the human being's fascination with flying: "As birds and insects were constantly around for him to observe and admire, he must have longed for wings of his own so that he, too, might take off and experience the rush of cool air as he swooped and turned in the skies. Unobstructed and free, he would escape the constraints of his earth-bound existence." That's why Doug and I traveled cross-country time and again to see the last Shuttle launches: our longings. Astronauts fulfill humanity's longing by escaping our Earthly existence.

Controlled flight—that of a bird, an airplane, an orbiter returning to the runway after a mission—depends upon the relationship of four forces: lift, drag, thrust, and gravity. The shuttle was designed with just enough stubby, Delta-shaped wing to provide a little lift, or the upward aerodynamic force generated when a wing or any airfoil passes through air. Newton's law explains that for every action, in this case air pushed down by a wing passing through it, there's an opposite and equal reaction, in this case lift of the wing. Lift offsets some pull of Earth's gravity. That way, the orbiter's landing could be controlled instead of allowing gravity to work unchecked, pulling the spacecraft back to Earth's surface in a drop, as it had with Apollo capsules. But the returning orbiter doesn't so much fly under its own power as glide, as a bird glides when not flapping wings.

Neither the shuttle's wings nor its legs—its landing gear—are as graceful or as deftly maneuverable as those of the wading birds we saw in Florida. The shuttle's landing gear—a wheel under the nose and one under each wing—have just enough strut and tire to cushion touchdown and provide braking. Once the gear deployed, when the orbiter had slowed to below 345 miles per hour and was just 250 feet or so above the ground, they couldn't be retracted from onboard. With no ability to generate thrust—no engine power, no wing flapping—to rise for a go-around or do-over, an orbiter had one shot to land. Later, shuttle workers pulled up the gear manually as part of preparation for the next mission—until there were no more missions scheduled.

Birds, according to Dalton, represent "perfect harmony of form and function." A shuttle orbiter, on the other hand, was an incongruous negotiation of form, function, and government committees that seemed to work in spite of itself. An orbiter couldn't take off on its own; instead, it required two strapped-on solid rocket boosters and an enormous fuel tank. Once descent from orbit began, it could not ascend, nor land wherever the crew might have desired to end up. An orbiter was no bird.

Had humankind never seen examples of flight by birds, would anyone have imagined a way to leave the ground? Had he not been curious about how birds managed to stay aloft, would Leonardo da Vinci have taken human flight seriously? Had wings not evolved in birds and insects, would a couple of guys who ran a bicycle shop in Ohio have thought to construct an airplane that could fly for a few lofty seconds? In a letter he wrote in December 1941, Orville Wright talks of birds as inspiration and reference point: "Learning the secret of flight from a bird was a good deal like learning the secret of magic from a magician. After you once know the trick and know what to look for, you see things that you did not notice when you did not know exactly what to look for."

When we planned our trips to Florida, we didn't know to look for birds and hadn't heard of Merritt Island. We noticed elegant birds standing in the water. We couldn't help but be curious about any flying thing.

The flights of the machines we'd come to see on the Space Coast seemed, at times over the previous three decades, almost as mundane as the commutes of those of us living ground-based lives. Even Doug and I didn't always notice when a shuttle launched or landed. After all, we don't pay much attention to the daily takeoffs and landings at O'Hare airport in Chicago, where more than a hundred airplanes might arrive in a single hour. By comparison, the shuttle had only 135 missions, so it was never commonplace.

The miles the shuttle logged offers another way of measuring. Some birds fly more than five thousand miles without stopping as they migrate; for a bird species flying that distance, the shuttle's mileage would be one hundred thousand migrations, or fifty thousand years of there and back. The shuttle's speed and flight path was like no worldly migration.

Only three functional orbiters—*Discovery*, *Endeavour*, and *Atlantis*—remained at the end of the Shuttle program. As soon as each completed its last mission, it was decommissioned, no longer fit for its intended purpose and readied for display at museums, taxidermied for exhibit and study like the last specimens of an extinct bird.

When we visited the Space Coast for the last-ever shuttle launch of *Atlantis*, Doug and I saw *Endeavour* already undergoing such refitting, which was really a sort of un-fitting. *Endeavour* was having its Orbital Maneuvering System pods, those bulbous protrusions near the shuttle's empennage, removed. Stephanie Stilson, a United Space Alliance employee and NASA's Director for Shuttle Transition and Retirement, gave us a personal tour of the Orbiter Processing Facility, where *Endeavour* was shrouded in scaffolding. Had *Endeavour* been getting ready for another flight when we saw it there in July 2011, the orbiter would have been in exactly this same position in the OPF, many of the same swap-outs and repairs occurring. We saw this rare specimen in its technological habitat, but we knew this time was the last-ever visit for *Endeavour* to the OPF. Extinction can be hard to see unless you're looking for it.

As soon as we walked through the double-doors inside the OPF, Doug and I were already standing under the orbiter. When we looked up, we could read the numbers printed on the thermal tiles of *Endeavour's* belly and note the little markers placed on the tiles by the debris team to designate dings and scratches that needed to be repaired. This time, though, the tiles were being repaired to look good for museum-goers of the future, not to protect a crew from the forces of re-entry once more.

We walked under the nose and around the nose gear. Stilson gave us footies to cover our shoes and fasteners to secure our glasses so that they wouldn't fall into some crevice of the orbiter. Then, she took us up top. The temporary staircase was situated in front of the orbiter, with the walkway over the foreword part of its nose like a bandage. The windows looked like close-set eyes, inches from my feet, smaller than I expected, though I knew that windows on a spacecraft were a human luxury more than a technological necessity. Each window had a black covering that read, *DO NOT REMOVE WITHOUT AUTHORIZATION*. I didn't touch *Endeavour's* eyes, though I was tempted.

While the orbiter's belly is covered with black thermal tiles, some surfaces up top that didn't take the brunt of re-entry heat were covered in stiff, white, quilted blankets. The side of the orbiter invited me to run my finger around the NASA logo and the lettering *United States*, but I had been told not to touch anything. I didn't dare.

Some of the orbiter's insides—red and pink pipes, metal brackets, wires, foil-wrapped objects, something bright green—were visible through openings. *Look*, I said to Doug, as if he were not looking, as if one of us might miss something. The machine's innards looked like a mess of vessels and organs, complicated in the extreme. The cargo bay doors were open, a process that, when the orbiter is on the ground, must be done carefully with support beams. The doors were designed to function gracefully in zero-gravity and are incapable of supporting their own weight on Earth. This shuttle was most itself in space, its fragility and awkwardness laid out in the OPF. The cargo bay sat empty, its interior sides covered in a shiny foil. I imagined what had been carried there: most recently, the Alpha Magnetic Spectrometer 2. This space would be forever empty; the orbiter would never move again of its own volition.

I knew that the emptiness I saw, the lack of momentum I observed, was my own as much as it was the orbiter's. Science tells me that the pathetic fallacy—attributing emotion or action to nature, to the non-human—is a terrible thing, a misrepresentation that clouds clarity of meaning, and it can be. I experienced, instead, what I think of as the pathetic insight, a heightened awareness of my own emotion elicited through my interaction with a machine. I noticed some things and, surely, not others. The word *pathetic* comes from a Greek word meaning *suffering* but also from a later word meaning *sensitive*. As I stood under and over *Endeavour*, I felt more human—more aware of my own heartbeats, my own breaths—in its presence. Doug and I squeezed each other's hands a few times, wordlessly, and I was newly cognizant of the shape and firmness of his hands. Within inches of a space shuttle, with my hand in Doug's briefly, I understood the shape of my hand differently too, as if I were inside myself and also observing.

The pathetic insight—and perhaps even the dreaded pathetic fallacy—is a way to become sensitive to what is beyond oneself, including suffering as well as joy. Somehow, because the shuttle was made by human hands or because humans flew encased inside, my affinity for this flying machine was, I realized, greater than my kinship with living birds. I got closer to this orbiter than I ever had to a bird.

Across the river from Titusville, where we stayed during our trips, lie both KSC and the Merritt Island National Wildlife Refuge. Geographically, these seemingly diametrically opposed government entities are one and the same. In 1963, as the Space Race geared up, the US government bought one hundred forty thousand acres of land, which make up the refuge. Ten thousand of these acres are used for NASA's launch facilities and supporting roads and buildings. In other words, the area is mostly a wildlife refuge, but seven percent is also used by NASA.

Birds outnumber all other vertebrate species in the world, and the wildlife refuge on the Space Coast is a protected home to hundreds of species of birds. So it's no wonder birds inserted themselves into my experiences there, forced me not to take them for granted. I close my eyes now and see an American avocet, its brown and white body atop two white legs, knees bending—to my mind—the wrong way, the bird's white head, its long, thin beak. One day, a heron stood in the waterside brush as if posing for my camera, turning its head for a better shot.

Feathers are birds' distinguishing feature, the amazingly light, aerodynamic, and shape-shifting attribute that humans have tried to emulate—even adding winglets to modern commercial aircraft like those feathers at the tips of eagle's wings—but have not figured out how to replicate. The bird's wing itself, much more complicated than the fixed wing of an airplane or shuttle orbiter, is, according to Dalton, "an incredibly complicated structure of muscles, tendons, blood vessels, and nerve tissue, which, by a combination of muscular movements and feather bending, is capable of flapping and changing its shape in a bewildering variety of ways." A bird, whose wing can change shape and size, reminds me of the limits of technological advances, constraints on flight that are also our constraints as humans.

It's odd that birds lived in the shadow of the shuttle. Technology, after all, threatens birds' well-being; too many birds are disappearing. The wood stork, the only stork to spend its breeding time in North America, is endangered, yet it's likely the first bird Doug and I noticed wading by the shore as we drove across the Indian River on NASA Parkway. The bird towered two or three feet, its white plumage a downy wrap, its movements careful, unhurried. At our first sighting, we didn't see the wood stork's pink feet, nor imagine its more-than-five-foot wingspan. Later, we saw wood storks in flight, beaks stretched forward, legs stretched back, soaring sight for our eyes. We saw an eagles' nest from a tour bus. The refuge's roseate tern, which dives for fish; the small piping plover; and the Florida scrub jay, the only bird endemic to (only existing in) Florida—all are threatened, on the path to becoming endangered.

The American alligator is also threatened and therefore protected from legal hunting in the United States, though judging by the number of alligators we saw in the ditches along NASA Parkway (and those that KSC workers had to chase off the landing strip before a shuttle return), I'm not as worried about this species. When I returned to the launch pad to see *Endeavour*, I edged over to the small roadside pond for a look. Indeed, two alligators, their snouts poking through brackish marsh water, stared back at me. In hindsight, I encroached closer than I should have, the creatures' lazy look lulling my sensibilities. Alligators are known to be territorial, and one volunteer claimed an alligator is faster than a horse for the first fifty feet of its run. Granted, I didn't inch farther than the other reporter gaping at the gators; I made sure someone else remained a more proximate meal. But I was within that first fifty swift feet. One of those gators could have clamped down on my leg and dragged me into the pond, tearing me into consumable chunks. All this death-roll thrashing I imagined in hindsight, weeks later, when I wondered how these creatures survived the sound and heat of a rocket launch that would kill a human being at that distance.

One day, Doug and I drove over to the beach, pausing for turtle after turtle crossing the road. I'm even less expert about turtles than I am about birds. Of the species of turtles wandering the wildlife refuge, I learned that the leatherback, green, Kemps Ridley, and Atlantic hawksbill are all endangered. Sea turtles such as these four are especially susceptible to mistaking garbage—floating plastic dumped into their ocean home—for food, which causes an array of health problems.

The loggerhead is threatened. Loggerheads, which we saw swimming in shallow water now and then, grow to roughly three feet long and can live more than sixty years. They aren't quick reproducers, maturing in their late teens or even later (like humans); females then lay eggs in a few nests only every two or three years.

Female sea turtles of several varieties crawl onto Florida beaches to lay their eggs in several clutches or batches, sometimes more than a hundred in a clutch, before returning to the sea. The eggs—probably 75 percent of those laid—hatch a couple of months later, and the tiny turtles, with shells less than an inch long, called carapaces, try to find the bright horizon that is the ocean before a bird, a lizard, or a fox gobbles them up. Since the 1980s, conservationists have placed screens over turtle nests on Merritt Island beaches to protect the eggs from predators. Still, the Office of Naval Research estimates that only one or two hatchlings per clutch survive the first year, and some conservation groups estimate that only one in several thousand hatchlings lives to maturity. In human terms, that's a heart-stopping mortality rate. Even in the countries with very high infant mortality, one or two babies in a hundred will die in their first year, according to *The World Factbook* from the CIA. When I think as a human being about sea turtles, the statistics of our lives flip-flop in my mind.

As Doug and I stood on the pristine stretch of beach across from Titusville's northern end, where languorous cranes and pelicans and the occasional eagle drifted overhead, children bent and peered at the wire grids that protected recently lain sea turtle eggs. We could see in the distance launch pad 39A, the spot that launched Apollo and many space shuttle missions.

Another day, we drove across Titusville's sweeping bridge to see the locally renowned manatees, sometimes called sea cows and weighing up to three thousand pounds. One-third of the nation's manatee population lives in the coastal waters of Merritt Island, and their ancestors swam in those shallow waters forty-five million years ago. At first, viewing from the observation deck, I was frustrated that the huge, dark blobs rolling occasionally to the water's surface were difficult to photograph, only partially visible for split-seconds at unpredictable intervals. Then, I let the camera dangle from my wrist and watched, calmed by the creatures' undulations.

A manatee can cruise at five miles per hour, with bursts three times that fast. At rest, a manatee can stay submerged for about fifteen minutes. Those we saw swimming came up for air every few minutes, flaring their nostrils as they rolled back under the surface. When I was five years old, my city-dweller parents took me to the zoo to see giraffes, sea lions, a cow. In those childhood years, I had inklings that animals were more moral, more comprehensible than people. I wanted to be a veterinarian and read *All Creatures Great and Small*. I remain fascinated that manatees, who are almost completely herbivorous, can consume one-tenth of their own body weight in the form of underwater plants and algae in a single day. They hold such a presence in Brevard County that the minor league baseball team, which plays at Space Coast Stadium in Melbourne, down the coast from Titusville, is named the Manatees.

Manatees are, like dolphins, mammals that spend all their time in the water and have shown signs of what we call intelligence. Manatees can be taught to perform some simple tasks, according to University of Florida researcher Roger Reep, though they're more difficult to motivate than dolphins because they don't find fish particularly tasty. Reep and colleagues elsewhere have also discovered that a manatee's brain and hairs form "a highly developed sense of touch" that indicates "evolution's shaping of an animal perfectly adapted to its environment," according to a *New York Times* article. In fact, manatees use their mouths and lips, just as elephants use their trunks (I'd wanted to be a big animal vet, working with elephants), to "distinguish differences as small as 0.05 millimeters" in grooves on underwater panels. That's better tactile awareness than humans. They're more in sync with their physical environment than we are with ours.

Yet, manatees are endangered. Changes in food sources, including proliferation of toxic algae, fell these creatures. Manatees hear only at a high frequency, which makes boats a hazard; large boats have motors that emit a low frequency, and recreational boats have motors with un-encased propellers. Reep estimates "collisions with boats account for about 25 percent of roughly three hundred manatee deaths" every year—that's seventy-five manatees killed by boats annually. Other manatees are scarred, sometimes again and again, from boat incursions; there are thousands of boats in Florida's waters. While the space industry has changed the region's ecosystem over the last five decades, tourism, spring break, and beachfront living pose this mammal's greatest immediate danger there. NASA, in fact, has gone out of its way to keep manatees from harm, equipping the two ships that retrieved spent solid rocket boosters from the ocean with water jets, not propellers.

That day at the refuge watching manatees—and many other days at the space center—the skin on my arms and legs became a blood-dappled, welted canvas of mosquito success. The eighty species of mosquitoes in the United States (there exist more than thirty-five hundred species worldwide), with genus names like *Aedes, Anopheles,* and *Culex,* seem to me the least endangered species in Florida. The Merritt Island refuge acknowledges them with an area called Mosquito Lagoon. One widespread Florida mosquito has the apt genus species name of *Aedes vexans*—they vexed me indeed! Suddenly, those threatened piping plovers—insect eaters!—seemed all the more worth saving in this world.

Some people argue that space exploration is important enough to overrun the natural landscape in the name of human progress. Others argue that technology should get out of that natural habitat entirely. Neither seems plausible or, at this point, necessary. In fact, both stances seem deeply flawed to me, for they depend on the false premise that humankind is not also a creature of nature, that humanity is necessarily in conflict with Earth rather than part and parcel with it. Surely, technology poses dangers and threatens species. And we are one of those species, threatened. *Accomplishment,* though, stems from a Latin word meaning *to complete,* and standing next to the orbiter forced me to consider that technology might complete humanity.

As a kid, I'd heard that NASA's rocket launches punched holes in the ozone, and damage to the environment remains one of my concerns about space exploration. The United States ditched aerosol cans years ago, and, more recently, as part of the Montreal Protocol drawn up in the 1970s, this country banned medical inhalers for asthma, like the albuterol inhaler I'd used for years. If those tiny metal tubes—one fits into the palm of a hand—pose a problem, big rockets must be awful for the environment.

In 1990, however, the space agency reported to Congress that, based on a schedule of nine shuttle launches and six Titan IV launches—both use solid fuel rockets that release dangerous chlorine into the atmosphere—NASA's release of halocarbons would represent only 0.25 percent of the annual worldwide total. Rocket launches are a mere smidge in the worldwide output of the dangerous chemicals.

Still, we shoot rockets right into where the ozone resides, far up in the stratosphere. A more recent study by the University of Colorado at Boulder and Embry-Riddle Aeronautical University predicted ozone depletion based on a growing space industry and more frequent rocket launches. With launches on the increase and aerosols and inhalers no longer contributing to ozone depletion, the space industry will become a larger percentage of the problem. The researchers recommend regulation. This research, importantly, was funded by NASA itself, along with the National Science Foundation and The Aerospace Corporation. NASA hasn't turned a blind eye to its environmental impact.

In fact, NASA keeps an eye on Earth's environment like no other entity can. The goals of the Airborne Science Program from Armstrong Flight Research Center in California include gathering accurate atmospheric measurements, both horizontally and vertically, over a given area. In other words, NASA uses aircraft to measure fine distinctions in the atmosphere, noting whether the mix is different closer to the ground (vertical) and farther from an urban area (horizontal). This program also calibrates the instruments sent into orbit on satellites used to observe Earth's atmosphere.

NASA's commitment to studying Earth's environment is nothing new. The Landsat program began in 1972, when I was just seven years old, with a satellite that circled the globe for almost six years. Landsat's satellites continue to provide data about Earth's surface to scientists and anyone else who wants it. So, for instance, data from Landsat helps commercial airlines as well as private pilots to avoid bird strikes. As NASA's website for Education and Public Outreach puts it, "Our goal is to enable you to access and use the entire Landsat Program's data, imagery, and associated science content for your own purposes."

One of the most recent discoveries by Landsat 7—a satellite launched in 1999, the immediate predecessor for the newer Landsat 8—is of Antarctic penguins. Scientists, of course, already knew there were penguins in the Antarctic, but they didn't know how many or whether they migrated. Though Landsat 7 doesn't have resolution good enough for scientists to count individual penguins on Earth's surface, researchers at the British Antarctic Survey used Landsat images to measure the extent of penguin poop that stained the ice when the creatures gathered during mating season. Decades-old data was updated in 2009; researchers located ten new colonies of emperor penguins and determined that six previously existing colonies had moved. In other words, we have penguins running around here on

Earth, but we couldn't see them in their totality until we looked at them from space. NASA didn't design Landsat to find penguins, but researchers were looking for penguins and could use Landsat's perspective to find them.

Not long ago, European Union leaders were looking at the wine-growing potential of each member nation, so they used Landsat. Leaders in the western United States wanted to see where precious water was going, so they peered through Landsat's eyes. To *see* and really understand what's going on in our own environment on Earth's surface, we stepped away to look from afar, from space.

I live relatively removed from nature, having grown used to the non-native, water-guzzling palm trees that, even though I expected them from years steeped in television viewing, took my Midwestern self by surprise when we first moved to California. Most days, I don't think about the paucity of squirrels compared to my Illinois childhood, and I'm less often struck dumb by squawking green parrots, though they'd been an audible reminder of our changed life at first. When I think of technology and nature coexisting, sharing the same land on Florida's coast, I'm reminded of Robert Frost's poem "Mending Wall"—the one that gave us the catch-phrase, "Good fences make good neighbors." Indeed, the character who utters these words is adamant that separation is necessary for society. People must be separated, this character says, and not muck about in each other's lives. Indeed, NASA maintains a secure government facility. A person can't meander onto the launch pad unescorted to see rocket or alligator. But the alligators aren't fenced out; only people pose security risks.

NASA doesn't need alligators or eagles, and alligators and eagles don't have use for rockets. And yet, the US Fish & Wildlife Service, on its Merritt Island National Wildlife Refuge website, boldly states, "[R]emember, if it were not for NASA, the land would not have been purchased by the federal government and the wildlife habitats protected by this purchase would likely [have] been replaced by [a] subdivision, or commercial land use." The Florida scrub jay lives only in Florida. Without NASA keeping non-space workers out, where would it have gone?

Frost's poem ultimately posits that walls are no good:

Something there is that doesn't love a wall,
That sends the frozen-ground-swell under it,
And spills the upper boulders in the sun;
And makes gaps even two can pass abreast.

That something that doesn't love a wall is nature; nature connects us to each other. In visiting the Space Coast to develop my affinity for an extravagant flying machine, I noticed nature, became more observant and sensitive, developed a kinship for birds that I'd not known before.

CHAPTER 16
LAST CHANCE
DOUG

> From here, though, it was just open ground between us and it.
> We stayed here for a few minutes to watch and photograph it.
> If any closer approach did in fact scare it off, then this was our
> last opportunity.
>
> —Douglas Adams and Mark Carwardine, *Last Chance to See*

After a year of planning, weeks of being on the road, and mere moments of watching *Endeavour* climbing on its pillar of fire only to disappear much too soon through a low cloud deck, Anna and I returned to the Space Coast. I had to be there the last time, for a last chance to see a shuttle launch.

In 2011 (and to this day), Anna and I were living the life of twenty-first century academics. Once graduation draws the curtain on an academic year, professors—a poet-professor like Anna or a scientist-turned-librarian like myself—turn to the work that doesn't fit into the regular school year. Summer means reading journal articles to catch up on what's going on in our disciplines; preparing future classes, as many of us professors and librarians don't teach the same class twice or don't teach the same class the same way exactly; writing grant applications to support our research or creative activity; and honing an article or book proposal. Instead, I prepared to leave town for the second time since spring classes ended.

Not all our colleagues understood why we spent so much time trying to catch a shuttle launch, but Anna and I had encouragement from key people in our lives. My boss, the library's dean, looked me in the eye shortly after I returned from the *Endeavour* launch and said, "You're going back for the last launch." The words could have ended with a question mark, a slight rise in her voice. They didn't.

Even if no publication emerged from our efforts, the experience changed for the better how Anna and I approached life together. We'd moved to California to make big changes, to see what would happen to us in a place and future we didn't know, to live down the freeway from where shuttles had been built. We'd turned this move into a fulcrum, used this spot in geography and time to leverage our lives. We exerted a small force over a long distance and over a few years because we were positioned at the exact point of balance for what we wanted to accomplish. We didn't move to California to follow the space program, but we wouldn't have embarked on this project if we hadn't moved, shifted time zones, climates, and mindsets. This adventure became part and parcel of who we were and who we wanted to be. We couldn't not go back for *Atlantis*.

When I took a few minutes to dwell upon it, the looming end of Shuttle depressed me. America's ability to launch its own astronauts into space was coming to an end. For all of my adult life, I'd been a card-carrying member of Generation Space. In fact, the only credit card I've regularly used for the past twenty years—my very first credit card—has a picture of the space shuttle on it. It's my last attachment to my first job after college, three years working at NASA's Center for AeroSpace Information, where I cultivated the interests in computer science and librarianship that led me to where I am now. I joined the NASA employee credit union as soon as I landed that job and have kept five bucks in a share account ever since in order to to keep that card.

That job at NASA CASI was an extension of my boyhood dream of being an astronaut. Throughout my adult life, I felt satisfaction knowing that shuttles were still being launched from the Space Coast. As long as the shuttle was launching, the possibility existed that, at any given moment, someone with whom I had much in common—another member of Generation Space—was roughly 250 miles above me, hurtling along at about 17,500 miles per hour, existing in that fine gravitational tension between crashing to Earth and being spun out into outer space.

When Anna and I left California to see *Atlantis* launch, the weather predictions for the Space Coast said cloudy, stormy, and wet on Friday, a poor combination for the complex, surprisingly fragile shuttle. The atmospheric odds-makers put the chances for me to see the final shuttle launch at 40 percent. Those odds left me with a sick feeling.

Science-fiction writer Douglas Adams, whose words begin this chapter, once said of the modern air travel experience, "No one ever said, 'As lovely as an airport.'" That quote came back to me while I was trying and failing to get my bearings at 4:30 a.m. on Thursday morning during our layover at Atlanta's Hartsfield International. A sleepless redeye flight from the West Coast left me with sore legs, a stiff back, and a foggy mind. Anna slumped forward with her elbows on her knees, staring emptily at the floor. More than two decades of traveling together have taught me that this is her end-of-the-line posture. She was done in.

With earnest effort—water, walking, stretching—my fog lifted a bit. In a clump of people who had gathered around the gate for the flight to Orlando, I recognized some faces from the redeye. I began to see the NASA logo and shuttle mission patches on hats and t-shirts. The same interests and experiences that brought me carried them along too.

One Southern California aerospace engineer waiting in the gate area planned most of his vacations around shuttle launches. He wouldn't reveal how many he'd seen (nor how many not-launches), but he admitted that his wife was happy for the end of the Shuttle program because she wanted to vacation with him again. Next, I spoke with a young engineer from NASA's Jet Propulsion Laboratory, little more than an hour up the road from my own California home. This was his first chance to see a shuttle launch. We didn't talk about the fact that it was also his last chance. So many people in his work group had asked for time off to go to Florida that his supervisor instituted a lottery. He and his friends were going to view the launch from the causeway, a road running from the mainland into KSC, a favored public viewing area.

On the short flight from Atlanta to Orlando, Anna and I downed caffeine to rally ourselves. We also looked around; we weren't in this alone. Though we didn't know their names, we recognized fellow space nerds. Thousands of us—Generation Space—headed to the Space Coast for the last launch. As we neared, I knew we might never return again, and, though that didn't turn out to be the case, this thought motivated me. We'd take in every experience as though it would never occur again. It wouldn't; experience isn't repeatable like an experiment, which ideally has the same result every time. The inherent goal of experience is new effects, new consequences.

When Anna and I arrived at the press credentialing office, a 1960s government-standard building, the parking lot was full, a confirmation of fears I'd kept to myself. A quick, shared look with Anna told me she was thinking it too. So many people, including members of the press—mainstream, social media, otherwise—were headed here that I might be jockeyed out of my experience, might not find the best spot. Projections for crowds were running at a half-million, and the actual count ended up almost twice that. The press line stretched out the door.

We made our way inside the office, showed our two forms of ID, and received STS-135 badges. The quick drive past the Visitor Complex and through security didn't prepare us for the parking lot at the News Center: acres of cars, satellite trucks, and several temporary studios in various stages of construction. The media extravaganza hadn't started yet—launch was set for tomorrow—but international hubbub was building.

Most of the press—Anna and I included—opted to watch launches from the wide, flat expanse of grass and weeds down the hill from the News Center itself. Higher on the slope offered a good perch for the studio tents and scaffolding we were seeing for the first time. The viewing area abutted a small body of water known as the turn basin, large enough for barges and tugboats to turn around after dropping off their cargo. The turn basin was originally created for Apollo, where the first and second stages of the Saturn V were hauled in from the Banana River on barges. It had been used for the delivery of the shuttle's external fuel tank for the last time on September 28, 2010. In the eight months that Anna and I had been coming to the Press Site, the only users of the turn basin that I'd witnessed had been bottlenose dolphins. The gliding gray bodies of the graceful mammals occasionally drew reporters and photographers up to the edge of the murky brown water; they often seemed surprised to see a sea creature in the heart of so many technological miracles.

I looked around, trying to predict where I might situate myself the next day. This viewing area's most recognizable accoutrement remains the iconic, digital countdown clock and the nearby flagpole. The two items had been added to the US National Register of Historic Places five years to the day after the launch of Apollo 11. For the ceremony, the large clock had been set to 9:32 a.m., the instant when the countdown ended, when Neil Armstrong, Michael Collins, and Buzz Aldrin became a moment in history in addition to being people.

Three days prior to the *Atlantis* launch, the countdown clock had been set to T-43:00:00, and the Shuttle Test Director set the countdown in motion by calling the launch controllers to their stations. The forty-three-hour countdown took three days to accomplish because of the seven built-in pauses, called *holds*, in the process: T-27 hours, T-19 hours, T-11 hours, T-6 hours, T-3 hours, T-20 minutes, T-9 minutes. The holds in the countdown process allowed launch personnel the extra time needed to finish tasks while still targeting a precise moment for launch.

For the *Endeavour* launch, I'd been less than twenty yards from the countdown clock. The storied machine's past of marking time before and during all of the Apollo voyages and again for Shuttle missions was now linked with my own history, my own sense of how time can be counted. I wanted another chance to watch the numbers tick down—T minus—to that instant when nearly seven million pounds of thrust overcomes gravity, when the clock starts counting mission elapsed time, *up* one second at a time.

The shuttle wasn't the only retiree in the news. Another retirement that hung in the air was Mark Kelly's. The STS-134 commander had announced two weeks earlier he'd be leaving NASA in the fall to continue supporting his wife, Congresswoman Gabrielle Giffords, during her recovery from the January shooting.

I'd wanted to be an astronaut, and I was once again reminded by Kelly's image and story in the news that I was the right age to have been in his shoes. When STS-134 was funded as the last mission, *Air & Space Magazine* noted that four of the six astronauts on *Endeavour*'s crew "weren't even born when the first shuttle commander, John Young, joined NASA in 1962." He flew the first shuttle when he was fifty years old, my age now. When Young started his forty-two-year NASA career, I hadn't yet been born. Neither had Anna. Neither had Mark Kelly. Kelly was a couple of years older than I and retiring from the career I'd wanted. For STS-135, only its commander Chris Ferguson was born prior to Young's joining NASA.

There exist many gradations of being left out, of not being in the shoes one might have worn well. I wondered how Ferguson, the actual last-ever Shuttle commander, felt about being left out of the media hoopla that had enveloped Kelly—first as the mistaken last-ever commander on magazine covers, then as the hero who set life's tragedy aside to fly. Did they rack up such goings-on to serendipity, the force I've come to understand as one of the most powerful in the universe, the force that led me from becoming an astronaut and to this adventure as witness to the Space Age?

Following the end of Shuttle had become a strange way of coming to terms with the choices I'd made and those that had been made for me, of understanding who I was and what I might do in this world. In some way, this book chronicles how I let go of second guesses and accepted my life with Anna and my role. In Generation Space, we can't all be the astronauts we might have dreamed of being, but we find happiness despite, or perhaps because of, shifts in our plans and desires.

While many journalists were at KSC for the first time, there were no first-time astronauts on STS-135. Pilot Doug Hurley, a Marine Corps pilot before his work for NASA, had the least experience, with one previous flight. Mission specialist Rex Walheim and Commander Ferguson each had two previous space flights. Sandy Magnus, the last woman to fly on a shuttle, had been a part of three prior missions but only two round-trips. She helped construct ISS in October 2002 on STS-122. She rode STS-126 to ISS in November 2008 to be a part of Expedition 18. But when Anna and I saw STS-126 end with its California landing, she wasn't onboard. Instead, she stayed on Station and rode home on STS-119 after 132 days in space.

Having met a few astronauts, I assume that most crews are quirky. This crew's wakeup songs embody idiosyncrasy: fellow Illinoisan Magnus requested "Tubthumping" by Chumbawamba and "Celebration" by Kool and the Gang, the latter a staple of Midwestern county fairs in my early years, while others chose songs by artists ranging from ELO to Coldplay to Keith Urban. NASA had also arranged special greetings: a message from REM frontman Michael Stipe accompanied "Man on the Moon," and a message from Beyoncé prefaced "Run the World (Girls)" to honor women in space. It's easy to think NASA is driven solely by science, engineering, and budget, but the space agency has always been steered by personality and pop culture, too. The shadow of Shuttle has a melody.

Anna and I waited, and we could have used a wake-up song. We hadn't slept. I perused press materials and ran past facts and future plans through my mind. The plan for the final Shuttle mission was an odd amalgam of routine and extraordinary: a resupply mission to ISS, the thirty-seventh shuttle trip there. *Atlantis,* known to NASA internally as OV-104 (Orbital Vehicle) or merely 104, made twelve of those flights and, in doing so, delivered a range of components: laboratory space, an air-lock, and several pieces of the Integrated Truss Structure, the backbone of ISS.

This time, *Atlantis* was carrying the Raffaello multi-purpose logistics module, a large, pressurized container for ferrying cargo. The STS-135 press materials summed up the Italian-built Raffaello—capable of handling 7.5 tons of materials—and its role in the mission: "This is the equivalent of a semi-truck trailer full of station gear bringing equipment to and from the space station." Though written in 2011 about a module, it could as easily have been written forty years earlier as a central objective for the shuttle itself: *a space-going semi-truck for delivering the goods to your space station.*

At times, as Anna and I listened to that day's press briefing about the manifest, it seemed as if *any thing* that might ever be of *any use*—realistic or otherwise—was being sent uphill: a host of supplies, potential replacement items, surplus gear. The mission was a perfect fit for a space truck, the vehicle NASA had touted decades earlier. Astronauts, like interchangeable drivers, might be considered secondary to cargo. If there were an on-orbit emergency during STS-135, there was no backup shuttle for a rescue. Instead, the four STS-135 astronauts would be stranded on Station and return to Earth on Russian Soyuz-TMA space-craft when necessary or convenient. *Atlantis:* a life spent as an ordinary working stiff. But the road that *Atlantis* and the other orbiters had trav-eled was 250 miles above our heads, not ordinary at all.

As of June 2011, before this last Shuttle launch, 538 humans had already travelled higher than fifty miles above Earth's surface, the metric by which the United States defines an astronaut. The Shuttle fleet carried 355—almost 66 percent—of those people. As a fleet, the five space-worthy shuttles had delivered 3,513,638 pounds of stuff to orbit. That accounts for more than half of all mass ever trucked into space, starting with Sputnik.

Even more impressive, shuttles, with their cavernous cargo bays, had returned 97 percent of all mass ever trucked *back* from space to Earth, some 229,132 pounds. Not much has come back, but that which did almost always came back on a shuttle. Many returned materials were studied for their response to the space environment, and some were disassembled to learn how they'd performed in space or, in some cases, failed to perform. This scenario would be the case for the final mission, too. In July 2010, an ammonia pump, part of the space station's Active Thermal Control System—the station's air conditioning unit, vital for cooling fragile electronics and astronauts—had failed. *Atlantis* would return the pump so that engineers could determine the cause of the failure and avoid it in the future. Weighing almost eight hundred pounds and measuring five feet by four feet by three feet, the ammonia pump was machinery that the shuttle—and no other spacecraft—was designed to haul.

Atlantis had already traveled more than one hundred and twenty million miles. That's equivalent to all the way to the Sun and about a third of the way back. While racking up those millions of miles, *Atlantis* carried, on two separate missions in 1989, two interplanetary probes into low-Earth orbit, where special booster rockets then launched the probes into deep space: Magellan, which began the first high-resolution mapping of Venus in 1990 and was sent to its demise into that planet's atmosphere in 1994, and Galileo, which reached Jupiter in 1995 and studied that planet and its moons and met its own atmospheric end on Jupiter in 2003. *Atlantis* also delivered one of NASA's Great Observatories, the Compton Gamma Ray Observatory, to low-Earth orbit. Science-oriented missions like these, with long-term goals, struck me as not merely the space-truck (or cargo-ship) variety—quite appropriate for *Atlantis*, a vehicle named after an ocean-faring research ship operated by the famous Woods Hole Oceanographic Institute for the nearly forty years before I was born.

At the end of Shuttle, NASA had finally achieved some original goals for the program, but not to the degree that the dreamers from the 1950s and 1960s had promised. Cost savings never materialized. Turnaround times got shorter, but not down to two weeks, as initially dreamed. With the last mission, the shuttle became the space truck that had been envisioned. As such, it stands as one of the least interesting missions ever flown. Yet traveling into space is never uninteresting, and this launch generated the most public interest in the program since the *Columbia* tragedy, simply because it was the end.

Everything was going according to plan, so the T-11-hour hold—the longest of the built-in pauses—was set to last between thirteen and fourteen hours. One major task during this hold was the rollback of the RSS. In May, I'd missed *Endeavour's* rollback because I was wearing shorts; for *Atlantis*, I was prepared.

Word circulated quickly and efficiently among the press corps: "The buses are loading." The press corps migrated, mostly en masse, with slowpokes in dribs and drabs, into the parking lot. We dutifully lined up for the security search next to the buses. We placed all of our cameras, bags, and other gear on the ground in a line that preserved our place, then stepped back out of the way. But the security team seemed in no hurry to emerge from their vehicles. The sweat trickled down our backs as Anna and I waited patiently in the Florida heat and humidity. A noxious brew of bug spray, sunscreen, and diesel fumes filled the air. And then, it started to rain. At first, a few drops. Then, hard, pelting. We stood, not sure what to do, not wanting to lose our spot.

A team from Japan's NTV reacted first. They dashed to their dizzying array of electronic wizardry sitting snuggly inside of ruggedized plastic cases. For the inspection, though, cases were all open, with the precious gear sitting unprotected, out in the rain. Up and down the line, teams followed the Japanese crew's lead and covered gear with raincoats, plastic bags, anything. The meager amount of gear that Anna and I had—a tiny, handheld video camera, a digital audio recorder, and a couple of digital cameras—was precious to us. We walked over to our bags, retrieved our handfuls, and huddled them under our clothes to wait out the weather. No one rushed back to the News Center. We all stood in the rain. The security personnel sat in their vehicles; they had no intention of getting wet. Anna and I would remain soggy for hours.

Eventually, the rain passed, and the search took place, but the effort appeared lackluster. On the ride to launch pad 39A—the pad from which Apollo 11 had left for the Moon—my engineer's mind began thinking about *Atlantis*. I was about to see a soon-to-be-up-close example of what it takes for thrust to overcome gravity.

When I got off the bus, my mind emptied. I was as close to a living spaceship—it seemed to breathe—as I'd ever get, and I wanted to know all that I could about how it functioned as machine, as a system. Instead, all I could do was stare slack-jawed and try to comprehend its beauty. Whatever doubts I had about the future, whatever ennui had been infecting me, it all faded into nothingness the moment I experienced *Atlantis*. The orbiter sat on the launch pad, looking for all the world as if it were ready to go any moment. It took me several moments to realize that the rollback had already occurred, that I'd missed part of the process and been bequeathed *Atlantis* itself.

Machines can be beautiful. This is a fundamental belief so deep in my value system that I rarely try to articulate or understand why I hold it. The skin of *Atlantis* was worn from work. Its white thermal protection blankets were smudged, streaked from the fiery heat of reentry during previous missions. These imperfections made beauty all the more evident as function: this was a machine for doing things in space. Now, it stood in front of me, resolute, pointed toward the sky as if to say, *That's where I'm going. Come along.*

Anna tapped my shoulder and drew me out of my reverie. "Don't you want to take some photos?" And I did. For the next several minutes, I battled mosquitos and other journalists for the best vantage. The sound of people slapping blood-sucking insects on their skin was nearly as loud as the clicks of cameras (professionals kept the shutter click, even in the digital age). In my notebook, I wrote snippets of overheard conversation and what I thought were profound observations. Mostly, I stared at the white monolith. If all went well, in twelve hours, *Atlantis* would carry Ferguson, Hurley, Magnus, and Walheim—real human beings like Anna and me—into low-Earth orbit: the final time any shuttle would do so. *This* shuttle, the one before my eyes.

The engineer in me took a breath. I welcomed him back. I examined the crawlerway under my feet, two paths of crushed stone that ran three-and-half miles from the VAB to the pad. In these river rocks, I intuited the enormity of the burden—the crawler-transporter and shuttle—they'd carried. I'd expected that these thickly spread rocks would pack tightly, having born seventeen million pounds of weight: 2.75 million for the stacked orbiter and 8.23 million for the mobile launcher platform upon which it sat, in addition to the crawler's weight of six million pounds. Instead, they had give; individual rocks moved even as the swathe remained stable. My mind teetered on some meaning of life I couldn't quite grasp. Years before, a software engineering professor told me, "All life is allegorical." Everything that day on the Space Coast meant something more than itself.

I lifted my head to look out at the intricate maze of pipes and tanks that carried LOX (liquid oxygen) and LH (liquid hydrogen) to the shuttle for fueling prior to launch and, in more cases than I'd realized before we started our adventure, away from the shuttle after a scrubbed launch. Would I mind a scrub tomorrow, if it were merely an extension?

Bloodied and bemused, the last-ever group of writers and photographers at the last-ever photo op for a shuttle on the launch pad rode quietly back to the News Center.

Sated with techno-majesty, Anna and I made our weary way back to the motel, showered, ate, and tried, but largely failed, to sleep. We'd been awake for thirty-six straight hours, but sleep eluded us. We hoped lying down would get us through another day. When the alarm went off the next morning, my mind and body were so sluggish that, at first, I wasn't sure what the sound was—or where I was. When I found my phone, I couldn't make my fingers swipe the screen to turn off the clanging. We hadn't expected our adventure to test our physical limits and comfort zones, but we discovered ways that the mind can push the body beyond itself, ways that the nausea of sleep deprivation can be subdued by adrenaline and the desire to be somewhere to witness something. We knew not everyone had the chances we'd had; we felt a responsibility to these moments.

Even at 3:30 a.m., the drive out to KSC made it clear that something important was going on. During previous early mornings, we'd had US 1—the road from downtown Titusville along the coast—mostly to ourselves. This time, the roadside was lined with RVs and campers, some with their owners already sitting outside to chat in the cool, wet air. Pickup trucks and cars, people lying in truck beds and on hoods, huddled under blankets, filled in the gaps. Small groups of people moved back and forth across the highway, headed to and from the enterprising donut shops and gas stations pushing coffee, soda, and sweets—caffeine and sugar—to keep people awake. I felt elated driving past them, knowing I was a part of this mass of humanity swelling in celebration of a machine, of something humans had made, something we'd done.

Early that morning, chances of a scrub were at 70 percent. Launch wasn't likely, but Anna and I dragged ourselves closer. The possibility—however small—existed for a clear window at launch time, and NASA was confident enough that tanking—filling the shuttle's external fuel tank with LOX and LH—had started just after 2:00 a.m. Anna and I are somewhat superstitious and also creatures of habit. The previous day's sogginess lay fresh in our minds, so we pulled into a gas station complex, as we had for *Endeavour*, to purchase a pair of umbrellas under the rule that, if you bring an umbrella, it won't rain. As we paid, the clerk told us to park close enough to walk back there to hear the live music they'd start in a couple of hours. The party was on. We had backstage passes!

As we drove across the NASA Parkway, I wondered whether Anna and I were already late to the party. For fifteen minutes, we waited in several miles of traffic without moving—the cars were not full of members of the general public, but others heading to KSC. Then, without warning, cars began to move steadily toward the security gate. As we passed the Visitor Complex, it was obvious they were preparing for the big send-off party, too. As we showed our badges at the gate, Anna surmised that traffic had been held there, because we were then sent forward in a wave. The entire day went like this early stint: masses of confused people, little explanation at hand, and besieged KSC staffers doing their best to keep everyone safe and happy.

The walk from the parking lot to the News Center felt like a Super Bowl Sunday. Satellite trucks from every major news outlet occupied the acreage nearest the press building so as to be as close to the electrical power sources as possible. Generators were lined up in a row that had been empty every time before. Their diesel motors pumped out enough heat to chase away the cool of the morning and likely enough electricity to keep on the lights in a medium-sized town. This is what it must have been like for Apollo, I thought, as if the pre-dawn darkness allowed decades to collapse briefly in my mind.

The networks and their temporary studios had expanded since the previous day. Cables, lights, and cameras were strewn everywhere, and reporters hunched over tables and hunkered down in broadcast chairs. On the way into the News Center, we saw Anderson Cooper in the CNN studio, and Anna couldn't resist stopping to take a few photographs. As the day wore on, we'd cross paths with actor and Twitterati space nerd Seth Green, as well as John Oliver, then with *The Daily Show*.

As with the press viewing area, activity inside the News Center was also ratcheted up. Blue-suited astronauts and their NASA public relations handlers were talking to journalists and checking itineraries to see where they were supposed to be five minutes ago. There weren't any lines for sign-up sheets as there had been in the past; instead, masses of reporters—many of whom had never been there before— jostled in large clumps around desks. Anna and I quickly wended our way into the fray and signed up to interview two astronauts. We were about to sign up for the astronaut walkout, trying to maneuver around our last human obstacles, when a staffer shouted, "The buses are just about to leave for the astronaut walkout. If you're going, you'd better go NOW."

Our adrenaline kicked in, and Anna and I knew what we were doing. The crew walkout was a deeply enshrined part of NASA culture, having taken place before every human spaceflight since 1968, and we'd seen it before ourselves for *Endeavour*'s crew. Crammed into an area between buildings, Anna and I—along with hundreds of others, press, KSC workers, and DC dignitaries—waited for the last shuttle crew to emerge from the Operations & Checkout building in their orange flight suits to pause, smile, and wave.

For me, the star of this show was the iconic, silver Astrovan, and waiting for the crew was opportunity to peruse it from a short distance. Its sole mission in the vast machinery of NASA's human spaceflight program was to carry the astronauts and some of their gear—for Shuttle, the astronaut's helmets, delivered in their own procession of NASA employees prior to the astronauts—the few miles from here to the launch pad. This Astrovan—with its big NASA logo and darkened side windows—was put into service at the request of the astronauts themselves, an explicit visual and nostalgic tie to the Apollo era. In its twenty-four years of Shuttle-era service, it zipped twenty-four thousand miles around KSC.

At 7:36 a.m., the four astronauts—Ferguson, Hurley, Magnus, and Walheim—walked out. They stopped; they waved; they pointed, as if recognizing people in the crowd. Cameras clicked away, a farewell song. Our own photos show the four smiling, and that's how I remember these moments. The walkout seemed short. The Astrovan drove away. If everything went well, the next time that the press or public saw them would be after the landing of *Atlantis*, when Shuttle would be over.

After returning from the walkout, I felt fully back in the swing of things. Anna and I wrote two pieces, one for our local newspaper, the *OC Register*, and one for a segment called *Your Voices* with the BBC Online. After that, we headed to our interview with Mike Massimino, or @Astro_Mike, as he is known on Twitter. He became famous as the first astronaut to tweet from space (sort of, as he'd emailed his tweets to Johnson Space Center, where staff then posted them on the social media site) and the first astronaut to reach a million followers.

In October 2010, Massimino had visited our university via Skype for a showing of *An Article of Hope*, a film about the loss of the shuttle *Columbia* and its crew. That documentary honed in on Israeli astronaut Ilan Ramon, and Massimino, a friend of Ramon, answered questions afterward. One young woman—a college student—asked, "How do I become an astronaut?" Massimino quipped quickly, "Learn Russian." He went on to give a more detailed answer, but his initial remark reflected two things that resonated the day we interviewed him at KSC: 1) The only immediate destination for American astronauts is ISS, and Russian is one of its two official languages. 2) Once Shuttle ended, Americans would ride into space only on Russian rockets.

In 2011, at KSC, Massimino told us that he "was six years old when Neil Armstrong walked on the Moon" and that, though he didn't know what he wanted to do early on, he "liked math and science." I wasn't yet three for the Moon landing, but otherwise Massimino seemed a lot like me. He made it sound as if he'd hardly planned his future, even as he finished college, by which time I'd known that I'd never be an astronaut and wasn't sure what to do. Massimino thought becoming an astronaut was impossible but figured the space program employed a lot of people. He wanted to play some role in that dream he'd had as a kid. I pictured myself, for a moment, in his shoes. Massimino had applied four times before he was accepted to the astronaut corps. As much as serendipity matters in the arc of a life, perseverance is the necessary follow-through. Faced with obstacles in my path at nineteen years old, I had walked away and started over. I'd persevered differently, but here I was anyway at KSC talking with an astronaut.

Massimino flew two Hubble servicing missions and considers the Hubble Space Telescope the greatest accomplishment of Shuttle, and I have to agree. In 2009, his second mission marked the four hundredth anniversary of Galileo's use of a telescope for astronomical observations. On that mission, Massimino viewed the stars through "a really good replica" of Galileo's telescope that they'd carried aboard in commemoration. As he viewed the stars with it, Hubble, the observatory that altered the way we understand the universe, sat in *Atlantis*'s payload bay.

The space telescope was named after astronomer Edwin Hubble, who inferred from observations that the universe is expanding. It looks into the cosmos with instruments that discern near ultraviolet, visible, and near infrared light. The versatile Hubble shows us images we've never before seen of different types of stars in different stages of development in different regions of the universe. Using Hubble, scientists study how stars emerge and perish, how a given star's formation makes planet development more or less likely, and why one star becomes a black hole while another forms a neutron star. Rich with color and vigorous shapes, these images depict a universe in motion, changing on small and large scales for the last thirteen or fourteen billion years. This eye-in-the-sky also confirmed that the part of the universe in which Earth sits is typical of the universe as a whole, that what we see here is what we get pretty much everywhere, so that studying a part offers clues to the whole. That's the sort of science I adore, knowledge that ripples out in all directions.

One of Hubble's most important discoveries came in 1998, when it observed far-off supernovae that showed the universe had expanded more slowly in the past, that expansion is accelerating, and something must be causing this—the predictions of Hubble the scientist had been confirmed by his namesake telescope. That something is called dark energy, and it's the largest component of the universe. Hubble pointed astrophysicist Adam Reiss to dark energy. He shared his Hubble-based insights, and the work of this group was awarded the 2011 Nobel Prize in Physics, months after Shuttle ended.

That story is emblematic of what's most heartening about Hubble and about all federally funded science: it belongs to everyone. Anyone can submit a proposal to request Hubble's time (though time is limited, so it's competitive) to investigate a particular scientific question. Though some data remains proprietary to the principle investigator for a year, the answers that Hubble finds are shared relatively quickly among scientists and with the public. That's part of why Hubble has led to publication of more than ten thousand scientific papers. Nonscientists benefit too. The Hubble Heritage Project is designed to share with the world Hubble's strikingly beautiful pictures of galaxies—the telescope sees ten thousand galaxies at a glance—and various celestial bodies that no one can see from the surface of our globe.

As I listened to Massimino wax nostalgic about having his hands on Hubble, I was disheartened to be reminded that, after Shuttle ended, Hubble would not be able to be serviced. Though the telescope is providing data, its parts will stop working one by one. Without the shuttle to nudge it up occasionally, its orbit will eventually decay, probably after 2020. I'm saddened to think that, once its mission ends, Hubble won't find its way home in a shuttle's payload bay to be preserved and displayed in the National and Air and Space Museum, an inspiration to future generations. Instead, it will fall into Earth's atmosphere and burn up, just as Skylab did years ago.

When Anna asked @Astro_Mike a kooky question about Italy and ISS as a global effort (we prided ourselves on coming up with at least one question no one else would ask), he revealed that he'd flown the Sicilian flag (he describes its iconography as "grotesque," but "it grows on you") on his first mission and that he'd recently been knighted by the Italian president.

Listening to him and all the other astronauts with whom Anna and I talked during our time in Florida, I didn't feel jealousy, as I'd expected when I'd considered encountering astronauts on this adventure, but, rather, an appreciation for the varied ways an individual's opportunities and decisions lead that person where he—or I—didn't plan to end up. Each person is the sum of his or her parts and also more than others might surmise at first glance. I was where I was supposed to be—wanted to be—at that moment: talking with an astronaut at KSC, waiting to watch a rocket launch.

As Anna and I and everybody else waited to see if the weather would clear, I doubted that day was the day that Shuttle would end. I wanted to see a launch, but part of me looked forward to a scrub, to one more day.

Anna and I stayed close together as we headed to look for a spot in the viewing area for the possible launch. The countdown clock had just hit T-15 minutes and counting. I was anxious in more ways than I could track.

We looked around for Margaret Lazarus Dean, another writer. I'd seen Margaret at a writer's conference a few years before, on a panel about using science in fiction. She'd discussed the research necessary for her novel, *The Time it Takes to Fall*, a coming-of-age story about a girl growing up on the Space Coast at the time of the *Challenger* disaster. We'd been in contact with Margaret, a younger member of Generation Space born in 1972, on and off for the better part of the previous year, and she'd texted us that she'd arrived at KSC. I had mixed feelings about sharing the last launch with anyone but Anna, but we were amidst a crowd as it was. Generation Space was full of our kind, to one extent or another, so I decided—difficult and partial as this thinking was for me—to consider this a shared experience with, not a throng, but individuals in ensemble. So Anna and I sought out Margaret through a smartphone-based version of Marco Polo ("I'm near Anderson Cooper!").

Positioning ourselves was like billiard balls deftly played by an unseen hustler. Clumps of journalists moved around, consciously or subconsciously driven to find the best vantage, whereas photographers dug in and held their ground. Maneuvering was a complex mathematics of balancing the number of the people in front of me, factoring in the average height of those directly in my line of sight, and anticipating the likelihood that individuals—or perhaps a whole group—in front of me would raise their hands and clap or jump up and down at the moment of launch. I called that the effusiveness factor.

After Margaret joined us, we pinned ourselves as a group to a spot near the water behind some photogs. Over the noise of the crowd and light wind, I couldn't hear the PA system well. I lost track of the count-down. Ten minutes? Three? I tried small talk but stopped short, my mind focused on machine and time. I stared out over the turn basin and across the three miles that separated us from the astronauts in *Atlantis*, seated on their backs, and pointed up, ready.

There existed few moments like this in a person's life. Even if by some miracle, through all the scrubs, you managed to witness every launch, you would have done it only 135 times. And that would have taken thirty years. Other than reporter Jay Barbree, I've never heard of anyone who's claimed to have done such a thing. I wondered, *Was the weather really good enough? Was that a break in the clouds above?*

Four minutes? One? I did what I imagined other engineers and scientists do in this situation—or maybe people on their deathbeds—I thought about all I had learned that was directly connected to this experience. I thought about how NASA had nearly failed in the 1960s (largely as a part of the Atlas-Centaur missile program) to use liquid hydrogen—a substance which needs to be kept at -423 °F, just 36 °F above absolute zero, the point at which all molecular motion stops—as a rocket fuel. If NASA had failed in that effort, astronauts wouldn't have reached the Moon. Diligent application of research and dollars had tamed the substance in time to be used in the second and third stages of the Saturn V. Given the success of Apollo, it was a natural step for the combination of liquid hydrogen and liquid oxygen to be used for the Space Shuttle Main Engines. When the two cryogenic substances combined and burned, the result was a nearly clear and intensely beautiful blue-tinged flame. That exhaust was mostly water vapor. I wanted to see that vapor, the orbiter's last breath in the sky above my head.

As launch approached—T minus what?—an engineer's thoughts kept running through my head. The shuttle's solid propellant rocket motors also had a tortured—and as in the case of Challenger, disastrous—development history. They produced an angry flame. Reds, oranges, yellows, and dirty browns commingled in twin columns of light and fire that extended one-and-a-half times the length of the shuttle itself. Where the fire ended, the escaped exhaust gases turned to caricatures of puffy white, clouds of nearly perfectly distributed density and dozens of miles long. These exhaust trails were a witch's brew of hydrochloric acid and other chemicals that resulted from burning solid fuel: aluminum, ammonium perchlorate, iron oxide, PBAN (polybutadiene acrylic acid acrylonitrile terpolymer), and an epoxy curing agent. I waited to see these last, angry breaths, too. I thought ahead because, as was the case at the launch pad the day before, I knew that, in the rush of emotion, I would be unable to parse details of what was really happening.

When the launch happened that July day, it took me by surprise even though I knew it was coming. "Ten...Nine..." The part of the crowd that could see the clock started to count down aloud in unison. "Eight... Seven—"

As happened at Endeavour's launch, I was momentarily stricken by the thought of Challenger. What if the shuttle exploded? What if the whole program ended in disaster?

The main engines ignited at roughly T-7 seconds, and all thoughts failed me. I experienced it with my body, my senses. The first white clouds gathered around the base of the launch pad. Atlantis was going to launch. I stole a quick glance at Anna, her unblinking eyes already filled with wonder. That we were sharing this moment wedded our lifetimes together, something we had hoped when we made our move to California even though we had no idea how it might happen.

The SRBs' flame—*fire*, my mind called out—grew brutish, almost pre-historic. The flame of the main engines was just visible, a perfect blue, a flame of science, of progress.

Atlantis passed the top of the launch tower at 11:29:10 a.m. EDT on the morning of July 8, 2011. At that second, control of the orbiter transferred to Houston's Mission Control. For all the NASA civil servants and contractors in the KSC fire room, their job was done. Their task would never be repeated.

I stared across the water as the shuttle rose. I listened. Ripping. Shredding. The heavy, humid Florida air was torn apart by heat, shoved out of the way by the passage of the shuttle's bulk and its exhaust. The sound washed over me in staccato blasts, claps of air. Changes in air pressure rose and fell in waves, reached into my chest. My body—and Anna's too, I knew—shook.

The crowd cheered. "Go!" and "Godspeed, *Atlantis*." I couldn't speak.

And still, *Atlantis* rose into the sky. The shuttle moved faster than I'd imagined the sweeping curves in the wings, arrow-shaft cylinders for the boosters, and cigar-like fuel tank could. *Atlantis* disappeared into a cloud layer. It was gone. Its shadow traced an extending line on the tops of clouds: *Atlantis*'s progress toward orbit. The sound of engines kept going, kept coming at me. For as long we could, Anna and I—and much of the crowd—listened. We looked, too. Though we could no longer see the orbiter, we watched the sky. I couldn't look away for a long time.

Even after we couldn't hear the shuttle's roar any longer, we lingered, watching the exhaust trails climb, then disappear. I retraced the shuttle's arc with my eyes, again and again. Finally, Anna and I turned to each other to hug. As much as we'd shared this experience, it was also mine alone and hers alone, each of us separated by skin and air.

I'd forgotten about other people until I became aware of myself again. The humid air and my own sweat made my face a drippy mess. With an enormous smile stretched over my face, I don't think that anyone but Anna could tell I was crying. The wonder in my eyes had created a few tears. A photographer—a man who'd been to many launches but who always turned his back to the pad and instead photographed the faces of people watching—walked in a half-circle around us, snapping pictures. Had our moment after launch ever been seen by anyone other than that photographer? I've hoped not. Even surrounded by thousands of people, I felt that this was my moment and our moment.

After *Endeavour's* launch, I'd felt energized, alive. After *Atlantis*, I was spent, wiped out in a way I'd never before known. Still, Anna and I held out for the post-launch press conference. Sitting in the small room, filled with rows of chairs and elbowing journalists (not nearly big enough for the fifteen hundred registered media), Anna leaned over to whisper in my ear: "I'm going to clap when the two Mikes come in. It's that kind of moment."

I rolled my eyes and half-hoped, half-knew she would then be Generation Space first and journalist second. Eventually, the two Mikes in charge of launch—Mike Moses and Mike Leinbach—walked into the room, along with NASA Associate Administrator Bill Gerstenmaier, KSC Director Bob Cabana, and press officer Mike Curie. How had Curie been the one to host the last shuttle launch news conference? Did he have seniority, or draw the long, legacy-rich straw?

Before the men were seated, Anna started clapping. The whole room followed in a standing ovation, not realizing who'd started it. Anna, I know, often feels most herself when she remains the invisible instigator, and the rest of us needed the merest excuse to release our enthusiasm and gratitude from beneath our journalist shells.

By the time that Anna and I made our way back to the motel that evening, we'd slept for about three hours of the previous fifty-six. We were bleary-eyed and groggy, and the events of the day, the past two months, and the previous year felt chaotic and heady.

For the second time in my life, I'd felt as much as heard the sound of the shuttle's liftoff hammer on and in my chest, and, even on a hot and humid Florida day, I'd experienced the radiant heat of the inferno beneath the shuttle's tail, the maelstrom of speeding, burning gases that carried the shuttle aloft and into a tenuous purchase above Earth. We would never witness it again. No one would. Anna and I had witnessed something extraordinary. Even her t-shirt spelled it out: *I WAS THERE.* Our happiness and sadness could not be teased apart. We slept for the next fifteen hours, and it was good.

CHAPTER 17
THE MOURNING AFTER
ANNA

All men live envelopec in whale-lines. All are born with halters round their necks; but it is only when caught in the swift, sudden turn of death, that mortals realize the silent, subtle, ever present perils of life.

—Herman Melville, Moby-Dick

Two nights after the last shuttle launch, Doug and I went out to the canal to wait for the second of two ships, which we'd heard was scheduled to come into view at about 8:00 p.m. with the left solid rocket booster. The SRBs had been attached to *Atlantis*'s external fuel tank to provide enormous propulsion from burning solid fuel during launch. They'd separated from the shuttle assembly at roughly two minutes into flight, after it had moved beyond the cloud cover and out of our view. The boosters had continued their upward trajectory until Earth's gravity slowly diminished the cylinders' momentum and ultimately drew them back downward. The SRBs had parachuted to the ocean, where two ships—*Liberty Star* and *Freedom Star*—had found them, their noses bobbing vertically above the surface far from shore. Divers inserted a plug into the nozzle of each booster, and then pumps aboard the ships forced water out of the tube that had been a rocket until it rose under its new buoyancy and tipped into a horizontal position. We'd missed *Liberty Star* and the hauling in of the right SRB earlier in the day because we didn't understand how events might unfold. When we rushed off to do an interview with the mayor of Titusville, it turned out that we missed that ship by ten minutes. Now, *Freedom Star* was hours late.

As we waited, a very large cruise ship departed, happy throngs waving and toasting on its deck. In no hurry ourselves, we strolled up and down along the wide canal and peered out over the blue expanse of ocean, wondering whether some dot on the horizon was what we'd come to see. The sky darkened. The raccoons of Jetty Park began peeking out at us from the rocks next to the canal. We grew tired; we didn't hold out.

Had we not developed enough patience these last several months? We'd convinced ourselves that we'd gotten this hurry-up-and-wait down pat. I was still coming to terms with the fact that we couldn't catch every event; no one can, and that's a hard lesson. The word *exhaust* means to completely use up. The boosters had been exhausted, drained of their very selves. Maybe I didn't really want to see that aftermath. I'd become exhausted in a way too, facing the end—the endings—of Shuttle.

By the morning of July 11, 2011, three days after the launch of *Atlantis*, we'd heard more about how the booster retrieval process worked. We skipped the canal where we'd walked the night before and headed straight to Canaveral Lock. A few other locals and reporters gathered there, too, but it was a small enough crowd that Doug and I felt we were insiders, in the know. Later, I'd see reports that the day before drew a much larger crowd. We appreciated the relative quiet, a private viewing of sorts.

Freedom Star, gleaming clean white with blue lettering, arrived at the lock just before 9:00 a.m. The ship pulled into the lock, the SRB floating light in the water, strapped horizontally to the boat's port side. Pelicans, with their unwieldy bills, paddled slowly in the greenish water, and a few manatees, dark grey blobs, lolled about. A heron stood near us, watching the process, and an eagle perched on a light post overhead. A large water bird, its arced wings spread, glided over the SRB. The lock's gates closed, the water level adjusted, and the transition from Atlantic Ocean to Banana River began.

Had we seen that first SRB come in the night before, would we have put such effort into seeing the process a second time? *Yes*, I thought. Watching *Endeavour* lift off the ground and into the sky hadn't been enough. Seeing *Atlantis*—seeing the last launch—felt necessary, too, and seeing the *last* SRB in its *last* official moments in the space program was part of this last chance to see as much as we possibly could.

Three crew in each of three small zodiac boats—not much more than inflatable rafts—detached the SRB from *Freedom Star*. The diameter of the booster was double the height of any of the crew in the boats next to it. Those in the zodiacs worked methodically and continuously to undo the few lines—tied with simple knots—from the larger boat and still maintain control of the SRB. The pace of this process was funereal.

These workers dragged the booster behind their boats through the locks. Such a large object for three small boats to maneuver. Like pulling a car over a frozen lake with a few strings, a small jerk could lead to a large slide. The booster was close enough to us as it passed that we could make out scratches on the metal casing; someone had etched *Sea Slug* near the joint at the top of the booster's bottom segment. We could see the battered insulation inside its nozzle. To accomplish orbit takes a lot of energy, and this metal casing had contained much of the previous day's energy in the form of solid fuel. Now, it looked raggedy. I was witness to reusability, the concept that was supposed to make the shuttle more affordable.

As I put my hand in Doug's, I knew that's how any relationship works too—it takes and gives energy. Life leaves us sometimes tattered and frayed, but mostly we keep each other intact as we get where we need to go.

As we watched, Doug and I assumed that this process happened this way all the time, though we wondered why *Liberty Star* was sitting in the Banana River and *Freedom Star* didn't sail right on through. *Liberty Star* had come through the lock and into the river fine the day before, we discovered later—always learning in hindsight as well as in the moment—but NASA had concerns that morning, at lower tide, about the river's water level just beyond the locks. *Freedom Star* had eleven feet of draft, too much of itself under the water's surface to traverse the shallow shoals just inside the lock system, so the SRB was taken over the shoals by the smaller zodiacs. This more complicated transfer reminded us that, with the space shuttle, seeing something once isn't seeing it all. I also thought about the behind-the-scenes people involved and how they adapted day to day, how we're all part of the big picture without usually stopping to think about the lives of others. Every observation we'd had over the previous year had helped us understand more about how the Shuttle program worked—had worked—and who we were in its shadow.

Once through the locks, the crew attached the SRB to the waiting *Liberty Star* to cross the remaining distance and be brought ashore at Port Canaveral. We ambled to the end of the concrete walkway along the locks, as close as we could get to the *Liberty Star*, to peer through a chain-link fence as the SRB was dragged out of sight. A dolphin followed the ship, breaking the water's surface with its fin and curling back under.

Usually, recovered boosters are refurbished—the segments separated, cleaned, and refilled with solid propellant—for a future launch. Not this time. There would be no future shuttle launch. The shuttle's reusable boosters—which had never become as cheap to reuse as NASA had hoped—were left without a use. Seeing the last booster dragged in from the ocean felt to Doug and me like an end, even though *Atlantis* was orbiting overhead. I characterized what I felt as grief. I was grateful to share these moments with Doug, to work through the various endings together. The meaning of any story is rarely discerned while you're still enmeshed in the plot, wondering what's next. Even after the last launch, we were trying to figure out what had happened these last fifty years and how we were a part of it, for we surely were. Seeing the orbiters after they'd written their stories seemed key to our understanding of technology, history, culture, and ourselves in all of it.

The transfer of *Discovery* to the National Air and Space Museum showed NASA at its most organized and official. The word *funeral* stems from the Latin for *corpse*, and funeral rituals take different forms in different cultures. This transfer unfolded like a formal state dinner. We were both lucky to attend.

We weren't both lucky enough to attend every event, though. Early on Saturday, April 14, 2012, Doug took an overnight flight from California to Florida. Riding on adrenaline, he headed to KSC and was bused over to the runway with other reporters and photographers to see *Discovery* mated to (attached to the top of) the Shuttle Carrier Aircraft, a modified 747 usually used to ferry an orbiter back to Florida after a landing at Edwards Air Force Base in California. I missed this event.

Doug also celebrated the fortieth anniversary of Apollo 16 at KSC without me. He took a public bus tour with Apollo 13 astronaut Jim Lovell, at the time eighty-four years old. I imagined the jaunt, Lovell's hands emphasizing his excitement. Doug, still lacking sleep, then attended a panel discussion that included Apollo 16 astronaut Charlie Duke, Apollo 14 Moon walker Ed Mitchell, Lovell's Apollo 13 crewmate Fred Haise, and shuttle astronaut and Director of Johnson Space Center Mike Coats. I still wasn't there yet.

The Apollo era had ended forty years earlier, and the Shuttle era was heading into history, too. I've come to believe that, just as energy can be neither created nor destroyed, there exists a law of conservation of experience. Experience takes a different form almost as soon as it reshapes us; experience becomes memory and commentary. Nothing that has happened is lost but, rather, transformed and transforming. That's part of why I became wrapped up in these sorts of events and why I was sad not to be there with Doug.

I'd been in Illinois on and off all spring. On March 1, my mother was diagnosed with pancreatic cancer, but that news was confirmation of what she and I knew. I was with her and my sister and my aunt for the failed surgery on April 10. My mother insisted I keep my date with Doug and *Discovery*. She remembered the news of Sputnik in 1957, and she'd watched Alan Shepard's fifteen-minute flight from a hospital bed in 1961. My mother knew how important following the shuttle had become for me. She was sick and still in the hospital, but she wasn't dying in the immediate sense, not yet, though we all knew that was coming. She told me, *Go!*

So, I arrived in Florida late on Sunday, April 15, and, the next day, Doug and I headed to the Mate-Demate Device at the Shuttle Landing Facility so that I could see that contraption—the objects, if not the process he'd seen—with my own eyes.

To see *Discovery* mounted on the top of a large jet airplane remains an odd image in my memory. Piggy-back planes, I thought, though technically the shuttle didn't fly of its own accord, not close to Earth anyway. When I arrived, the configuration was positioned with noses still inside the scaffolding that had been used two days before for the mating process. The configuration began to be backed out with a tug like those at airport gates, at first imperceptibly, then noticeably moving backward onto the tarmac.

Discovery's last crew stood on the tarmac to watch, too, separated from the press—from us—by a flimsy rope. The STS-133 crew seemed to have cohered especially well. As questions started to be lobbed their way, Doug and I became quickly irritated with much of the press. Though we were still relatively new to this part-time NASA life ourselves, we'd become judgmental. How easy it was for us to disapprove of others' naïve, though earnest, questions. How much we wanted to think of ourselves as insiders for a few minutes. How hard we'd worked to build that confidence. Reporters that day seemed lazy, spending their precious moments with this orbiter and this crew eking out the word *bittersweet*, which, to us, had become a dull earworm in mainstream media about the end of the Shuttle era. This crew would be happy to take another flight but had come to terms with *Discovery's* retirement.

In fact, Commander Steve Lindsay defined the day as epilogue: "I already said goodbye to *Discovery* [...] when we walked off the vehicle." He was more interested in talking about the cool T-38s astronauts flew from Houston and how important "talking between the seats" in that standard-issue training jet had been for the interplay among a crew on the shuttle. We seemed among only a few who wanted to hear what he wanted to talk about. His enthusiasm for the jets reminded us of Apollo astronaut Charlie Duke's excitement when talking about his test pilot days. We'd immersed ourselves in this story enough to make connections over time and to enjoy astronauts' quirkiness. Other reporters moved on to elicit the next utterance of *bittersweet*.

Bittersweet reminds me of the chocolate chips my great aunt used for cookies when I was a kid, and there's little bitter in those memories. Those two words together—*bitter* and *sweet*—originally referred to the taste of an apple. This word refers to taste, to a savoring of the sharp and the pleasant, that quickly became hackneyed that day—that year—by reporters wanting readers to eat it up. Traci Brimhall's title poem from her book *Saudade* captures part of the meaning I'm trying to convey:

[...] If you want
to know what I long for, I'd say a world of my own
making where changing destinies is a phrase away,
where everything is true but retreats when you try
to touch it. [...]

I felt—still feel—saudade toward the shuttle.

Steve Bowen echoed Lindsay's sentiments: what was done was done. He noted lockers that, after all these years, needed some shoving to close, like kitchen cabinets slightly askew after the house has settled for decades. But, he said, "On that last landing, [...] she was pristine." He added of STS-133, the last mission for *Discovery* and for him, "It was harder walking away from it after it landed." I was thinking something similar about all these endings: it's easier to leave when you think you'll be back. My own returns to this place were surely winnowing. I thought about my mother, too, and wondered how many times I could return to her before she was gone.

Mission Specialist Michael Barratt, with whom we'd had an exciting interview in a closet at the News Center, explained what we already knew but what most reporters seemed surprised to learn: most of the STS-133 crew wore two mission patches on the shoulders of their blue flight suits. The new one—with Bowen's name replacing Kopra's—was sewn over, slightly askew of the old one. This, too, was a symbol of the mixed feelings toward their former crew member, whom they were sad to see drop out, and the one who took his place, whom they were happy to have join them.

On January 15, 2011, Mission Specialist and lead spacewalker for STS-133 Tim Kopra had a bicycle accident and injured his hip. (Less than five months earlier, former astronaut William Lenoir—veteran of STS-5, *Columbia*'s "We Deliver" flight—died from injuries suffered in a bicycle accident.) Because this accident occurred between *Discovery*'s not-launch, which we witnessed in person, and its launch, which we didn't, the timing of Kopra's accident was terrible for him. Rumor had it that Kopra's hip had been broken, but, as with the rest of us, astronauts' medical records are private. Though astronauts have always been chosen with health and fitness in mind, we wondered why this sort of negative occurrence didn't occur more frequently among astronauts. Astronauts were a risk-seeking bunch. Michael Barratt, who had been set to work with Kopra to operate the robotic arm in space, said as much. He didn't come right out and say that an accident could happen to any of them, but that was our inevitable conclusion.

NASA's spokesperson said that Kopra thought of himself "in the penalty box [...] for getting hurt before the flight." Doug remembered when the military physician told him he'd never fly to space, and I imagined Kopra was as devastated as Doug had been. Or maybe he was even more grateful for his time on ISS, that he lucked out in becoming an astronaut at all, when so many of us who'd dreamed of that life—even for fleeting, unrealistic moments like I did—never left Earth.

Kopra's previous trip to space was on STS-127 in 2009 for a two-month stay aboard ISS. He thought he'd have another chance to see Earth's curve, to do the work he's trained to do, to be part of *Discovery's* last-ever crew. As we worked on this book in May 2016, Kopra was on ISS again, having flown up on Soyuz.

"It was quite an impact to our training," Barratt said to us, acknowledging Kopra. "We understood each other. [...] Steve [Bowen] was very accommodating. He knew his stuff very well." Only a few of the regular reporters knew what to make of this lengthy story about a man who'd *not* gone up on STS-133. I had a sense. Some attachments became stronger than others; history matters and so do individual people. But most reporters that day didn't know one astronaut from another. They needed their inverted pyramids and wanted their *bittersweet*, whereas I wanted story and image, character and texture, that layering of mission patches into meaning.

Someone asked Barratt about Bones McCoy, the physician from *Star Trek*. "He was my hero. Now I get to do that." That's what everyone wanted to hear, a reference we all understood that marked many of us there as Generation Space. Doug and I smiled too.

I was scribbling notes, trying to keep up with all the information. We asked Barratt about radiation and Mars. We knew from our earlier interview with him in the storage closet that he got enthused when he talked about the effects of radiation on the human body. Another reporter leaned over to tell me, "That was the smartest question anyone asked today." It was. I knew it. And I was pleased someone had noticed.

Pilot Eric Boe put the Shuttle program into a larger perspective, as our generation's dream-become-reality: "I like to call it the dream machine." He meant the dreams of the people who made it and kept it running for thirty years. Bowen extended that thinking and wasn't cheerful about the transition happening before our eyes. "The workmanship and the expertise," he said, will be impossible to capture in a museum exhibit. "That's the part we're losing. People make it special. People make it work." People matter.

Mission Specialist Nicole Stott put the most positive spin on *Discovery's* move to Udvar-Hazy, asserting that this orbiter will touch "people who didn't know they were interested." In fact, the next day, our novelist-friend Leslie Pietrzyk saw our blog post about *Discovery's* last flight to the museum and on that whim, went to the Potomac River to watch the shuttle aloft above her. What most surprised her was how many other people did the same thing, went outside to look up at that symbol of who we are, of what we can make and do.

While many there were busy weaving *bittersweet* quotes into news stories they'd already drafted for deadlines, Doug and I had decided in the midst of the previous year that we wanted to write a book, that the story of the end of the Shuttle program needed an in-depth treatment, and this day defined why: only a few of those who covered Shuttle events as news were experts, and daily deadlines and short word counts limited journalists' ability to ask complicated questions, follow lengthy answers, and understand the story over time. Even among the knowledgeable and dedicated space reporters, few connected the minutia with which they were fascinated to their own lives or the culture's attitudes. We'd heard Rebecca Skloot, author of *The Immortal Life of Henrietta Lacks*, say at a writer's conference a few years before: "People need stories in order to read science." News and science reporting provided important versions of the story, but our version explains who Doug and I are as a couple and also as part of a generation. It's a personal and cultural memoir.

That next day, Doug remained back at the News Center, hoping to get the orbiter and the Vehicle Assembly Building in the same photographic frame as *Discovery* departed. The lack of sleep and preponderance of exertion had added up, and he wasn't feeling very well. We'd learned to each go when and where we had the chance, so I left Doug behind, trusting he'd be okay. In our early years together, there had been stretches when we'd tried too hard to guess what the other wanted or needed, but we'd learned, sometimes painfully (as I imagine most couples who stay together must), that we each didn't always know ourselves and often misguessed each other. Maybe he wanted the option not to look too close at this ending, for he and I each wanted to see and know in different ways. I wanted to situate myself as close as I could, watch as long as possible, even if it was uncomfortable.

It was still dark when I boarded a bus with other reporters and photographers to go to the runway. I had to choose a position. Would I sit in the stands in front of the control tower, which was higher up and would provide a longer unobstructed vantage but which was set back from the runway? Or would I stand alongside the runway, which was separated by only a ditch from where the SCA-*Discovery* contraption would roar by and lift from the ground? I wanted to be as close to the action as possible. I followed the News Center volunteer who had the camera with the longest lens, who'd done this dozens of times. Beside the runway, the ground was uneven, and the mosquitoes tickled my ankles right away. The area remained unlit until, eventually, the sun started rising.

Finally—how many minutes or hours did I spend enduring this terrible waiting that marked the process of following a space shuttle—I glimpsed the Boeing 747 in the distance to the left. With the sky still pinked with sunrise, the mated orbiter started moving toward us. I focused, snapped, refocused, snapped. NASA was so aware that this process was a great last photo opportunity that the SCA, with *Discovery* atop, stopped directly in front of us for several minutes, posing for its last pictures at KSC, barely fitting into the frame for those of us this close. Then, it headed on to line up for a takeoff from right to left.

The SCA revved its engines, its wings spread wide, the orbiter's wings draped over them for a doubled effect. The configuration remained fully on the ground as it passed me, wheels rolling, gaining speed. When it was perfectly situated in my photographic frame, the wheels lifted from the ground, the forces of nature syncing exactly with my ability to capture forever the vision. If I hadn't known how orbiters worked, I would have wondered whether *Discovery* were lifting the larger jet, pulling it into the air.

The mated orbiter flew off south, then circled back, flying over the VAB, then low along the runway from left to right. An official fly-over, a gesture of good-bye. The vortices off the 747's wings trailed the vision as it flew into the distance. I watched until I couldn't make out the craft at all.

Wednesday, April 18, was a travel day for us and for everyone heading to Washington, DC, for the induction of the orbiter into the nation's premier aviation museum. Because Doug and I had flown to Florida from different places on different days, our planning had put us on different flights from Orlando to Dulles Airport, too. Before my flight, I thought a man in the waiting area looked familiar, but I couldn't place him. As I boarded, I knew that the man in Seat 1A—the best passenger seat on the aircraft—was Bob Cabana, Director of KSC. I didn't expect a KSC bigwig—a former astronaut—to take a commercial flight like the rest of us. When the flight attendants came around with the beverage service, I asked one of them to deliver my note to seat 1A: *Thank you for your service to our nation*. Before following the end of Shuttle, I wouldn't have been this brash. I signed my name so that he'd know who was stalking—had recognized—him; I wanted a reply, an acknowledgment that my noticing mattered. Of course, my noticing is making sense for myself; my note was proof to myself that I knew what I was doing. It had little to do with Cabana, and not getting a reply didn't matter. When we landed at Dulles, I snapped photos out the window of my plane; the mated orbiter sat inert on the tarmac.

On Thursday, April 19, Doug and I drove the short distance from our hotel to the Udvar-Hazy Center. We met up with Margaret Lazarus Dean, who, like us, was writing a true story about the end of Shuttle. The three of us were negotiating, as relative strangers, how to support and compete with each other as space writers. Inside the enormous building, we—a makeshift journalist team—stopped at the press check-in table for our bright bracelets, as if at a music concert with proof we were old enough to drink and wondering whether our

IDs would pass scrutiny. Doug and I had registered for media credentials, but there wasn't much scrutiny that day, and all three of us were ushered in.

Once outside again, we found our way to the secure press area. I slipped the temporary bracelet—intentionally left loose—off my wrist. Margaret took it out of the fenced area (or maybe to the fence), and her friend, Omar Izquierdo, wore it back in to join us. He deserved to get as close as he could to the orbiter for as long as he wanted. He'd taken a day off work at KSC to fly up to DC and see the end of *Discovery*'s journey. He'd been working with the shuttles for six years, keeping them safe from harm on the ground. If the man from India who'd wanted to touch a space shuttle actually made it to the launch pad that Halloween in 2010, Omar would have stopped him from putting his hand on *Discovery*.

Margaret remembered this exchange differently. Though I left my Tyvek wristband loose on purpose (I say it was yellow; she says, orange), it may well have been her own wristband made from NASA spinoff technology that she passed to her friend. His extra access was certainly her doing.

We each took notes; we each wrote books. Margaret and I sometimes watched the shuttle simultaneously within a few feet of each other. Undoubtedly, we each wondered then, at least briefly, whether the other had better access in a given moment or would have greater success in the future. Psychologists define two types of envy: malicious envy covets and wishes ill for another, and the benign type motivates one to strive all the harder. Only for split-seconds have I ever wanted something Margaret had; instead, I realized that we each earned and grew from our own moments of success and failure.

In addition, each version of the same event matters. Often, someone of Generation Space responds to what I say about this book with, *Me too*. Every *me too* is a way to share an individual story. When someone shares a memory of the Space Age, we find intersections, but the perspectives we bring to the conversations are always slightly different. Experience and interpretation require a specific point of view. Each of us has only our own voice and life, our own story to live and tell. Never have I wanted for another space writer, especially the one with whom we've corresponded and toasted, anything less than great things. Never have I wished to alter experiences and opportunities—the great things—Doug and I had during these years.

Enterprise—the test-flight shuttle that had been on display since 2003—had already been pulled out from its exhibit hangar. The test orbiter ceremoniously stood on the concrete road in front of us, behind a stage. Then, John Glenn, the first American to orbit Earth, arrived. The ceremony really kicked into gear when a US Marine band in red jackets led *Discovery* along the road to meet *Enterprise*, nose to nose like heads of state shaking hands. Astronauts who'd commanded *Discovery* over the years walked along the orbiter's left side, more than a dozen men and women in their blue flight jackets. Opera singer Denyce Graves sang the national anthem. The speeches were both solemn and congratulatory.

All this pomp and circumstance served as prelude for getting the orbiter into the exhibit hangar. The press shuffled into the hangar and arranged itself along an interview line. The VIPs followed and stopped to answer questions. When Doug asked John Glenn whether he believed NASA had stopped flying the shuttle too soon, Glenn cut him off. It wasn't NASA who'd made that decision; it was Congress, a body in which he'd once served. He called the shuttle "the most intricate, complex machine people have ever made." Glenn took hold of Doug's mis-question and wouldn't let go. He expressed earnest frustration that NASA had been given marching orders to go to Mars without being given the funding necessary to make that happen.

In contrast to Glenn, Charlie Bolden was as slick as ever, perhaps a necessary trait for a NASA Administrator negotiating a tight budget at the end of a program that some people thought had never been worth it. Bolden didn't want to "put words in Senator Glenn's mouth" but said that the former senator was fully supportive of NASA's current program of exploration and research. He rattled off his customary talking points: he was passionate about manned space exploration, the work on ISS continued to be important, and it was time for the private sector to take over low-Earth orbit. We smiled and nodded because he left no room for challenge, and the day's ambience was all decorum.

It's easy for Doug and me to go deer-in-headlights when we see astronauts. We'd learned to fight paralysis early on, when we ended up in that room full of astronauts after *Discovery*'s not-launch. When Eileen Collins approached at Udvar-Hazy, I took a deep breath and asked my Stephen Colbert-esque question: "*Discovery*—great shuttle, or the greatest shuttle?" Collins smiled; her eyes revealed her quandary about whether to play favorites. "I flew *Discovery* for my first mission and my last mission." Was that an admission that the orbiter waiting to come into this hangar was her favorite? "But I will say I have a special place in my heart for *Columbia.*" Someone had actually said it aloud today, right here at the state dinner for *Discovery*. Only three of the orbiters that went to space survived, and Collins made audible the loss of a shuttle and, on this day of seeming celebration, put a name to tragedy: *Columbia.* I went deer-in-headlights.

The most enthusiastic conversation we had was with Wayne Clough—pronounced *cluff*—the twelfth Secretary of the Smithsonian Institution. Of course, he was happy; NASA had given him a space shuttle, and not just any orbiter but the workhorse of the fleet, what would now be the shuttle of record for serious study. Growing up in a small town in Georgia, Clough had been unaware that artifacts like the ones he now oversaw even existed. "That's a shame," he reflected. His mission, as he saw it, was to ensure that people have more access to the artifacts of the century of flight and the objects of the Space Age than he did. As a kid, my parents had taken me to the Museum of Science and Industry in Chicago, time and again. Those artifacts—including airplanes and spacecraft—shaped my understanding of the world around me. No one at NASA had been as good a spokesperson for why this state dinner was a good thing as was Clough. The shuttles belonged to the American public, to Generation Space. We didn't really want them to stop flying when no spacecraft could take their place, but now they belonged to history and to those who will succeed us.

The orbiter had to be pulled into place by a tractor, a tug like the one at the Mate-Demate Device we saw earlier in Florida. This exacting maneuver—every part of the orbiter had to line up with the opening in the building perfectly—is not something for the faint of heart. The wiggle room for the tail through the slit at the peak of the wall was just a few feet wide. If the tug miscalculated, the tail would rip into the building, and the irreplaceable orbiter would be damaged. At the very least, if the man driving didn't turn the corner and line up the orbiter exactly, he'd have to back up and try again with dozens of us watching. He drove slowly. He welcomed direction from several spotters. Doug would be good at this task; I would not.

The orbiter eased in slowly, steadily. The tail split the hangar wall's opening beautifully. *Discovery* hit its mark. I gave the driver a round of applause; others joined in.

After some flimsy barriers were in place, the press walked around to photograph the machine where it would remain. The words *United States* and the American flag—blue field in its upper right corner, stripes flowing away from the orbiter's nose as if unfurling in flight—ran along the orbiter's side. The orbiter was scuffed in places, a bit dirty, evidence that it had gone to space, that it had been a workhorse. A yellow arrow with the word *RESCUE* pointed to the escape hatch on the left side under *Discovery's* windows. On the right side under the cockpit windows, a yellow rectangle with back lettering: *CUT HERE FOR EMERGENCY RESCUE. As* if rescue might be simple. These details were a shuttle's minutia, the small items that people made and maintained, the bits of knowledge that people carried in manuals and in their minds.

Doug wandered off to shoot a photo from two stories above. Margaret and I waved to him from under the orbiter's bulbous nose. The big picture, the whole of it—me in the story. The word *museum* harkens back to the muses, the nine goddesses of the arts and sciences, of inspiration. Here were two women writers with our shuttle muse. A museum is a house for the muses, and the archived shuttles were inspiration and memory.

Doug and I felt sated, filled up with overindulgence, replete with our proximity to power. As we headed out of the museum, weary from hours of intense observation, hundreds of people—the general public—were let in to see *Discovery* in its new home. They'd been waiting behind a fence, viewing us—bigwigs and press—from a distance for several hours, many of them depleted from standing outside in the sun.

The transfer of *Discovery* was a highly orchestrated event for the politically powerful, a state dinner, an extravagant handshake. The gesture was a *Thank You* from Washington, DC, the seat of the federal government, to NASA for its service of more than six decades. These few days, especially the last day, had been a chance for the key VIPs to tell each other that the space shuttle had been important. The symbolism—especially the two orbiters nose to nose, with the recognizable faces of NASA on the stage in front of the nuzzling beasts—exuded significance.

The installation process for *Discovery* had gone flawlessly as a denouement, a word that means *to unknot*, a tying up of the story, a letting go. But it was also a beginning, a dry run for the more difficult transfer—cross-country in the sky and across Los Angeles on streets—of *Endeavour*. And so Doug and I felt as entangled with the shuttle as ever.

CHAPTER 18
JOURNEY'S END
DOUG

All good things must come to an end.

—Q, *Star Trek: The Next Generation*

Right after *Atlantis* had launched, Anna and I saw *Endeavour* in the Orbiter Processing Facility. I'd walked under the orbiter's belly and on the scaffolding over its nose. I'd peered into its cargo bay. I'd seen some of its hidden insides. I might have thought this orbiter was being readied for its next launch. Instead, it was being embalmed for its final procession through the skies and through the streets of Los Angeles and Inglewood.

If *Discovery*'s transfer had been a solemn, official state dinner, *Endeavour*'s transfer was a spectacle, an event for the masses. *Endeavour* was *our* orbiter, too: the one we saw at Edwards Air Force Base in 2009, when we first moved to California; the first we'd seen launch in person; and the one that would reside permanently in our backyard in the California Science Center.

On October 11, 2011, Anna and I drove to that science center for the transfer of title for *Endeavour* from NASA, a sort of reading of the will. For the sign-over, children from the charter school on the same grounds filed in, squirmed, and cheered. At the ceremony, we sat behind June Lockhart, star of the 1960s television show *Lost in Space*, a reminder of how space exploration had shaped our culture and a reminder that this simple event was the beginning of the spectacle. Nichelle Nichols from the original *Star Trek* was there too. Two years earlier, before Anna and I started our quest, I couldn't have predicted I would hang out with the Dr. Maureen Robinson and the Uhura of my childhood imagination.

We chose this chapter's title because *Endeavour* was ending its journey. "Journey's End" is also the title of an episode of *Star Trek: The Next Generation*. (It's the title of a *Doctor Who* episode, too, but that's too convoluted for analogy.) In this *TNG* episode, the Federation has agreed to return several planets to the Cardassians. Starfleet must, as part of the title transfer process, relocate colonists of these planets, though not every planet's residents want to leave their chosen home. This *TNG* story is about history and territory, about who gets what and who decides, about how a new status quo emerges even though it's not ideal for all involved. To my mind, those issues—relocation, resistance, and vying for objects—were what I was sorting through as Anna and I followed the orbiters to their museum homes. Los Angeles had beaten out Chicago, Seattle, and Houston to get a shuttle, even though the latter was the home of astronauts and Mission Control.

In addition, the character of Wesley Crusher finds a spirit guide that leads him to quit Starfleet and explore the universe. So this story—and my story—is also about acknowledging who I thought I would be (an astronaut) and discovering who I'm still in the process of becoming (a writer, a husband, someone I didn't know I might become but am happy to be). In fact, the whole story of Shuttle and Generation Space can be seen as one of potential, of finding our way, of setting goals as if they can be reached and then reaching them, of discovering other means and creating an end out of those.

The last time we'd seen the last *Endeavour* crew had been at the astronaut walkout before sunrise on May 16, 2011. I'm always excited to be in the company of spacefarers, so I was happy to see Mark Kelly, Greg Johnson, Mike Fincke, and Andy Feustal again at the Science Center. (Roberto Vittori and Greg Chamitoff couldn't make the title transfer event.) The group was relaxed, joking that, on the space shuttle, M&Ms are worth fighting for, but, as Greg Johnson said, "You don't have Diet Coke like I'm addicted to here on Earth." He waxed nostalgic about the positive effects of zero gravity on his height; indeed, this particular bunch could have used an extra few inches. This reunion was chummy, with an aura of *hey, remember that time when we*—. Fincke said, "We need our toes, our big toes especially, to push off" and move around the shuttle or ISS. "Imagine you feel like your normal self," he said of being in the zero gravity of space, "except you can fly." The men became captivated by the video footage of their journey, sometimes whispering in each other's ears or pointing at a corner of the screen. I was privy to the home movies of what looked like a Space Age family vacation I'd imagined as a kid. "We had fun morning to night," Andy Feustal said. Of course, morning to night occurs more quickly in orbit, when one circles the globe every ninety minutes.

After the press conference, Anna and I walked down the stairs with Fincke, close enough to touch his shoulder (though I didn't), while Johnson joked around on the escalator beside us. The proximity to this sort of astronaut camaraderie was what I'd wanted since I was young. I wasn't one of them, as I'd planned when I was growing up, but, for a few minutes, I felt as if I understood what being an astronaut might have meant in day-to-day terms. More, I understood that life's goal is to each find our careers, our buddies, our fit with the world. Though I found those moments deeply meaningful, it was never more clear to me that my life was as a writer and with Anna.

Jeffrey Rudolph, director of that science center, was the (non-astronaut) man of the hour, assuring everyone that *Endeavour* would be in good hands and not too Hollywooded-up. He expected the California Science Center to become one of "the world's great science centers" and had reminded us just before *Endeavour*'s launch that his museum was already "the only place in the Western United States who has *flown* Mercury, Gemini, and Apollo command modules." He calls the shuttle "the crowning jewel." Frontman Rudolph believes, as we do, "Air and space has a great potential to inspire people to dream about what's possible."

It's easy to become jaded as one ages; before we'd moved to California, I was somewhat world-weary, stuck in a rut, exerting a lot of effort to accomplish not enough. Following the shuttles reminded me that I'd had childhood dreams, that life is full of potential. As spiritual as that may sound, I'm thinking like an engineer here. Potential depends upon mass, position, distance. Potential energy is the relationship between an object and gravity. The idea goes back to Aristotle's notion that an object holds possibilities that become realities only under the right conditions and when impediments are removed. What is potential, then, but inspiration and motivation, a quickening heartbeat when I see a space shuttle or an astronaut and imagine?

On September 14, 2012, Anna and I, donned in a navy blue NASA t-shirt, ate burritos and clinked bottled beers at El Leoncito back in Florida before following *Endeavour* home to California. Out the window, across the water in the darkness, stood the empty launch pad at KSC.

The next day, a Saturday, we spent at the Visitor Complex. The new building for *Atlantis* and the Shuttle Launch Experience was well underway. Anna and I snapped photos: us in front of the NASA meatball logo, us under a Soyuz capsule. Anna wore her first-free-man-in-space t-shirt commemorating Alan Shepard's Mercury flight. And we snapped more photos: each of us in front of a photo of the original Mercury Seven astronauts, Anna with President Kennedy, us on the orange scaffolding arm used by Apollo astronauts to access the capsule atop the rocket, us sitting on a mock-up of a lunar jeep. We played tourist. We played field trip. We spent the day making sure we had an odd visual record of what matters—of what might have been in addition to what had been—before it was over and we went back to our regular lives. These images became part of our family photo album as a couple.

On September 16, Anna and I were at the Shuttle Landing Facility before sunrise. *Endeavour* had already been mated to the Boeing 747 for the flight to California. The STS-134 crew didn't come to KSC to see the departure; perhaps, they'd moved on with their lives. Astronaut and Navy officer Kay Hire showed up to talk with reporters that weekend. Hire had been the first woman assigned to a combat aircrew and the first KSC employee—she had worked as an engineer there—to be selected as an astronaut. She wanted to be at KSC when the mated orbiter pulled out of the Mate-Demate Device that day because she had flown on STS-130 aboard *Endeavour* in February 2010. But she was the lone *Endeavour* astronaut there. The lack of fanfare allowed me to think of *Endeavour* as more mine; I cared about *Endeavour* enough to be here when even her last crew wasn't, and I'd see this orbiter home with me.

Later that day, Anna and I took the "up close" bus tour of KSC. After we'd been inside the immense VAB—its vast expanse like a vacuum that made me gasp—the tour guide announced that *Endeavour*'s ferry flight had been delayed a day. When the bus let us off to view the Apollo 8 launch reenactment and Apollo artifacts, including the enormous Saturn V rocket hanging horizontal above our heads, we called the special phone number for media updates and learned that the ferry flight was delayed because of probable weather issues between Titusville, Florida, and Houston, Texas. It takes only a little rain to keep the mated orbiter on the ground; at jet speeds, rain—and ice aloft—can damage its thermal tiles. A bit queasy from the news and from lack of sleep—up again at 4:00 a.m.—we grabbed a couple of caffeinated beverages, sat down under the looming Saturn V rocket, and tossed around possible ways to handle the news. We switched from tourists to writers.

Anna had to be back in California on Tuesday—in two days—for the kickoff of the poetry reading series she directs. "I can go back with you," I said. "We can see *Endeavour* land together at Dryden." Weeks ago, we'd discussed this possibility.

Endeavour's ferry flight was the last ever for a shuttle. We wanted to see it, but we'd grown used to planning for contingency. Unexpected circumstances like these were the reason we worked hard to function as a team, to hone our styles and story together, to be able to pick up where the other left off. We'd done this sort of thing before; we'd managed various kinds of separation over the years. I knew she'd say, *Stay!* And she did.

Endeavour departed KSC for the last time on Wednesday, September 19. For the takeoff, I chose a different perch than Anna had for *Discovery*—we always looked for breadth as well as depth of experience. I stood raised in the stands under the control tower. From this vantage, I avoided the muck and the mosquitoes, but, mostly, I had more room for error. We differ in this way, Anna and I: I like planning ahead and having a margin for error, and Anna likes to get going as soon as she's committed to something, making it work as she goes.

I snapped photos of the SCA-orbiter configuration as it stopped for just that purpose on the runway. Then, I shot videos of the configuration gently lifting from the ground. In the first snippet of this video, the configuration sits at the end of the runway, the SCA obscured by trees, the orbiter visible, ready to go. The configuration begins to roll forward, gains speed. The SCA-*Endeavour* combo zips past, its nose rises, and the whole thing moves into the air, slowly gaining altitude. I kept the orbiter perfectly framed, perfectly focused for the thirty-eight seconds the departure took. Viewing with my own eyes was the important part of all these experiences. This time, though, I was especially conscious to capture the experience as perfectly as I could on video, too, because Anna would watch it secondhand later, on a computer screen.

I saw *Endeavour* take flight from the Space Coast this time, and Anna didn't. We'd be together on the other end. A lesson we'd embedded in ourselves following the shuttles: how to always be together on the other end of anything. That requires trusting oneself as much as each other. Two years following the shuttle taught us trust.

I adjusted my travel plans more than once during that trip and flew back to California the day *Endeavour* departed. I flew to an airport on Anna's way to Dryden Flight Research Center, so that we could see *Endeavour* land together.

Anna and I met the orbiter at Dryden (now, Armstrong Flight Research Center) in the California desert on September 20, 2012. We'd been there once before, in November 2009, the day from which this book ultimately emerged.

Endeavour had made stops along the way and limited the legs of its journey for refueling, sleep for the crew, and weather conditions, so we arrived before the shuttle made its way across the country. Several reporters—fewer than at KSC, fewer than would be at LAX—parked at the direction of the Air Force escorts and milled about next to the runway. Our access was unusual, getting within a few feet of an active runway, and the MPs requested that we not photograph military aircraft. But no one checked.

The SCA-*Endeavour* configuration approached in the vast blue sky and circled above. It floated, banked gently into its turns, looking top-heavy enough at times that it might tip over. Mostly, though, it looked as if the two crafts had become one thing, permanently coupled and dependent on each other. If it had stayed aloft, I could have watched this circling for hours, lingering, observing engineering at work in this strangely elegant form. The pilots set the configuration down gradually.

The rear wheels of the 747 gave off a puff of smoke, and then the nose wheel touched ground. The configuration whisked in front of us, braking slowly under its heft as it extended down the runway.

After landing, the configuration taxied off and sat on display for an open house of sorts, a thank-you to those who had built and tested the shuttles. To get to this exhibition, we drove around Dryden's main set of buildings and walked through the one sporting the NASA entrance that television astronaut Anthony Nelson used in I Dream of Jeannie. Out on the tarmac, we walked 180 degrees tail to nose around Endeavour as it sat atop the 747. Nose over nose, not all that different from each other in shape. Delta wing over straight, slightly swept wing. Simple tail over complex tail, and me right there under both. The shuttle was smaller than the jumbo jet; the shuttle's nose not quite as far forward as the 747's front cabin door, its tail not reaching the jet's rear cabin door. Even so, the shuttle was a large, heavy object connected to the 747 by three pairs of small support bars. I squinted to study those three attachment points, noting the results of precise engineering decisions, pondering aerodynamics and the certain ways in which the shuttle is so fragile on Earth that strapping it down willy-nilly would damage it.

As if the landing and that full view of the SCA-Endeavour combo weren't enough for one day, I convinced a press officer to take us to see a couple of SRBs that I'd seen lying around on the property. I walked right up and put my hand on one of them. Across a fence stood Dryden's Mate-Demate Device, now defunct. No one seemed to know what would happen to all these artifacts. Probably, they'll be scrapped, the consensus seemed to be. The shuttles were prized, but much of the material evidence of this space program would never be seen by the public. I later mentioned these abandoned SRBs to Endeavour's caretaker, and I learned the plan is to add them to the ultimate exhibit.

The next day, Anna and I stood by the runway to watch Endeavour taxi and depart from its birthplace in the desert toward Los Angeles. It took off from left to right, from west to east, gaining speed. It raised its nose as it passed us. Endeavour lifted into the air for the last time ever. We watched as the 747 pulled its landing gear into its belly, as the configuration circled back around to head west.

Though others hopped into their cars and drove as fast as they could, we didn't rush to LAX for the last landing. We had planned to; we could have. Aristotle, the Greek philosopher, thought about two kinds of potential: one, the chance to happen, and the other as doing something well. In my own life, I transformed the chance to be an astronaut for the chance to do other things well: to help the next generation—college students—achieve their goals; to write this book and others; and to build an intellectual, physical, and emotional life with another human being. Chance is not real; doing is. I wanted to remember the orbiter aloft as long as I could. It had the chance to land, and I knew it would, but I didn't want to see that myself.

Because of a lag time built in for weather delays and to complete preparation for its travel from LAX to the science center, it took weeks for the final unveiling to occur. But eventually, *Endeavour* wended along urban streets toward the California Science Center. The journey was dubbed "Mission 26," since *Endeavour* had flown twenty-five missions and this would be its last journey. Streetlights and signs had been removed along its path. Trees—sometimes large, old trees—had been cut down, with the science center agreeing to replant two trees on its own dime for every one that had to be removed. The orbiter couldn't take the shortest route, for it had to avoid going under overpasses on freeways (*free* is the ironic term for roadways in Los Angeles). And the orbiter didn't—couldn't—avoid an L.A. neighborhood where riots had set the place on fire years earlier. Now, jubilant crowds gathered, hanging out of windows and clumping on corners to celebrate the spectacle of a space shuttle traveling down their street. At one point on the journey, in a cushy deal planned months ahead, a Toyota pickup truck pulled the orbiter across a bridge for the cameras, creating a commercial I would see again and again. The juxtaposition between this slick segment carefully crafted to sell something and the photographic images of surprise and joy on faces of L.A.-area residents lining the streets still leaves me awash in cognitive dissonance I don't even attempt to reconcile.

On Saturday, October 13, delays crept into the twelve-mile process quickly. Anna and I had gone to the science center that day to wait for the orbiter's arrival. Its first stop was on time; at the Forum in Inglewood, people cheered *Endeavour*. After that, it was supposed to arrive at a shopping plaza at the corner of Crenshaw and Martin Luther King Jr. boulevards for a half-hour dance extravaganza choreographed by Debbie Allen and involving dozens of students at her dance academy. But the orbiter was running late. At KSC, these glitches were expected, but Hollywood likes to roll camera when the lighting is right.

Anna and I gave up our vigil when the online updates said that the tractor carrying the shuttle had broken down and the earliest it would arrive was 6:00 a.m. When we woke at 4:00 a.m. the next morning to check its progress only a few hours after we'd gone to bed, the ETA had been delayed further, and we slept a little longer.

We drove back to the science center to wait for *Endeavour's* arrival with others who'd garnered press credentials. The weather was perfect, a phenomenon not lost on us native Midwesterners. When we had to use the restroom, a volunteer walked us over the path *Endeavour* would take, right through the off-limits hangar that had been built to house the orbiter. I stood in the empty space exactly where *Endeavour* would stand a few hours later, another lesson in potential and transformation around the corner.

Back under the trees, after waiting some more, we saw *Endeavour* moving slowly along a street a couple of blocks away. An outrageous visage. Mounted on a roving platform given the literal name Overland Transporter, the orbiter turned the corner to head our way. Rounding that street corner looked normal compared with the zigzagging action of the final two blocks, avoiding a light post on one side of the street, then a tree on the other, then another light post and another. How the orbiter didn't clip something that day—not anywhere on its twelve-mile, obstacle-ridden land journey—depended on trust that such a thing could be achieved. Southern California, of course, is the home of suspension of disbelief.

And then the orbiter was right there in front of us, its wing sweeping right over our heads, the wing's leading edge, that delicate curve of black, almost within my reach. The underside of the wing revealed the familiar, numbered tiles, the varying shades of gray, the streaks left from its last launch. Anna posed for a photograph as if kissing *Endeavour's* nose in thanks that it had finally arrived, and I posed as if punching it in the nose for being late. As the orbiter continued toward its hangar, the outer edge of its left wing came within six inches of the trunk of the tree next to us. Not every possibility—good or bad—comes to fruition as we wend our way along life's path.

The whole process for *Endeavour*, from title transfer to installation, was designed as all show. The crowd at the museum was chaotic, meandering in various positions over an area of several blocks. Children slipped into the press area to get a better view, imperiling expensive cameras that reporters had set up and left unmanned during the long wait. The sound system was terrible, muffling whatever ceremonious words the center's director had to say. Whenever Mayor Antonio Villaraigosa was around, it was clear that the most dangerous place in Los Angeles was between him and a camera. People were having fun.

While we were hanging out that day, we found the biggest space nerd around, the man who put together the proposal requesting a shuttle from NASA. When Ken Phillips was hired to curate aerospace science in 1991, he told his boss Jeffrey Rudolph that, if another shuttle accident were to occur, the program would undoubtedly be shut down and, when that happened, he wanted to bring an orbiter to their facility. That idea was incredibly forward thinking. When Phillips was hired, *Endeavour*, the replacement for *Challenger*, hadn't yet made its maiden voyage to space. In subsequent conversations with Phillips, we understood why he'd thought about this idea—the potential—for so long: he'd gone to college in North Carolina with Ron McNair. The two had remained friends through McNair's astronaut training and right up until the astronaut's death in the *Challenger* accident in 1986. Phillips's personal reasons for wanting to care for a shuttle fueled the proposal that convinced NASA that *Endeavour*—*Challenger*'s replacement—should educate the masses for free under his care.

The National Air and Space Museum expected to be first choice for a permanent shuttle home and was ready for *Discovery*; it opened its exhibit of the newly acquired orbiter the same day it arrived. Rudolph, who heads the California Science Center, must have been somewhat surprised to get the phone call from Charlie Bolden about being awarded an orbiter. He was certainly not fully equipped financially, nor did he have the facilities to accommodate *Endeavour* as proposed. NASA made it clear that once the orbiter was at LAX, all responsibility for it was on the science center. The California Science Center met that challenge and orchestrated the strangest shuttle journey ever. The new exhibit opened to the public on October 30, 2012, and Anna and I have seen it several times. I like to show it off. I sometimes attract a small crowd as I'm talking about how the engines work.

Eventually—and ambitiously—the orbiter will be displayed upright, as if ready for launch. As we write this book, Phillips thinks a 2018 opening of that exhibit is within the realm of possibility—and Phillips knows something about turning potential into reality. It's going to be spectacular, and I'm ready to line up now.

CHAPTER 19
ALL GOOD THINGS
ANNA

> We shall not cease from exploration
> And the end of all our exploring
> Will be to arrive where we started
> And know the place for the first time.

—T.S. Eliot, *Four Quartets*

If *Discovery*'s installation had been an official ceremony in which power was palpable, acknowledged, and leveraged, and if *Endeavour*'s cross-country, cross-city transfer had been entertainment for the masses, the celebration for *Atlantis* was for family, for the people who were personally attached to the shuttle. *Atlantis* represented the program, the workers, and the end of the end of Shuttle in November 2012.

On November 1, Doug and I were back at the badging office for what we thought could be last time. My mother was growing weaker from cancer and its treatment and would die before the end of the year. Two years earlier, before my mother was sick, we'd come to KSC for the first time for *Discovery*'s last not-launch. We'd learned an incredible amount about space exploration and about ourselves in those two years. I didn't want my mother to die, and Doug and I didn't really want to face the end of the end of Shuttle, but, in life, we don't often get to choose endings.

The gaping hole in the newly constructed annex of the Visitor Complex made it look only half-ready for *Atlantis* to arrive the next day. Outside the News Center, on the lawn where we'd watched *Atlantis* launch more than a year ago, the countdown clock loomed dark.

Reporters—we were reporters, we'd been reporters for two years—milled about in the News Center. Suddenly, Luke Wilson—the actor from movies like *Legally Blonde* and *Old School*—walked right behind the desk where I was working as if he belonged and into a room used by the NASA film crew, a room we'd never been inside. When Wilson exited about a half-hour later, we followed. Outside, Doug yelled, "Mr. Wilson. Excuse me, Mr. Wilson." Like me, Doug, already good at socializing when we started our adventure, had become more brash in the last two years. The actor turned around, and we introduced ourselves as part-time reporters and space nerds. In the photograph Doug took, the actor and I share the same surprised smile, with mirror-image front teeth, the same furrows in our foreheads as we squinted. Later, my department colleagues laminated a blown-up version of the photograph for me and said that Luke and I looked like brother and sister. He was born in 1971; he is Generation Space too.

November 2, Doug's birthday and the anniversary of first habitation of ISS, was the day of *Atlantis*'s big family barbeque. Doug's father, fond of corny Dad jokes, would have gone around telling NASA insiders that they needn't have gone to so much trouble for his son's birthday. Doug never said as much, but I could tell he didn't mind a bit that a huge space-nerd party coincided with his birthday.

The tasks at hand—following *Atlantis* to its resting place—required a 4:00 a.m. wake-up. Friday's alarm clock (our cell phones) wasn't set quite as early as during some other of our Space Coast adventures, but, with the coast-to-coast three-hour time change, we got up near to when we usually went to bed.

We arrived at the KSC News Center by 5:15 a.m., the whole area still cloaked in a deep, quiet darkness we never experienced at home in Southern California. The television news vans were already heading across the street to the VAB, and the pressroom bustled with journalists working on adrenaline and caffeine, us among them. Around 6:00 a.m., reporters were put through security, then we boarded buses and headed to the VAB.

As the press disembarked, we spread out along the media line, an area roped off for us. The VAB door was already raised, *Atlantis* inside. This first stop was our opportunity to see, for the last time, the orbiter with those individuals who worked on it. A group of shuttle workers gathered behind a banner celebrating their accomplishment. A commemorative song, complete with actual launch and landing commentary, played loudly—and then played again and again. The commentary on the recording was the voice of George Diller, a public affairs officer who'd done every launch commentary for STS-27 through STS-135, from the end of 1988 through July 8, 2011. Diller now stood just a few feet from us. *Atlantis*, atop a flat trailer, was backed out of the VAB for the last time ahead of schedule. It turned and moved slowly away into the darkness.

The word *ambiguous* is often taken to mean *vague* or *obscure*, and my feelings that day were difficult to pin down and label. The word, however, comes from Latin words meaning *to drive both ways*, and its first definition and the one I use as a poet is *to mean two or more things at once*. The day's events were ambiguous, and my feelings were too—not a jumble that couldn't be sorted out but, rather, a complex combination of distinct emotions. As Traci Brimhall writes in her poem "Saudade," "[...] If only the past will have me / now that I have / its answers—its griefs and inheritances." I was a witness, an observer, an interpreter of intertwined sadness and happiness. I stood in for Generation Space as a whole, carried its grief and inheritance, for the many of us who did not contribute directly to the space program but who grew up in its shadow. I had also become fully myself somehow and able to accept saudade as the state of middle age.

The press re-boarded the buses—I leaned into Doug in the seat next to mine—for the corner of Kennedy Parkway and Schwartz Road for an in-transit photo op. We milled around on the expanse of the corner. I'd dressed up for the occasion; the fabric of my skirt bore a repeated photograph of a space shuttle launch. Doug took my picture as I fanned my skirt. The sun had come up.

With the VAB looming behind the orbiter, *Atlantis* made its way past us. The space shuttle had a clear path and proceeded with certitude. This was its neighborhood, after all, though it had not traveled this stretch of road before. For an orbiter on the ground, it was moving at a good clip. Usually, the orbiter on a transporter travels at between two and four miles an hour. Later in the day, this orbiter set a land speed record of ten miles per hour.

The press re-boarded the buses—again. At this point, Doug and I knew that it was going to be a very long day, with no way to get back to our car. The bus drove on to the official handover of *Atlantis* from KSC to the Delaware North Corporation, which runs the Visitor Complex. At that next stop, we used the port-o-potties right away. We'd learned to take advantage of opportunities when they arose. Then, we milled about; shuttle days were still defined by hurry-up, then wait.

VIPs and the STS-135 crew showed up. I eyed astronaut Sandy Magnus, a fellow Illinoisan, standing with crewmates Doug Hurley and Rex Walheim. Donned in my shuttle skirt, which I'd ordered online for such occasions, I approached the group and boldly asked whether they would sign my skirt. I'd purchased metallic-ink Sharpies at Target the day before, and I'd worked for years—especially these last two—against introversion to be able to take advantage of chance occasions. The astronauts seemed a little confused—used to signing autographs, but never on a skirt. Yet after sizing me up, they were willing to give it a go. Their handler quickly intruded, saying bluntly, "No autographs today." Her concern was certainly that one autograph could lead to many requests, and, as members of the press, we were never supposed to ask for autographs. Even though there weren't that many people in the media and VIP area, the regular reporters among the KSC press are huge space nerds and might have surrounded autograph-signing astronauts. Within a minute or two, two male members of the media got the male crew members to sign t-shirts they were wearing. I felt angry for letting male colleagues observe and steal my idea while I lost out. Magnus and I weren't the old boys' club, so we followed the rules.

Sandy Magnus, though, struck up a conversation with me, impressed by my most unusual request to autograph a skirt. Whatever anger I still felt about being slighted as a woman in this space nerd crowd, my heart was racing because an astronaut wanted to talk with me. Magnus thought her artsy sister might like the shuttle skirt. So she snapped a photo of me with her phone—a photo of me was on the phone of one of four of the last astronauts to ever be in space on a shuttle. How cool was that? I want to believe she still has that photo, even though she probably has no idea who was wearing it, even though she probably no longer has that phone. That request was the first and best of several that day to photograph the skirt or ask where it came from.

When excitement about my skirt died down, NASA started the retirement ceremony. I hadn't been to a community parade like this since I was a kid, when at the state fair in Springfield, Illinois, my family would line the streets to watch school marching bands and waving politicians. The title transfer ceremony for *Atlantis* was short and to the point. *Atlantis's* first and last commanders, Karol Bobko and Chris Ferguson, spoke. Bill Moore from Delaware North spoke too. KSC Director Bob Cabana and NASA Administrator Charlie Bolden had their uplifting say about the shuttle program's end and this orbiter's new role to educate and inspire. Bolden noted about NASA, "We are not in the history business. [...] We are in the business of making science fiction into science fact." The words were a good catch phrase designed to encourage the people who worked at KSC—the community right there—not to get discouraged, not to dwell in the past or on the layoffs.

As buzzards circled closer and closer overhead—an oddly symbolic occurrence that day—the VIPs on stage then signed the care of *Atlantis* over to the Visitor Complex. This orbiter officially remains the property of NASA, the only orbiter indefinitely on loan to its museum home. Bolden was wrong. NASA does make history as much as it makes engineering and science. That history is the context in which Generation Space—Doug and I—grew up. History is the wake of objects through time, like the shuttle through air, physical and emotional memory rippling after the wing slices through.

Doug and I re-boarded the press buses. Friday still had miles and hours to go before we could sleep. At Exploration Park, the KSC public affairs representatives handed us off to the Visitor Complex public affairs representatives, and we were free to wander around the area as we waited. This park, situated on the secure government facility, was brimming with families. The hustle and bustle was cheerful, like a county fair. The food stands—the ones with caffeine—were an especially welcome sight for us.

Doug and I circled the silver Astrovan on display. NASA no longer had a need for the Astrovan, which had transported astronauts to the launch pad, so here it was for us to see up close. All the while, speakers on a central stage regaled the crowd with pep talks and memories. NASA Administrator Charlie Bolden and KSC Director Bob Cabana took the stage, repeating some of what they'd said earlier in the day. They also shared something we didn't know: not only did they both serve in the Marines, but their sons served in the Marines, and their sons had served together at some point. We'd never seen these two men more relaxed than during their friendly banter with a crowd of Shuttle workers and their families. This wasn't the slick Bolden we'd seen before; it was a more genuine Charlie.

Before too long, the orbiter's tail was in sight, rising above the tree line like a shark's fin breaking the surface of the ocean. People gathered on the sides of the road, as security walked up and down in a futile effort to wave people back behind the sidewalk. Slowly, *Atlantis* rounded a bend and emerged. At the turn where the crowds had gathered, right in the middle of this backyard barbeque, the orbiter stopped, and we all swarmed the vehicle.

I stood under a wing. Doug and I walked around to stand under the orbiter's nose. We couldn't believe that we could get close enough to touch it. A Visitor Complex media representative indicated that this was the closest that the public had ever been allowed to get to a space shuttle. Adults pointed to different parts; they'd worked on this or that shuttle. Kids wriggled with excitement; it's amazing when their small bodies can barely contain the emotions that adults like me hold inside ourselves. NASA let everyone hang out with *Atlantis* for a good, long time that afternoon.

When we had soaked up as much as we could as relative outsiders in this mix of KSC family, we headed to our next bus. We hadn't eaten much, it was getting warm, and we wanted to spend a few hours wandering around the Visitor Complex before the next press event. The café was busier than we'd ever seen it, and the French fries were hot and salty—*best ever*, my mother would have sworn. The rocket garden offered a nice breeze, and there were special exhibits set up in the Debus Center for the day. That's where I tried on a spacesuit glove and met a man who trained shuttle astronauts for Extra Vehicular Activity, or spacewalks. I convinced Doug to ride the Space Launch Experience with me (the ride cost $60 million to build but was free to ride), and I could have twanged, shuddered, and g-forced for hours longer than the less-than-ten-minute experience. On the Space Coast, even in the hurry-up-and-wait process, we never really found downtime, never stopped soaking it all in.

The day was proceeding on schedule. Next up, *Atlantis* would traverse the last leg and end up where we stood. We gathered by the ditch between the Visitor Complex and the road we'd driven to KSC many times. This part of the day was another hurry-up-and-wait stage, something by now familiar to our journalist selves, though we usually didn't wait this close to alligators. Finally, *Atlantis* rounded the last corner and headed toward us.

Thirty astronauts—Apollo veterans as well as shuttle astronauts—led the space shuttle. Each was acknowledged by name as the group made the long pass in front of the large crowd of cheering onlookers. Buzz Aldrin, Alan Bean, Gene Cernan, Charlie Duke—though not necessarily in that alphabetical order. Fred Gregory, Kathy Thornton—astronauts we had interviewed before. Mary Cleave, Eileen Collins, Mark Lee—astronauts with whom we'd talk the next day at the Astronaut Autograph and Memorabilia Show. This group of former space-travelers led *Atlantis* all the way around the corner to the door of the orbiter's new home, a short jaunt for a large orbiter but a long walk for some astronauts in their eighties.

The media scurried over to greet orbiter and astronauts in the construction zone. The men and women in their blue flight jackets gathered loosely in front of the orbiter for a photo op. They didn't function as an organized cohort; some avoided others. Several treated this as a family reunion, not a press event. We all mingled for a few minutes, not sure what to do or what would happen next. Some journalists pressed for interviews, and some astronauts proceeded quickly into the gaping building to get out of the fray.

I introduced myself to Eileen Collins, the first female commander of an American spacecraft, and Doug shot a photograph of the two of us together. I'd asked her my go-to Colbert-esque question back at the *Discovery* transfer. I had little energy for small talk, and my cheeks were sore from smiling hard, something I couldn't help but do during this last leg. Our conversation was brief. These interactions take a lot out of me; I need to be geared up to do a good job, and, though I'd made myself better at public socializing, I don't always have the energy I want to muster. The next day, I was in better form, in a more familiar setting, and Collins would sign my shuttle skirt for a donation to the scholarship fund.

Doug and I searched for a decent perch among the construction materials and waited for dusk. A few bright lights illuminated the orbiter as the day began to wind down, Earth rotating toward nightfall. Finally, it was dark. The fireworks began bursting in air behind *Atlantis*. Pops and bangs. Green sparkles and silver steaks. Red, white, and blue, of course. Doug and I were both spent. After we had turned to leave: one late burst of sound and sparkle in the dark.

We caught a bus back to the News Center to retrieve our car. Our writer friend Margaret had already contacted Omar Izquierdo, her KSC insider friend. We all met at El Leoncito in Titusville to eat our fill of good Mexican food. We toasted the events of the day; we drowned our sorrows.

Omar told us that folks at KSC had taken to saying, "Don't cry because it's over. Smile because it happened." That's what a shuttle worker had said over the microphone at the beginning of the day, when *Atlantis* was emerging from the VAB in the pre-dawn darkness and chill. That's a quote often attributed to Dr. Seuss, though it's tough to track down where he might have said it, and it's also been attributed to the novelist Gabriel García Márquez. The sentiment is a version of lines from Alfred, Lord Tennyson's long poem *In Memorium*: "'Tis better to have loved and lost / Than never to have loved at all." Omar was irritated, even shaken up, by this attitude. Folks shouldn't be smiling about the end of US manned spaceflight, he asserted. You can't take the bitter out of bittersweet, I thought. Margaret agreed with Omar. It was okay—maybe even good—to be angry that Shuttle had ended. I admired their conviction; I nodded and took a sip of my beer. It was logical to resent the end of Shuttle when no replacement was in place.

Yet I had relished this more-than-two-year effort—the numerous cross-country flights, the expenses, the scrambling to keep up with our day jobs, the scurrying to get somewhere before sunrise, the waiting even after we had arrived for one event or another, the exhaustion from trying not to miss anything for fifteen hours at a time or for days in a row. My memories were vivid, sensory, complex. Of course, I was sad. And I was happy too. I couldn't muster resentfulness myself, though I understood it in others. For me, these couple of years had been full of spontaneity and excitement, brimming with new knowledge and un-imagined experiences. I'd reshaped myself, and Doug and I had become closer than ever before. The shuttle—a complex machine—had made me feel more human, more compassionate, more open to possibility and loss.

In a way, Doug and I had lived two lives simultaneously those two years: the regular life that most people who knew us saw, and this other, intermittent life with the space shuttle and people who didn't know us. In a commencement address in 2012, science-fiction writer Neil Gaiman said, "Nothing I did where the only reason for doing it was the money was ever worth it. [...] The things I did because I was excited and wanted to see them in existence have never let me down." Doug and I had put everything we could into following the end of the space shuttle program because we were excited and wanted to see it in existence. We were never let down. NASA never let us down, and we never let our-selves down. We understood Omar's position. But I couldn't feel angry. I had grown up in Shuttle's shadow. Its end wasn't an erasure. Grief, I've come to learn, contains both sorrow and joy, at least for me. And I knew that what I felt about the space shuttle was a version of what I felt about my mother, that the two losses were intertwined in time. I couldn't afford to be angry in the face of my still-impending loss. My mother's death would not erase the life I'd lived in her shadow. The multitude of moments that had shaped me existed vibrantly as history and memory.

So, though I never said it aloud to either of them, I saw these mo-ments differently than Omar and Margaret, as I could not separate the end of Shuttle in November 2012 from what was going on in the rest of my life. My mother was dying. Though her parents had lived into their nineties and though she was otherwise healthy, my mother had lived the average number of years for an American woman and had accom-plished amazing feats (including winning a Supreme Court case) for a woman of the Silent Generation born with bilateral club foot. She had outlived her parents, and I would outlive her, which is the way we think of the natural course of lifespans. She led a good life, and she came to terms, relatively speaking, with the fact that her life was ending. *Grief* comes from a French word meaning *to burden*; I wanted to carry the full burden. As sad as I was to be losing my mother and as much as I wanted to cry every day, I was happy and grateful that I'd shared my life to that point with her and that I carried on. 'Tis indeed good that I loved her, even though there was no way to not lose her. I remain grateful even for those painful moments during that last year of her life. And yes, I wish there'd been a few more moments or days to eke out.

As the writer Geoffrey Chaucer posited hundreds of years ago, "There is an end to everything, to good things as well." That's a proverb reiterated by Frank Baum in *The Marvelous Land of Oz* and the character Q in the series finale of *Star Trek: The Next Generation*. It's a version of what Omar had said in the blog post he wrote for us. It's one of the ways in which we deal with—rationalize—endings. As the philosopher Friedrich Nietzsche pointed out, "The end of a melody is not its goal; but nonetheless, had the melody not reached its end it would not have reached its goal either." In this way, the ending of Shuttle is part of Shuttle, as real and necessary as any other part of its song.

CHAPTER 20
DOMO ARIGATO, MR. ROBOTO
DOUG

Don't worry about Master Luke. I'm sure he'll be all right.
He's quite clever, you know...for a human being.

—C-3PO, *The Empire Strikes Back*

When I returned to the Space Coast in September 2011 for the launch of GRAIL, a mission to map the Moon, Anna did not go with me. I took notes and snapped photographs, while she led her day-to-day life as an English professor. I was like the pair of satellites I went to watch launch. Immersed in my own experiences, I sent home data via emails, texts, and phone calls. I returned to KSC as part of a NASA Tweetup; Twitter has made us all surveyors of this planet, collecting and disseminating data for each other. A human cartographer-probe, I mapped the landscape, recorded the events, and analyzed my surroundings in almost real time for Anna, thousands of miles away. Set to task, I moved around of my own volition and determined for myself what information was most interesting. I missed Anna, but it was definitely better for one of us to go—me this time!—than for neither of us to have the direct experience. I'd been thinking, though, about what *direct* might mean now and in the future, for NASA was sending machines not humans to the Moon this time.

The launch of GRAIL was delayed. By this point, delay had redefined Anna and me as a couple, teaching us patience, persistence, and trust, separately and together. The two launch windows on a given day for GRAIL were "instantaneous," meaning a one-second timeframe to *go* or *no go*, and thirty-nine minutes apart. What that really meant, in this particular case, was that the launch window on a given day was forty minutes long, but it took about thirty-nine minutes after the first missed launch to load the new launch information into the old Delta II rocket for a second *go* or *no go*. It's a fascinating way to look at time and how to build in a second chance from the get-go. That's a way Anna and I had begun thinking, building contingency into our lives, thinking together about back-up plans and moving on, moving differently, in spite of—or because of—the inevitable ways plans don't pan out. On September 8, high winds aloft scrubbed the two possible launches for GRAIL, less than ten minutes before launch. The next day, a problem with the rocket was discovered.

GRAIL, in NASA's method of producing acronyms, stands for Gravity Recovery and Interior Laboratory. Each craft also contained MoonKAM (Moon Knowledge Acquired by Middle-school students as part of Sally Ride Science), cameras that could take photos for educational and public outreach purposes. The mission was to place two nearly identical, washing-machine-sized spacecraft in the same orbit around the Moon in order to map our closest celestial neighbor. To do this, the two spacecraft had to travel toward the Moon and begin orbiting, then adjust their orbits—under NASA's instructions—until one was following the other in a low-altitude, nearly circular path of formation flying. These spacecraft had to travel roughly 2.6 million miles to get to the Moon via a low-energy trajectory toward the Sun. Then, they had to orbit in formation together; they could not be off-track more than 7.5 micrometers (a micrometer is one-millionth of a meter). In other words, for the Moon mapping to work, NASA tracked the consistent distance between the two spacecraft down to the diameter of a red blood cell.

By mapping the Moon's gravity, scientists could better understand the Moon's interior and its thermal history. By scrutinizing the Moon's lumps and bumps with sensitive instruments, its past would be revealed, a past that is part of Earth's history, too, and therefore part of the way humans understand ourselves and our place in the universe. The front and back—the near side we see and the far, dark side—of the Moon are radically different. Maria Zuber, the Principal Investigator on the GRAIL project, wanted to know why. And now, so did I.

232

Seeing the world and the universe in the form of maps means something deeper as well. Years before my family stopped during a childhood family road trip, I memorized the floor plan of the Air Force's museum in Dayton, Ohio, imagining the different galleries and positions of aircraft. I hadn't yet experienced the museum directly, but I knew it anyway. "We organize information on maps in order to see our knowledge in a new way," writes Peter Turchi in *Maps of the Imagination*. "As a result, maps suggest explanations; and while explanations reassure us, they also inspire us to ask more questions, consider other possibilities."

Much science proceeds by increments. An experiment offers an explanation, and that hard-won information spawns new questions, new ideas to investigate. The researchers carry out their work, passing down data and lore through laboratory lineages. They map and remap to welcome, even envision, possibilities, as well as to confirm our suspicions.

On the day of the third launch attempt, I was standing on the shoreline across from Cape Canaveral Air Force Base before sunrise. The first attempt that day was scrubbed at 8:21 a.m. The second launch opportunity was at 9:08 a.m. So I waited.

People say, *space is hard*, and that's what delays as well as the incredible distance and exactitude of GRAIL imply. Space exploration isn't especially hard, though, so much as it requires a great deal of human intelligence, calculation, and engineering. It requires both accuracy (hitting the right mark) and precision (consistently hitting the same mark). The catchphrase—*space is hard*—is sometimes an oversimplification that's used to get us off the hook for failures or mistakes. When efforts fail, it's because the machines and mission goals are complex and subject to statistical probabilities and mistakes, just like any other machine or task. Humans and especially scientists and engineers learn from mistakes, especially after they've calculated to avoid them. Mistakes and delays—the seeming hard parts—are integral to the process This wait was less than an hour.

Ignition! GRAIL lifted off from Launch Complex 17A, one of two launch pads at KSC dedicated to Delta rockets, a reliable type used since the 1960s. When the Delta II main engine and solid rockets fired, they produced a combined thrust of 1.2 million pounds. *Zoom!* In less than thirty-five seconds, the sleek configuration had gone supersonic. This was much faster than the shuttle ascends—a different sort of thrill. The rocket and its surveying probes disappeared into the clouds, leaving a rip and a streak like a Y in the sky above my head. GRAIL was the last Delta II launched from LC-17, ending a history that spanned 259 launches since 1960.

Within roughly nine minutes of liftoff, the first of the GRAIL probes separated from the second stage and was on its own way to the Moon. The second GRAIL craft followed several minutes later. The spacecraft, named Ebb and Flow by fourth-graders at Emily Dickinson Elementary School in Montana, started orbiting the Moon on December 31 and January 1. These spacecraft did almost all of their of their work in eighty-eight days.

GRAIL told scientists about the structure of the lunar crust, the Moon's thermal and magnetic history, the structure under the surface of basins and gravitational anomalies, and the possible size of the Moon's core. NASA released a GRAIL-based gravity map of the Moon less than a year later. These probes—engineered machines that sent data back home to people on Earth—provided scientists with more (and more accurate) information about our closest celestial body than had ever been known, more than Apollo astronauts had been able to gather directly on the Moon decades earlier.

Less than two weeks after that gravity map was available to the public, the two spacecraft intentionally crashed into the lunar surface within minutes of each other. Probes are expendable. Expendable probes are cheaper than something that has to be built and fueled to come back to Earth. The cost of GRAIL was estimated at almost a half-billion dollars. That's about $50 million more than a single space shuttle launch cost, even at the end of the program. It's less than one-quarter the cost of a B-2 bomber, if development and testing costs are included.

These comparisons and decisions are those with which Generation Space now grapples. Big science isn't cheap, but it's cheaper than war and a better way for humanity to define itself. Science is one way to be our most human, to understand the universe and humans' place in it.

After those first launches had been scrubbed on September 8, a day that marked the forty-fifth anniversary of the first airing of Star Trek, I hung out at the Tweetup. Nichelle Nichols, who played Uhura in the original Star Trek television series, arrived to tell the social media crowd, "If you can imagine it, you can dream it, you can do it." I was a kid who grew up believing her words, not only because of the Moon landing I remember watching as a toddler, but also because of that television series and the worlds I saw through Uhura's eyes (or heard through her interpretation of communication signals).

Also that day, real-life astrophysicist Neil deGrasse Tyson focused on the power of science to describe the world in a way that's both sensible and meaningful to us beyond our senses. Maybe what you see is not what you get, and there exist many ways of seeing. Mostly, he urged adults to take field trips like kids do, to keep learning about the world and the universe. I was on an adult field trip of sorts for the GRAIL launch. My two-year adventure with Anna on the Space Coast was a field trip to understand space exploration and also make sense of ourselves. We'd become a better couple because we learned things together.

For now, the United States is launching only unmanned spacecraft. GRAIL is one pair of probes in a long line of spacecraft that NASA has used both to survey other planets and to go beyond the solar system. Perhaps my own fondness for GRAIL is related to knowing that the first geodesic satellite, measuring Earth's size, shape, orientation, and gravity, was named ANNA.

ANNA 1-B, a joint military and civilian project, successfully launched on a Delta rocket on Halloween of 1962. Like a science disco ball, ANNA's primary tool was a series of four enormously powerful strobe lights arrayed on its spherical body. The lights flashed in a prescribed sequence in response to radio signals broadcast from Earth-side stations. Photographs taken of the flashes from known positions on Earth against a background of known stars allowed scientists to track new positions via triangulation (the use of triangles to measure relative distances between points). ANNA is still up there orbiting Earth, though the satellite no longer flashes in acknowledgement of received messages.

Message: missive and meaning. That's what my Anna would say. Earth emanates inadvertent messages in the form of natural and manmade radio waves. What do we—what does Earth—sound like? A few years ago, the news outlet Space.com reported, "Earth emits an ear-piercing series of chirps and whistles." People don't hear this awful sound because it's generated above Earth's protective ionosphere, where particles in solar winds hit our planet's magnetic field and send beams of radio waves outward. The sound of Earth's inherent dynamics—the movement of atmosphere and oceans—produces a steady drone as well. Lightning produces crackling, which scientists call *sferics*. You might not think sferics make much noise, until you consider that lightning strikes occur roughly one hundred times per second on our planet—that's a lot of crackling. People on Earth haven't thought much about what we sound like—what we're saying—to the universe. One of the few concerted efforts to hone our cosmic voice was the Voyager Golden Record. The Voyager program, with its two probing spacecraft, had message very much in mind.

In 1977, NASA, with a committee headed by astrophysicist Carl Sagan, designed two phonograph records. Then they put each aboard its own Voyager spacecraft, whose mission was to go out into space and keep going and going, perhaps happening upon intelligent life somewhere out there. I didn't really know who Sagan was until his novel *Contact* was published in 1985; I was an engineering student then, and all my peers were devouring it. I was hooked on his ideas and the search for extraterrestrial intelligence (SETI). When SETI@home was released in 1999, I rushed to answer the call for the public's help to analyze radio signal data. My home computer became part of the large, public, distributed computing project to search for extraterrestrial intelligence. Anna remembers Sagan from *The Tonight Show* in the early 1980s, when he was also doing the PBS show *Cosmos*. In those appearances—in Johnny Carson's parody—Sagan popularized his phrase *billions upon billions of stars*.

The Golden Record aboard Voyager contains greetings in fifty-six languages, natural sounds like thunder and crickets chirping, and music from around the world, all of which are in audio. The disc also includes, in analog form, 115 images, from planets to fetuses. Perhaps the most interesting information to be included in Earth's official, communal voice is an hour-long recording of the brainwaves and heartbeats of a woman named Ann Druyan. Hooked up to machines, she was given a list of things to ponder, starting with the history of Earth. This woman went on to marry Sagan, with whom she'd work on the television series *Cosmos*. When we saw Druyan at PlanetFest (hosted by The Planetary Society) in 2012, she described her contribution to the Golden Record as the heartbeat of a young woman in love. Though nothing can be comprehensive, I sometimes think the Golden Record and even just one woman's heartbeat might be somehow representative of all of us on Earth.

My own loose connection to the Golden Record came about through the serendipity that marks the most interesting moments of my life. I spent part of the two years after Shuttle ended collaborating with software pioneer Ted Nelson. In addition to teaching a course with him, I planned a conference and co-edited a festschrift book, which is written by those he influenced to honor him and his life's work. One of the contributors to the book was electronic music innovator Laurie Spiegel. Spiegel's rendition of "Harmonices Mundi"—Latin for *the harmony of the world*—by seventeenth-century astronomer Johannes Kepler is stored on the Golden Record. In mathematics, there exists the Erdös number, which is basically the six-degrees-of-Kevin-Bacon game to understand one's relationship to ultra-prolific mathematician Paul Erdös. I edited that festschrift with mathematician Daniele Struppa, whose Erdös number is three, making mine four. I'd like to suggest a variant, the Voyager number for a person's relationship to someone who has contributed to the Golden Record. My Voyager number would be one, and that has me thinking that the Space Age has been so encompassing that perhaps each American—and certainly every American engineer or scientist—is only a few degrees separated from someone directly involved in a mission to explore space.

Voyager 1 has already crossed beyond the edge of our solar system into interstellar space, and both spacecraft will carry humanity's voices farther away toward the billions and billions of stars. Sagan had said of the mission, "[T]he launching of this bottle into the cosmic ocean says something very hopeful about life on this planet." The meaning is in the sending of the message as well as in the potential of another entity receiving it. That's the way Anna and I—as part of Generation Space—have come to understand ourselves. Following the end of Shuttle was not only a way for Anna and I to share the story of the Space Age, but also became a way to understand how the Space Age had shaped us and told us who we are.

As William Taber, the supervisor of JPL's Mission Design and Navigation Software Group, recounted to us, "On Valentine's Day, 1990, long after Voyager's cameras could return any more science images, the mission controllers at JPL honored the request of the late Carl Sagan to command Voyager 1 to turn its camera back toward the inner solar system [...]. These images show the sun, Venus, Earth, Jupiter, Saturn, Uranus, and Neptune as seen from the edge of the solar system." The Voyager Family Portrait. That's what the image is called at JPL. Our solar system's meaning shifts when we see it from somewhere else. Taber said of that photograph, which held no scientific value, "The reality of how tiny we are in the universe and of the vast emptiness between the stars was seared into my mind. And with this sense of smallness was sense that I was witness to a piece of humankind taking one last look in the rearview mirror, before heading out on a voyage to the stars, carrying postcards from earth into the cosmos." Humans explore space to understand the universe but also to better understand who we are in this vast expanse. When Voyager looked back at us, we were able to look back at ourselves.

NASA has a long history of unmanned missions, and, without Shuttle, that's the only kind of space travel NASA does at the moment. NASA considers probes a kind of robot. The cognitive prototype of *robot*—the default image most of us think of when we hear or read *robot*—is probably something like Marvin from *The Hitchiker's Guide to the Galaxy*, C-3PO from *Star Wars*, the maid in *The Jetsons*, or Robby, the nearly ubiquitous robot, who first appeared in the 1956 film *The Forbidden Planet* and then popped up in *Hazel, Columbo, Gilligan's Island, The Addams Family, Wonder Woman*, and *Mork & Mindy*. Thirty years in the future, if, like in *Lost in Space*, a family were going to check out a planet circling the star Alpha Centauri, Robby seemed like a perfectly reasonable solution, with his elliptical glass head, flexible arms, rotating trunk, superhuman strength, amazing calculation aptitude, claws that could shoot laser beams, and the ability to laugh and sing. And robots are perfectly reasonable—in fact, part and parcel—for space exploration.

NASA has a robot reminiscent of these popular culture icons: Robonaut 2. Anna saw a version of R2 in person. Its ready-to-work-in-space version was aboard *Discovery* on STS-133. R2 looks like a person from the hips up, not finely featured but with a torso, arms, and head with a faceplate. This robot was installed in ISS so that it could slide back and forth along a taskboard to turn knobs, flip switches, push buttons, and lift handles and, thereby, perform the jobs controlled by those devices. The human-like hand was this robot's great asset. Mostly, though, NASA uses robots that are not humanoid in form and that use a computer, instruments, and tools to gather information.

The Mars rovers are these sorts of robots. JPL in Pasadena is the birthplace of four of these rovers. In 1971, the Russian space probes Mars 2 and Mars 3 reached the planet Mars within a week of each other, but the missions were plagued with problems. While Mars 2 was the first human-made object on the surface of the red planet, it crashed there, and Mars 3 stopped sending signals seconds after it started sending signals. I was too young to understand what those orbiter-lander-rover failures meant for my chances—human chances—to go to Mars, but, as I grew up and read more about space exploration, I understood that unmanned missions had been necessary first forays to the Moon, preparation for the Apollo astronauts landing there, and we weren't yet doing unmanned missions successfully on Mars.

It would take more than a quarter of a century after that to finally land a roving robot on Mars and get some data back to Earth. Sojourner was a twenty-three-pound, six-wheeled rover that spent almost three months—twelve times longer than the planned seven-day mission—in 1997 examining the composition of the soil and rocks on Mars.

The amazing success of Mars rovers, however, really took hold with the four hundred-pound, six-wheeled twins Spirit and Opportunity. The primary science goal of the project known as Mars Exploration Rover Mission was to study the environment, particularly the geology, of two locations that scientists suspected had once been wet and possibly conducive to supporting life. Spirit left Earth on June 10, 2003, and landed on Mars on January 4, 2004. Opportunity, which studies wind and radio signals in addition to the planet's crust and terrain, followed three weeks later. Spirit was designed to work for ninety days but exceeded that mission goal by twenty times; the rover then got stuck in soft Martian soil in 2009 and stopped responding to commands the following March.

Opportunity was, likewise, designed for ninety days of active work on the Martian surface. In July 2014, it set an off-Earth driving record when it surpassed 25.01 miles (though some of that was wheel-spinning when it got stuck in sand) and is still (as of December 2016) roving the red planet and examining pebbles after twelve years, having completed the equivalent of an earthly marathon (26.2 miles) in March 2015. Opportunity—a robot—functions as an on-the-ground mapper in detail.

These roving robots set the stage for Curiosity, the six-wheeled, car-sized explorer we saw in person at JPL as it was being built in 2011. At that year's JPL Open House, Anna and I stood looking down through the acrylic glass window as if we were observers of a complicated surgical procedure. Still, Curiosity looked like a high school experiment, made with fancy tin foil and spare parts. It was, of course, an incredibly complicated machine. The room in which Curiosity was being assembled was pristine, as dust free as possible. Engineers covered themselves head to toe in white protective gear—known affectionately as bunny suits and worn to protect Curiosity from its makers, not the other way around—to perform the meticulous assemblage.

As with long-lived, deep-space robots, a radioisotope thermoelectric generator powers Curiosity. In other words, this rover's battery uses nuclear power produced by 10.6 pounds of plutonium-238, which has a half-life of less than ninety years, as opposed to the more dangerous plutonium-239 used in nuclear weapons, which has a half-life of 24,100 years. That's more than twenty-four thousand years for plutonium-239 to become half as radioactive, and another twenty-four thousand years for its radioactivity to be halved again, and so on. The United States stopped producing plutonium-238 in 1988. Since 1993, the United States has been purchasing this radioactive isotope from Russia for its unmanned spacecraft. But that country is no longer producing it either. With the world supply limited, NASA and the Department of Energy have asked to restart production, and the first test batch went forward at the end of 2015. For deep space exploration to continue beyond Generation Space (and without international political entanglements), the United States must produce its own energy supply. And for deep space travel, there exists no straightforward alternative to nuclear.

Curiosity launched from Launch Complex 41 at Cape Canaveral atop an Atlas V rocket on November 26, 2011. Anna and I didn't attend the launch in person; we were celebrating our anniversary in Las Vegas with family. Just a few months after the last space shuttle mission concluded, we would have liked to be in closer proximity to the path toward the future, toward Mars. The decision to carry out our traditional anniversary plans and to miss a space launch opportunity signified that we'd started to come to terms with the Space Age and our aging within it. We decided to celebrate our relationship without also looking to the heavens this time.

We did, however, look to the heavens to celebrate Curiosity's landing with the rest of humanity. Anna and I didn't see Curiosity land on Mars, just as we hadn't seen the shuttle land two years earlier when we went to the desert to greet it. No one saw Curiosity land, not really. But we and many others around the world shared a view of that landing.

On August 6, 2012, we were watching the event on a big screen at Planetfest, surrounded by space nerds that included Bill Nye the Science Guy. Anna posed for a photo with a life-size image of the science nerd as if they were both holding a planet. Ann Druyan was there to. Her recorded heartbeats were traveling to interstellar space on Voyager. She announced to boisterous cheers from the crowd that the television show Cosmos would return. Folks affiliated with JPL, the place that built the rover and would run the mission, were tripping over each other with excitement. The fourteen-minute relay delay because of Earth's distance from Mars meant that whatever had happened to Curiosity had already happened by the time we saw it on the big screen.

While Curiosity was not the first rover to go to Mars, its landing, because of its heft, was the most complicated, dubbed the "seven minutes of terror," during which the rover had to slow from thirteen thousand to zero miles per hour. To start the deceleration, Curiosity deployed a supersonic parachute, and that parachute had to work properly. The rover also cast off its heat shield, and the heat shield had to be thrown far away so that the rover wouldn't land on it. When Curiosity was a hundred meters above the surface of Mars, the Mars Science Laboratory deployed a hovering crane. Spirit and Opportunity, the rovers that had preceded Curiosity, had been padded with airbags so that they could bounce around until they stopped, but Curiosity was too big and heavy to use this tried-and-true method. Even though I'd watched the animated version of the landing several times, this scenario seemed like science fiction to me. The hovering rocket-crane lowered Curiosity itself to the ground. All this was presumably happening as I waited at PlanetFest to know whether it had worked. The rover then cut the cables quickly so that the hovering crane could blast itself away instead of smashing down on the rover.

Tense viewers—Anna and I among them—wondered whether the rover had plopped down properly or smashed into the unforgiving planet. This worry was grave and valid. When an image of the touched-down rover appeared on the screen, cheers arose. People near me wept—with amazement, perhaps with joy—that a robot had reached the surface of another planet in our stead. The intense nervousness and excitement I felt surprised me. The distance and time delay didn't diminish my emotion, my joy. The experience seemed as direct as I could imagine, even though I wasn't on Mars.

Perhaps, people cheered also because—in the wake of the Shuttle program's end and in a terrible economy—a failure may have meant that NASA stumbled for the next couple of decades. In 1971, Apollo and its final three missions had been canceled. It was another decade before the space shuttle took flight and twenty-six before the first American rover went to Mars. In 2012, Generation Space wanted Curiosity to succeed. And it did. Hundreds of people in that large room in Pasadena, some of whom had touched Curiosity with their hands, felt relief along with utter joy.

What fascinated me most about the landing was that two satellites were in place to capture information and images as the rover landed. That we had three satellites orbiting Mars and two positioned to show us Curiosity's landing in almost-real-time astounded me. Satellites did not exist sixty years earlier, yet Generation Space now depends on them. The first man-made satellite ever launched was Sputnik; the Russians sent it into low-Earth orbit in 1957. Sixty-five years later, low-Earth orbit is cluttered with satellites, and people the world over depend on GPS, a satellite-based navigation system. One satellite orbiting Mars relayed data so that NASA could track Curiosity's landing, and the other passed over the landing site to snap a photo of the rover, its parachute deployed. Even though the first image that Curiosity itself relayed was a blurry black-and-white self-portrait, the picture made Curiosity's landing feel personal, as if I were there, in some way.

Who isn't moved by the photograph of the rover's own shadow on the pebbly surface of another world? As if it were humanity's shadow. Who isn't at least a bit intrigued that Curiosity found evidence of water somewhere else in the universe? I've lived to know what people had been wondering for generations: is there water—and therefore the possibility of life—elsewhere? Yes, there is.

Before the end of 2015, data from Curiosity convinced NASA that a very wet lake- and stream-filled Mars had once existed and that water might still flow on its surface at times. It wasn't buried where it'd be tough to locate but right there when we looked. Wind tends to leave rocks rough, with sharp edges. Water, on the other hand, tends to give rocks a smooth surface. Hundreds of rocks that Curiosity perused at Gale Crater were smooth. Conditions conducive to life existed on another planet and might be happening in other places far off in the galaxy too. Scientists think the water that shaped those rocks must have had a depth of between four inches and just over three feet, with a flow rate of just over two miles per hour. Curiosity tells scientists that the water was likely slightly salty and contained the stuff that microbes might consume. To me, Curiosity's discoveries are both Mars-altering and mind-blowing because they mean that life really might exist somewhere other than Earth and that it might not be too difficult to find if we keep looking.

The rover contains two onboard computers to organize tasks and perform scientific calculations. Its mast holds two cameras for color images and two more that shoot in black and white. When the rover moves its wheels or robotic arm, four pairs of additional black-and-white cameras look forward and backward for treacherous rocks and inclines. The robotic arm even has a wire brush for sweeping dust off a rock.

The computers and cameras, of course, are designed so that Curiosity makes the best use of its scientific instruments, including four spectrometers. The alpha particle x-ray spectrometer, for example, analyzes elements in a soil sample by irradiating the dust and pebbles with alpha particles and then mapping the x-rays the sample emits. Another spectrometer called SAM studies organic compounds like oxygen and carbon in surface soil and in the atmosphere. Another suite of instruments keeps track of the same sort of weather conditions we see covered on the local evening news: temperature, humidity, pressure, and wind speed. One camera, located on the rover's robotic arm, is science specific; the Mars hand lens imager snaps microscopic images of soil samples. Though Curiosity is far from humanoid, this rover is the epitome of robot, moving around in and interacting with its Mars surroundings. It's difficult to imagine that a person could do what Curiosity does better or more efficiently (never mind get there in the first place).

Curiosity's mission was planned to last two years, but, of course, the rover exceeded that goal, and NASA has extended its mission indefinitely.

Astronaut Mary Cleave is a tiny woman, small enough that Anna and I questioned, when we first saw her among astronauts at the Atlantis transfer, whether she actually met NASA height requirements for astronauts. She admitted to us that she had been too short to be a flight attendant. She took her first flying lesson before she knew how to drive. She applied to become an astronaut "not because of the spaceflights. I just wanted to figure out how to get into a T-38," the jets that all astronauts fly as part of their ongoing training. During her selection interview, Cleave told the board—which included John Young, the Apollo astronaut who flew the first shuttle mission—"I'll give you an almost-full-sized brain for half the payload price." NASA is always concerned with the weight and related cost of anything that goes to space. Her joke worked.

Cleave flew aboard two shuttle missions. On the first, she operated the shuttle's robotic arm while two fellow crew floated out in space under her control. On the second, she deployed the Magellan spacecraft that studied Venus. That remains her proudest moment as an astronaut. "It was just fantastic to watch it leave the payload bay and to know it was going to Venus."

She left the space program because what she saw, as an astronaut with a background in environmental engineering, was "how fast we [human beings] were changing things" on this planet. She became a manager of a thirteen-year project to study all the plants on Earth, both on land and in the oceans, and to study carbon dioxide in the atmosphere. "We made a difference in global carbon models." Cleave remains more proud of her contribution to understanding climate change than of her work as an astronaut.

Of *Atlantis*'s retirement, Cleave said, "It's just such a great-looking spaceship, and it looks so good. You're sort of going, *Oh*. I hate to see that thing get rolled into a museum." As a scientist, however, she knew the decision to retire the shuttle was the rational one, since NASA had spent decades buying down the risk of low-Earth orbit and can now spin that technology off to the private sector. "That's the way things are supposed to work," she said definitively.

Cleave pointed out to us, during our conversation with her in 2012, "I worked in unmanned spaceflight longer than I worked in manned spaceflight." I realized that that's true of NASA as a whole, too, and that unmanned spaceflight was not only necessary but also thrilling in its own right, as it allowed Generation Space to reach beyond our grasp. In the 1970s and 1980s, numerous space probes mapped Venus, and one of the landers survived more than two hours on its hot surface. New Horizons showed the world Jupiter in 2007 and the dwarf planet Pluto—growing up, I knew it as a full-fledged planet—in 2015. The European Space Agency's Rosetta landed on a comet in 2014; though no one is there, the spacecraft carries a tiny disc etched with microscopic text in twelve hundred languages. It's gathering information, but it's a message too. As I make final edits to this chapter, Juno, after its five-year journey, has started orbiting Jupiter, by far the largest planet in our solar system.

Cleave has worked with college kids, ones adept at video games, to build CubeSats, research satellites measuring ten square centimeters that can be deployed into orbit from the International Space Station. Of that work with students, she said, "Most of them have been members of robotics clubs in high school. And they are really comfortable with the idea of using extensions of humans that are not necessarily human to do their exploring." Was she asserting that there was no need to send humans to space?

Even here on Earth, scientists are studying how some of what we experience virtually becomes remembered as if it happened to us physically in the real world. Cleave believes that future generations will conceive of robots as extensions of our own bodies. In the United States, many people have already moved toward understanding that our perception and cognition—our brains—may not keep actual and virtual realities as separate as we might expect. As a result, she asserts that putting humans on another planet will not drive the future of space exploration as it has in the past. Robots may do the job, not just *for* humans, but *as* humans in our stead.

Generation Space thought—I thought, when I was a kid—that the United States, perhaps as part of a global effort, would have landed a *person* on Mars by now. The Mars rover Curiosity is a prime example of the focused questions we can answer and technological problems we can solve by sending machines into space. Curiosity and Cleave make a compelling argument that unmanned missions are smart science.

Still, as I remember how much as I enjoyed and learned from my trip to the Space Coast to watch GRAIL launch, I know that it wasn't the same for Anna as she received the data—emails, texts, calls—I sent back home. It wasn't the same as being there in person. As successful as GRAIL was, those cartographer probes weren't the same as sending human beings to the Moon. Watching GRAIL launch or reading the results of the data it sent back to Earth wasn't the same experience; it wasn't an adequate substitute for watching Neil Armstrong step onto the Moon when I was a toddler. Of course, it's possible this Generation Space viewpoint dates me, makes me a little old-fashioned.

In 1981, which marks the first shuttle launch and the last of those born into Generation Space, Sony introduced the floppy disk, which is no longer in use. Many of our college students have never seen one and don't recognize the *save* icon on their computers as an image of a floppy disk. In 1981, the first video game magazine was published; it was defunct within a few years. IBM introduced its first, clunky personal computer in 1981, with the Microsoft DOS operating system; Anna and I remember DOS, which makes us all the more grateful for Windows and iOS. Those born after Generation Space have a different, less complicated relationship with computers. In 1982, *Time Magazine* featured the computer as "Machine of the Year"; *man* of that year was absent, and the digital or virtual stood in. That same year, the movie *Tron* convinced viewers of computer-generated graphics as reality, and a hacker became the computer itself. Those born after Generation Space were born into a different time and see different shadows.

CHAPTER 21
INFINITY AND BACK
DOUG

I joke that Apollo 11 took me to the wrong planet, to the Moon instead of Mars, but it is true that my close-up look at the Moon has served only to whet my Martian appetite.

—Michael Collins, *Mission to Mars*

The long wave of fiftieth anniversaries of spaceflight is upon us. Both Anna and I will have turned fifty before readers see these words. Generation Space is middle aged.

The first-ever human spaceflights by Soviet Yuri Gagarin and of *Freedom 7*, which took the first American, Alan Shepard, to space, occurred in 1961. We're in the midst of the fiftieth anniversaries of the Gemini program, which flew ten manned missions in two years. The last, Gemini 12 in November 1966, launched Buzz Aldrin and Jim Lovell on a four-day orbital mission during which Aldrin walked tethered in space for two hours and, thereby, made walking and working on the Moon all the more feasible.

The publication date for *Generation Space* nearly coincides with the fiftieth anniversary of NASA's first great tragedy, the fire during a ground test of Apollo 1 that killed three astronauts. Within a couple of years, the fiftieth anniversaries of Apollo's lunar missions will unfold. December 2018 marks five decades since Apollo 8, the first manned lunar mission, in which three astronauts looked back at Earth for the first time from the other side of the Moon. Our calendars are already marked for July 20, 2019: the fiftieth anniversary of the first person setting his boots on another celestial body.

Of course, 2016 also marked the fifth anniversary of the end of Shuttle. In January 2016, Anna and I made two trips from Southern California to the Midwest. While not every American flies as often as we do—usually a half-dozen times a year—commercial aviation is a tried-and-true means of travel for roughly eight million people every day, according to the International Air Transportation Association. On one of those flights, turbulence kept Anna and me belted to our seats for most of the eighteen-hundred-mile journey. Yet, at no time were we fearful. Someone taking those flights in 1953, fifty years after the Wright brothers' initial accomplishment of powered, controlled, human flight—the fiftieth anniversary of aviation—might have felt differently.

In fact, late 1953 saw a spate of deadly aviation accidents. A crash outside Frankfurt in mid-October killed forty-four passengers. In early November, a DC-3 went down in Brazil; twenty-eight lives were lost. An early December accident saw twenty-three of thirty-three souls lost on the side of mountain in Spain. A C-47 crashed in India in December, killing thirteen people. Imagine four deadly airline accidents within two months. News channels now would show nothing else for months.

The de Havilland Comet—the first jet airliner—had been introduced the year before. Shortly after, Comets started crashing, and the aircraft was taken out of service to fix structural flaws before its reintroduction later that decade. Flight was not smooth sailing.

Yet more people wanted to travel by air. That year, 1953, marked a pivotal point in commercial aviation: for the first time, more than fifty million passengers took flight. That's roughly how many passengers fly every week now, and Denver International alone handled fifty-three million passengers in 2015. Aviation grew from two brothers in 1903 to tens of millions of people five decades later to more than three billion fifty years after that.

After a midair collision killed 128 people over the Grand Canyon in 1956, the Federal Aviation Administration was established to make aviation safer. In short, aviation's first fifty or so years were a time of enormous challenges and rapid development. The next fifty years got aviation to where it is today. Aided by improved passenger jets and national civil authorities dedicated to safety, the second five decades of aviation transformed flying from the *wild* blue yonder to part of the fabric of our increasingly traveled lives.

The fiftieth anniversary of human space flight, on the other hand, was marked by the end of Shuttle. The end, at least for the foreseeable future, of US manned spaceflight.

Until the end of Shuttle, I hadn't spent much time thinking about commercial space, the handover of low-Earth orbit from NASA to private enterprise. As is often the case with NASA, the commercial space programs are another alphabet soup of acronyms: C3PO (yes, like *Star Wars*), SAA, COTS, CRS, CCDev, CCDev2, CCiCap, all of which are hopes and programs-in-progress. Hidden behind all those letters is NASA's decision that hauling crew and cargo to ISS should, after fifty years of NASA-run spaceflight, belong to private companies.

The first time Anna and I got up close to commercial space was after the throngs of people gathered to watch the final launch of *Atlantis* headed home. Anna and I stuck around, having booked a longer trip in case the launch had been delayed.

We learned from fellow reporters that the SpaceX capsule was on display at the Air Force Space and Missile History Center. I set the air conditioner to full blast on the way to the center, which shared a small campus with SpaceX and Space Florida. We were excited to see what might be the next step in spaceflight. I expected SpaceX's presence in Florida to be big, a little flashy. Instead, it was a low, squat, beige brick building, surrounded by palm trees, shrubbery, and all manner of plant life—almost as if it was being reclaimed by native Floridian flora.

The Dragon capsule stood outside, shielded from the Sun's glare by a tent positioned nearer to the history center than to SpaceX, as if it were one more among dozens of pieces of used-up spacecraft and rockets of the Space Age. At first glance, the conical capsule was so reminiscent of Apollo-era designs that, after thirty years of the winged shuttle, I might be forgiven for thinking that this too was a historical artifact. But this commercial space capsule was very modern, still being refined for its tasks.

SpaceX—Space Exploration Technologies Corporation of Hawthorne, California—had launched this particular Dragon on December 8, 2010, just less than fifty years after the first human spaceflight. That event marked the first time any entity other than a nation had launched, orbited, and recovered a spacecraft designed to carry humans to space. It flew empty, except for a wheel of cheese as homage to a Monty Python skit. It orbited twice and returned for a splashdown in the Pacific Ocean. Dragon will hold as many as seven astronauts, but, as I peered inside it that day on the Space Coast, I imagined it would be a very cozy, even uncomfortable, ride—or all Dragon astronauts will have to be the size of Mary Cleave.

Dingy, soot-like streaks arced from bottom to top across the white painted surface on one side of the capsule. I was close enough to run my hand across the vehicle's surface; I was very tempted. The bright blue SpaceX logo had bubbled and peeled away. Though it was mostly hidden underneath, the Dragon's heat shield was rough and blackened, a sign of the tremendous heat experienced while reentering Earth's atmosphere. Spaceflight had been defined as something done by NASA (and by government agencies in other countries), but commercial space was indeed spaceflight. The evidence was right before my eyes that day.

Anna and I didn't return to Florida together for more than a year. We made the trip back in November 2012 to attend what was essentially a NASA retirement party for the space shuttle *Atlantis*. In addition to following the movement of *Atlantis* to its permanent home at the Visitors Complex, we had a chance to get up-close with mock-ups of three competitors in the commercial space race.

Despite the county fair feel that day, the equipment on display was far from the John Deere and International Harvester tractors of my Midwestern childhood memories but, instead, were the twenty-first century rides I'd imagined. Even the names were evocative of hope (Dream Chaser), wild animals (Lynx), and whimsy (Dragon).

Sierra Nevada's Dream Chaser, a lifting body whose looks made it clear that it carried the DNA of the space shuttle and 1960s-era lifting bodies like the HL-10 (the aircraft featured in the opening montage of *The Six Million Dollar Man*), wasn't selected as a finalist for the CCDev (Commercial Crew Development—astronauts) program. However, in January 2016, Sierra Nevada was awarded a Commercial Resupply Services (CRS) contract to carry cargo to ISS. Dream Chaser hasn't been to ISS yet, but that's scheduled for 2019, the fiftieth anniversary of the first Moon landing.

XCOR's Lynx, on the other hand, is intended for the space tourism market. We'd seen another—possibly the same—mock-up of Lynx on display at Planetfest in Pasadena a few months earlier, the day that Curiosity landed on Mars. Lynx, which has been under development since 2003, is designed for a quick, suborbital ride to the sixty-two-mile (one-hundred-kilometer) line above the atmosphere that differentiates Earth from space; reaching this distance is what qualifies a person as an astronaut. Lynx is a two-person spacecraft; if it works, one passenger will pay $50,000 for the privilege of becoming an astronaut, acting as passenger, and the other will pilot the craft.

I'd spoken with XCOR's then-CEO Jeff Greason at the University of California-Riverside's annual Tuskegee Airmen event in 2009. I recognized Greason from articles I'd read about what was then being called *New Space*, though, at the time, I admit I wanted Old Space to continue. Like my father, I rarely pass up an opportunity to introduce myself to someone that I recognize, even if he doesn't know me from Adam.

As a part of the day's program, Greason presented Tuskegee Airman LeRoy Gillead with a ticket for a suborbital flight aboard Lynx. The award was the first in XCOR's Legacy Flight program to recognize contributions to aviation. I told Greason how greatly moved I was that this event connected a group of African-American heroes I'd read about as a boy with the opportunity for spaceflight, which had been denied to them until 1983. Lynx hasn't yet made its first test flight, and Gillead is still alive and kicking, waiting to punch his ticket to space. I want them both to make it.

At the 2013 Space Tech Expo in Long Beach, Anna and I spoke with former astronaut Garrett Reisman, another astronaut with a compact frame and also a megawatt smile. A couple of years younger than I am, he's the Project Manager for Dragon V2—the updated version of SpaceX's crew capsule. We'd met him once before, when a colleague invited us to a celebration of the Ilan Ramon Day School in Los Angeles.

During our conversation, Reisman defined the Golden Age of aviation as having occurred between World Wars, roughly when the Silent

Generation of our parents was born. He pointed out that, at the time, designers and engineers hadn't yet settled even on the number of wings an airplane should have. He imagined these years to be an incredibly exciting time for an aircraft engineer.

Likewise, I thought, in 1953, commercial jet traffic hadn't yet taken hold. Almost all passengers flew on propeller-driven aircraft then. Once again, no one knew precisely what an aircraft should look like. Engineers experimented with types of engines (jet or piston?), number of engines (one, two, four?), and engine placement (in or under wings?). That period, too, must have been exciting for aircraft engineers. My father was a boy then, figuring out what he wanted to build in this world; he became an automotive engineer and now builds industrial screens.

By the early twenty-first century, Reisman told us, mature commercial aviation technology consistently looked like a slender metal tube with two jet engines slung under the wings. With his signature smile, he suggested that a trip to LAX would reveal that the only way to distinguish between Airbus and Boeing would be the very tips of the wings. Boeing has long favored winglets (the tip of the wing curved upward) to reduce vortices rotating off the wing as it moves through the air, while Airbus preferred fences, or delta-shaped metal pieces that extend both above and below the wing's tip. These distinctive features were hardly definitive, and Airbus is switching to winglets, making aircraft all the more the same and leaving less for the engineer to ponder.

Talking with Reisman, I began to see a timeline clearly: decades of simply figuring out how to keep an airplane flying, followed by decades of intense engineering innovation, and then decades of commercial adoption of a mature technology. I saw, too, that the rough timeline that applied to aviation might describe spaceflight as well: the intense decade or so of figuring out how to orbit Earth and get to the Moon and back, followed by innovation that resulted in a long-term shuttle program and ongoing habitation in low-Earth orbit, and then—now—a shift to commercial acceptance of a mature technology.

This way of seeing the end of Shuttle heartened me; Shuttle was the middle of the story. In a way, even I'd followed the same timeline; I'd spent a long time (nearly five decades) figuring out the basics and, on the old side of middle age, was ready for the next stage (another fifty years?) in my own life.

When I was in junior high school, a few years before the first launch of a space shuttle, I told an adult at a holiday party about my desire to be an astronaut on the new spacecraft. Armed with information gleaned from *Popular Science* and *Popular Mechanics,* I explained how the shuttle would reduce the cost of putting things into space and thereby usher in a new space age. After listening patiently, the adult explained to me how, in the 1800s, it hadn't been the first railroad businessmen who'd made railroads profitable; it'd been the second wave of entrepreneurs, those who bought out bankrupt early adopters, taking advantage of investments in equipment and lines they purchased for pennies on the dollar. At the time, I was frustrated by the discussion of trains and the past when I wanted to talk about spaceships and the future. I now see that, whether or not this adult had the details correct, perhaps all modes of transportation have followed a similar timeline of development before widespread use. Railroads defined the nineteenth century, and aviation defined the twentieth century—and we're only halfway through a century's worth of spaceflight.

Like Reisman, astronaut Michael Barratt had told us a couple of years earlier, before Shuttle had ended, that this was an exciting time for spacecraft designers. "We don't know what a spaceship should look like," Barratt had said. Focused on Shuttle and its past at the time, I hadn't fully grasped what his words suggested. Reisman amplified Barratt's comments, "We're in this Golden Age of spaceflight right now, where nobody knows exactly for sure what a spaceship is supposed to look like. So we're experimenting with all these different things. Sierra Nevada has their lifting body. Some guys are working with solid rockets. We're [SpaceX] working with liquid rockets and capsules. [There are] different methods of abort systems, new fangled pusher abort systems. And that's what's exciting from an engineering standpoint." Only then did I understand that the multiple designs for commercial spacecraft— winged Lynx versus lifting-body Dream Chaser versus capsule-based Dragon—signaled a new, exciting phase for spaceflight.

What historian Tom Crouch said of aviation can be said of space-flight as well: "The direct effects of aviation on society are easy enough to catalogue, but the deeper consequences of technological change are difficult to anticipate, frequently contradictory or ambiguous, and almost always impossible to evaluate outside a specific point of view." There exist plenty of catalogues of spaceflights, but few interpretations. Anna and I wrote this book from the shadow of Shuttle so that we could wend our ways through our own lives as well as the contradictory and ambiguous culture that surrounds us. We embody and are embodied by the Space Age—with all the disappointments and achievements—that has come into its own, just as we have. The future holds more for the two of us, we hope, and more for manned space exploration.

In his February 2016 "The State of NASA" address, which I watched at a NASA Social at Armstrong Flight Research Center, Administrator Charlie Bolden commented that the previous year had seen a larger influx of investment capital to the commercial space arena than the previous fifteen years combined. NASA had done fifty years of research and development, funded by the American taxpayer, and the private sector was ready to take advantage of that infrastructure.

Bolden is an early Boomer, born more than a decade before Sputnik. As he talked about NASA's infrastructure and building on those first fifty years of spaceflight, I reminded myself how important it is to work toward Mars now, while those engineers involved in Apollo are still alive and while the combined knowledge and experience of those who worked on Shuttle are at hand. Shipbuilding skills came close to being entirely lost in the United States, when one maritime company after another closed. South Korea and China provide most of the world's large ships, and the United States supplies a single-digit percentage. If the law didn't require that all ships transporting goods between US ports were American made, if federal grants and special funds to support that effort weren't in place, and if the military didn't require homemade vessels, I doubt any large ships would still be built in this country. The United States cannot afford to lose decades of wisdom, but that risk exists.

At the end of 2015, two remarkable achievements indicated commercial space might be ready to pay dividends. Both Blue Origin, founded by Amazon tech billionaire Jeff Bezos, and SpaceX, founded by PayPal tech billionaire Elon Musk, demonstrated reusability, the holy grail of sharply reducing the cost of and generating a profit from launches. Shuttle re-used the vehicle and also the solid rocket boosters, and, though NASA didn't reap the promised cost savings, private companies believe they can build on NASA's foundation to make re-use profitable.

On December 21 of that year, I watched, on a computer screen in my office in the library, the SpaceX launch that demonstrated potential reusability. A Falcon 9 booster rocket successfully delivered eleven communication satellites to orbit and returned safely to a landing zone on Florida's Space Coast. A working, revenue-generating mission. By the time that the booster touched down, I was shaking with excitement. The following April, after several botched attempts, SpaceX landed a spent booster on a small barge in the ocean. I have watched that video a dozen times and am still amazed.

In November 2015, Blue Origin's New Shepard booster rocket—named for America's first astronaut, Alan Shepard—launched from a test range near Van Horn in West Texas. The booster made a suborbital flight to above sixty-two miles, that astronautical dividing line between atmosphere and space, before returning to land safely at the same facility. It was the first time that an entire booster rocket and capsule had crossed into space and returned safely to its point of origin (the empty crew capsule parachuted to a safe landing). To demonstrate reusability, the exact same New Shepard booster was refurbished and refueled. It repeated the eleven-minute feat on January 22, 2016.

Though the two launches were demonstrations of the same concept—reuse—each was done under different conditions and toward different goals. Falcon 9 is a general-purpose booster that has delivered satellites to orbit and cargo to ISS via the Dragon capsule, whereas New Shepard isn't capable of delivering payloads to orbit, designed instead for the space tourism market. Falcon 9 missions have tipped the scales at more than 450 tons, more than ten times as heavy as New Shepard. Falcon 9 used nine Merlin 1D engines of one hundred and forty-seven thousand pounds of thrust each, for a total of 1.3 million pounds of thrust, nearly ten times as powerful as a single New Shepard. In other words, moving space technology into the commercial sector allows for entrepreneurship and variety. Though I'd needed time to cope with Shuttle's end, these achievements signaled that commercial space was headed in the right direction: UP! I hadn't expected to feel enthused about commercial space, but I am.

I understand why Apollo veterans like Neil Armstrong (first man on the Moon), Jim Lovell (of Apollo 13, NASA's finest hour), and Gene Cernan (last man on the Moon) expressed concerns to Congress about the direction of America's space program. They were worried particularly about retiring the space shuttle fleet before NASA had a replacement. At the time, I agreed with them.

I remembered talking with John Glenn, America's second man in space. Press lanyard around my neck, I asked him, "Did NASA stop flying the shuttle too soon?" I knew that I'd made a mistake the moment I heard the words. Instead, I should have said, "Was it wrong to retire the shuttle fleet?" In front of Anna and other reporters, Glenn lectured me on how it wasn't NASA's decision to stop flying the shuttle. He'd already issued a public statement that shuttles should fly until a replacement vehicle was ready. Glenn's voice carried a passion that made him appear decades younger than his ninety years. I tried to listen, but all that I could hear was my own internal voice telling me that I screwed up. But that exchange prompted me to look further into what was really going on for NASA and consider seriously commercial space.

Now, though, those actions and statements of several years ago seem to me more a clash of generations than of intentions. When I think of that timeline—development, innovation, wide use—from the perspective of Generation Space, SpaceX seems inevitable, necessary, and exciting. Commercial space, from my perspective (though I took a couple of years to get to this thinking), is the ultimate validation of the value of Apollo and Shuttle. Shuttle was not an end.

After all, Elon Musk, the de facto leader of the commercial space vanguard, started SpaceX with the intention of settling Mars. That's still a hope, not the reality I expected as a kid. He plans to turn humans into a multi-planet species. Garrett Reisman acknowledged that it would be "cool" to be among the first astronauts to Mars, and that's a big part of why he retired from NASA and joined SpaceX. Gwynne Shotwell, SpaceX COO, spoke emphatically with Anna and me: "We're not talking about joyriders [going to Mars]. We're talking about explorers, settlers." SpaceX may do cargo runs to ISS now, but Musk and his company recently announced plans for their own unmanned mission to Mars in 2018, the first step in realizing the biggest dream of Generation Space.

NASA isn't standing still either. Curiosity landed on Mars in 2012, and NASA is making plans to send humans to the red planet. NASA's most comprehensive statement about these plans is *Journey to Mars: Pioneering Next Steps in Space Exploration*. The thirty-six-page document, published in October 2015, lays out the case: "Why Mars? Mars is the horizon goal for pioneering space; it is the next tangible frontier for expanding human presence." Yes, that's what my inner child has wanted to hear! Exploring Mars will answer questions posed by scientists as well as by science fiction writers long before NASA existed or I was born. Was Mars home to microbial life? Is it today? What can it teach us about the beginnings of life on Earth or elsewhere? Can it be a safe home for humans? What can it reveal about Earth's future?

NASA doesn't yet have the details worked out, of course, but one of the most important pieces exists: the Orion spacecraft. At least in an early version.

Orion is NASA's human-rated (or to-be-human-rated) craft for deep space. I first encountered Orion through mock-ups and videos at the National Air and Space Museum in 2012 when the Udvar-Hazy facility received space shuttle *Discovery*. There, notebook in hand, I talked in person with Lockheed-Martin's Dr. Michael Hawes, the professorial-looking man with an expansive imagination who directs the development of Orion.

Hawes told me, "We need to do some form of Gemini again." That surprised me—or, I admit, I may not have wanted to hear, at my age, that that NASA still needs to test a lot of ideas and equipment closer to home as part of progress toward the longer-distance goal. He also suggested that, as part of this in-between stage, NASA needed a mission to a place from which it wouldn't be immediately possible to return to Earth. ISS, though astronauts may be stuck in a sense, is too close to understand the sort of away-ness required to get to Mars. Hawes suggested visiting a Lagrange point on the far side of the Moon, something I'd not considered before but that sounded pretty cool.

A Lagrange point is a location in space where two massive bodies—Earth and Moon, for example (or Sun and Earth, for another)—gravitationally balance each other out. Such a point can function as a kind of parking lot, with a spacecraft held in position by roughly equal gravitational forces. Until I imagined the white Orion in the blackness of space just then, I hadn't thought about a spacecraft out there not moving, not going somewhere. Hawes's idea exceeded what *Journey to Mars* described as a proving ground, but it would show how to "conduct complex operations in a deep space environment."

Such a mission would take humans farther from Earth than ever before. That alone appeals to my Generation Space sense of adventure. Hawes figured the mission would last for two weeks, perhaps a month, in part to evaluate the psychological effects of isolation in space. Jim Lovell and Frank Borman spent two cozy weeks together during Gemini 12, but they were generally acknowledged as having easier-going personalities than many other astronauts. I could do a month in space, I'm sure of it. I'm less sure that I'd withstand the much longer trip to Mars, especially if anyone but Anna were along for the ride (and I wouldn't be sure about Anna without these last few years together).

In December 2014, I braved traffic for the thirty-five miles that sometimes takes three hours to attend the EFT-1 NASA Social at the Jet Propulsion Laboratory (there were other NASA locations too) for Orion's first journey into space. Being with other space nerds for the early stages of the effort to get to Mars heartened me, even though I still harbored doubts it could happen in my lifetime.

Exploration Flight Test-1 launched from the Space Coast. The flight's two orbits took four hours. At 220 miles overhead, ISS takes three hours to orbit the planet twice, whereas Orion reached a maximum distance of thirty-six hundred miles and, therefore, had a bigger, longer orbit. During those hours, NASA tested Orion's systems: avionics, parachutes, and ocean recovery. The empty crew capsule reentered the earth's atmosphere at nearly 20,000 mph. EFT-1 and its heat shield were declared a scorching success.

Orion's next test won't take place until November 2018, a long time in some ways—at my age—to wait for yet another unmanned test. But that's the way this process works. SpaceX has incredibly optimistic plans to send its Red Dragon capsule, which could eventually carry heavy payloads, to Mars in 2018. The date widely circulated for NASA sending humans to Mars is the nebulous mid-2030s. I'll be seventy years old by then.

According to Joseph Pelton, in an article in *Space Policy*,

> After the Apollo 17 mission, reporters asked [Werner] von Braun [architect of Apollo's Saturn V rocket] when there would be a permanent lunar colony. He quickly responded he thought it would take about 37 years. His estimate was based on the time from humans first reaching the South Pole until the establishment of a permanent research base in the Antarctic.

Models—precedents—exist for exploring and inhabiting, just as the timeline for aviation serves as a precedent for spaceflight. Forty-four years have passed since Apollo 17, the last time a human stood on the Moon. No person has been there since, and there exists no lunar colony, let alone a Martian one, though ISS has been inhabited since 2000. Yet if humans set their minds to it—it's a big *if*—I've begun to believe that people may well live on Mars forty years from now. I'll be ninety years old by then.

To my mind and probably to NASA's as well, the biggest obstacle in getting to Mars is the radiation that humans would encounter along the way. With current propulsion technology, the time it would take to travel to Mars would expose humans to enough radiation to kill them. Curiosity was exposed to the equivalent of eighty-four hundred chest x-rays (or twenty-four CT scans) in six months. Imagine getting forty-six chest x-rays per day (or a CT scan each week) for half a year. In addition, on the red planet's surface, the radiation exposure the rover faces is higher and more unpredictable than scientists had expected.

As of 2015, NASA remained in early stages of assessing and modeling the risk of radiation. In fact, the *Mars Mission and Space Radiation Risks*

Overview focuses much on other, more well understood risks like altered gravity, confinement, and isolation. While the model for acute radiation syndrome in flight exists and such risk might be reduced with shielding, the model for cancer risk is still being refined, and the risks that radiation poses to the cardiovascular and nervous systems are being investigated. In other words, there's a lot we don't know yet.

Knowing more about how radiation affects the human body and how the human body can be protected from its effects could be a good thing even here on Earth, as CT scans, nuclear accidents, and air travel (yes, air travel increases exposure) have become more common. In some ways, that's the best argument for going to Mars; we'll learn a lot about radiation and cancer that can save lives here on Earth. Already, researchers have used the microgravity aboard ISS to improve predictions of radiation-induced cancer on Earth and to research improvements in microencapsulation for delivering cancer-fighting drugs. Whether or not humans take up long-term residence on Mars, as SpaceX's Elon Musk proposes, the effort to get there would answer practical questions and allow us to keep asking new questions. Boots on Mars is the bonus.

Michael Barratt agreed. Radiation is the greatest obstacle in putting live humans on Mars, and, as an astronaut-physician, he's studied the problem. "We can maintain bone and muscle quite nicely," Barratt said about progress made with Shuttle astronauts. "We've actually got a good modeling of radiation out there." But he emphasized, "Deep space radiation is a very different animal than we see in low-Earth orbit." We don't understand how the body responds to that radiation, especially given the time a Mars trip would take. "What we want to do more than anything is fly faster," he said, in order to limit exposure by getting to Mars as quickly as possible. Still, NASA must find ways to protect the body—perhaps a combination of shielding, genetic screening, pharmaceuticals, even vitamin supplements—and some of those protections would be useful on Earth too.

Ultimately, though, whether addressing the challenge of interplanetary radiation or the propulsion needed, Mars all comes down to cost.

How much will it cost to get humans to Mars? A reasonable estimate that often comes up is $100 billion. That number was posited by a panel of NASA, industry, and academic experts in 2014. In 2016, at the Armstrong Flight Research Center Social for "The State of NASA" address, someone asked the same question. David McBride, Armstrong's Director, gave an off-the-cuff answer: "Give us [NASA] $100 billion, and we'll get to Mars." The same number. That's also the figure Apollo 11 astronaut Michael Collins quoted in his book *Mission to Mars* in 1990, referring to an estimate by Russian physicist Roald Sagdeev. Ever the conservative engineer, Collins pointed out that there were many unknowns—the technology doesn't yet exist in its entirety—and posited that double Sagdeev's figure, or $200 billion, would do the job.

How much is $200 billion? In 2014, *Business Insider* pulled together costs of the war in Iraq (2003-2011). The estimated cost of that war was $5000 per second and $12 billion per month. The annual air conditioning cost for the war (often cited in these discussions because of its indication of scale and its suggestion of hidden costs) was $20 billion; over eight years, that's close to Collins's estimated cost for putting humans on Mars. And since I've been thinking in fifty-year increments, it's important to note that, according to the Watson Institute at Brown University, the interest payments on war costs that the United States will owe in 2053, fifty years after that war began, will be $7 trillion (not billion, but trillion). That's thirty-five times the conservative estimate for a Mars mission.

I'm comfortable making these comparisons or equivalencies in part because I want boots on the Moon and Mars instead of boots on the ground in foreign countries and also because Michael Collins made a profound observation in *Mission to Mars* before I did: "The only thing that I know for certain is that starting a human colony on a second planet will cost much less than the weapons we buy to destroy the first one." When I ponder the supposed lack of will to fund a Mars mission, how easily distracted people are even from what they see as a good idea, I'm left aghast at what that says about humanity, the United States, and the future. Mars is a reasonable choice in the big scheme of the world.

Perhaps a more immediate way to think about my point is to consider the F-35 fighter plane, supposedly America's latest and greatest stealth aircraft. An August 2015 GAO report estimated that program's total cost for its fifty-year lifetime at more than $1 trillion dollars, five times what Collins conservatively estimated for a Mars journey. One trillion for a plane that, even as it's being built (and eight years after its first test flight), still faces problems. Over the last several years, F-35s have been grounded with engine and software problems, among myriad others. It's expensive—the most expensive military weapons system the United States has ever had. And it doesn't work very well.

By comparison, during its first fifty years (1958-2008), NASA received less than $1 trillion from the federal budget. Think about that for a moment: $1 trillion for one overdue, over budget, less-than-effective aircraft program or $1 trillion for the Moon landing, Hubble Space Telescope, the Mars rovers and landers, the Voyager twins, everything else that NASA has ever accomplished, plus seed money left over to start the process of going to Mars.

Going to Mars should not be a difficult fiscal choice. In addition to all the practical reasons of science and spinoff technology, I want NASA to take humans to Mars because of what it says about who I am in this vast universe. I want individuals to go there in peace for all the rest of us.

Of course, as Collins pointed out in his earlier book *Carrying the Fire*, the federal budget depends upon a holistic view. Choices are rarely between two specific programs. I get that; I'm not naïve about politics.

At the same time, space exploration is more popular than ever before. NASA has more than nineteen million Twitter followers. Even after Shuttle ended, the character Howard on *The Big Bang* Theory traveled aboard Soyuz to ISS with real-life astronaut Mike Massimino. Americans like space.

At the end of 2015, NASA announced it opened applications for the next astronaut class. The United States has no operational and certified vehicle to send people to space, though ISS remains an important part of NASA's work. If Mars is a serious goal, continuity of the astronaut corps is crucial. The application form required transcripts proving a STEM degree, lists of education and work experience, and five references. The deadline for applications was in February. By October, NASA would ask "highly qualified" candidates to get an FAA medical exam.

NASA received 18,300 applications. That's right, thousands of people want to be in the next class of astronaut trainees. This applicant pool was more than double the number of applications that were received in the previous largest pool, eight thousand in 1978, the first year NASA considered applications from women. Americans want to go to space.

Mine was one of those 18,300 applications. It's a long shot for me, especially since I turn fifty before the selections will be announced in mid-2017. After all these years, after leaving that possibility behind in college and finding and making the life in which I now thrive, I still wanted my name to be in the mix. NASA, of course, has already given me my career, as my job at NASA's Center for AeroSpace Information in the early 1990s set me on the trajectory that's led me to where I am now. In that position as an abstracter and indexer, I learned librarianship and programming, and NASA CASI paid for the early computer science courses that I took at area community colleges. Those years became the foundation for graduate degrees in computer science and library science and, ultimately, for the job I hold now as the Digital Humanities and Sciences Librarian. To join the next astronaut class would, therefore, be icing on the cake that I've been eating for the last two decades.

I want a person—thinking, thoughtful, feeling—to step onto the surface of Mars. I know that person cannot be me—the timing is off, we've taken too long. But someone.

EPILOGUE
RETURN TO TOMORROW
BOTH

We travel, initially, to lose ourselves; and we travel, next, to find ourselves.

—Pico Iyer, *Salon*

It is good to renew one's wonder, said the philosopher. Space travel has again made children of us all.

—Ray Bradbury, *The Martian Chronicles*

In Southern California, August 25, 2012, was a beautiful Saturday, all blue sky, warm sunshine, and cool breeze. *Discovery* had been installed in its permanent museum home, and we had started to make plans to follow *Endeavour* and *Atlantis* to museums that fall. The semester was set to begin on Monday, and we were at home working. That day, Neil Armstrong died.

Neil Armstrong, the first human being to stand on the Moon, was eighty-two years old and living in Cincinnati. Armstrong and eleven other men had visited the Moon. Those of us who had been watching, as young as we might have been then, became the first wave of Generation Space. The first era of US manned spaceflight ended with his death: the Shuttle program was over, and Generation Space became the adults of this nation.

The time that had elapsed between the moment Armstrong left humanity's first lunar footprints permanently enshrined in the Moon's soil to the day of his death spanned our conscious lives.

Doug's first memory of life was that of Armstrong's bulky white form, gracelessly clambering down the lunar module's ladder. As toddlers, we may not have known what meaning that moment held, but even young children sense meaning, recognize when a thing or event holds meaning.

Armstrong had been just thirty-eight years old when he flew on Apollo 11. We've now hit fifty ourselves. We're past middle age. It's time we grow up—or admit that we've grown up. Just as we stood on the shoulders of the previous generation, we must ensure that our shoulders are strong enough to support those who will follow us.

Earlier on in the month he died, Armstrong had celebrated his birthday, and then he had heart bypass surgery. His arteries were clogged—not an unusual occurrence, not something that made the headlines. He'd shied away from the limelight after the initial hoopla over the Moon landing, so news of his health wasn't something we'd seen. On August 25, the reports on that sunny Saturday were that his recovery had appeared to be going well but that complications had arisen. Complications sound unusual but are not; complications are commonplace, and astronauts know that. Complications can even happen to the first person to walk on the Moon. Life is full of complications, and we die from some of those complications.

The news stories, public condolences, and commemorations began to pile up quickly. NASA Administrator Charlie Bolden issued the following statement: "As long as there are history books, Neil Armstrong will be included in them, remembered for taking humankind's first small step on a world beyond our own. Besides being one of America's greatest explorers, Neil carried himself with a grace and humility that was an example to us all. When President Kennedy challenged the nation to send a human to the moon, Neil Armstrong accepted without reservation."

Bob Cabana, Director of Kennedy Space Center, said, "Neil Armstrong was a true American hero, and one of the nicest gentlemen around. He was the epitome of what an engineering test pilot should be, and a role model for anyone who aspired to be an astronaut."

Astrophysicist Neil DeGrasse Tyson pointed to the grand nature of Armstrong's accomplishment, adding, "No other act of human exploration ever laid a plaque saying, 'We came in peace for all mankind.'"

Apollo astronaut Michael Collins, who orbited the Moon while Armstrong and Buzz Aldrin walked upon its surface, said simply of Armstrong, "He was the best, and I will miss him terribly."

John Glenn, the first American to orbit Earth, was going strong at ninety-one years old when we interviewed him that previous spring at *Discovery*'s installation at the Udvar-Hazy Facility. Now he is gone too. Glenn, who was not usually envious of others because of his own successes in space and in politics, once had admitted that Armstrong was the one person he envied. Of the twelve men who had walked on the Moon, six—Armstrong, Gene Cernan, Pete Conrad, James Irwin, Edgar Mitchell, and Alan Shepherd—are, as we write this, already gone. The oldest living Moon walker is Aldrin, born in 1930, and the youngest is Charlie Duke, born in 1935. The Silent Generation born between world wars is leaving us.

Armstrong knew that he was a "nerdy engineer," as he said in a NASA oral history project, who came of age at just the right time. Had he been born ten years earlier or later, he would not have walked on any extraterrestrial body other than Earth. Had it not been him on the lunar surface on July 20, 1969, it would have been someone else. But it wasn't someone else. We watched Neil Armstrong step onto the Moon. As he put it in his own words, "Looking back, we were really very privileged to live in that thin slice of history where we changed how man looks at himself and what he might become and where he might go."

We hope all the remaining Apollo astronauts live another decade. We'd very much like to have another good conversation with Charlie Duke when he's ninety. We'd very much like to meet Michael Collins, the best writer of the bunch and one of those few men who circled the Moon all alone. But the Apollo astronauts will not live forever. They made history; we were born into the history they were making. We grew up in the Space Age that they forged for us, and they are leaving us.

Sally Ride, the first American women to travel to space, had died a few weeks before Armstrong, and Mary Lee Leahy (Anna's mother), an achiever in her own right, was gone before the end of that year. Both died of pancreatic cancer, which is rarely caught early and has a terrible prognosis no matter its stage. The vast majority of those diagnosed with pancreatic cancer die within a year. Ride lived seventeen months after diagnosis, and Mary Lee survived eight months. Ride's legacy lives on in Sally Ride Science, an organization she founded with her partner, Tam O'Shaughnessy, and three others to inspire kids, especially girls, in science and engineering. Mary Lee's legacy lives on in her daughters and the legal precedents she helped establish. That year was one of losing those who'd come before us.

Upon hearing of Neil Armstrong's death on that August Saturday in 2012, we wondered how exactly we would see ourselves and where we might go. We are Generation Space, born into Apollo and then into Shuttle, and we—individually and collectively—must make the most of the thin slice of history in which we now live as adults. Our time, we suddenly felt palpably, was limited.

Mark Kelly, the commander of *Endeavour's* last mission, is fifty-two years old as we write this epilogue, an astronaut of Generation Space. He announced, only three weeks after completing the penultimate shuttle mission, he was retiring from NASA. His twin brother, Scott, also announced his retirement within two weeks of returning from nearly a year aboard the International Space Station in March 2016. These men are moving on with their lives, as are many astronauts we met over the last few years. Space exploration is behind them, memories for their old age—and contributions to history, culture, and technology as their legacy.

We're already nostalgic about the space shuttle. The two of us are especially nostalgic about *Endeavour*, made from spare parts to replace *Challenger*. When we visit *Endeavour* in its museum home, its scuffs are memories, a record of flight etched into skin, a spark of launch day in our mind's eye, a fire and vibration in the heart. We remember seeing it on the launch pad. One orbiter's presence is a reminder of another's absence, a hint left of that cold January day in 1986 when we watched the column of cloud-smoke split in the sky—a hint left of the people who have shaped our lives and are now gone.

Our response to seeing *Endeavour* now might best be described by that Portuguese word *saudade*, that emotional state in which memory is sensory, in which happiness and sadness cannot be teased apart. There exists a strange pleasure in coming to terms with heartache, of letting heartache settle in, of making do and making whole. The last few years, as we've worked our way through the story that is *Generation Space*, we've learned that love is both longing and contentment, both wanting and gratitude. At life's pivot point, we became positioned so as to move, balanced perhaps precariously. Just past middle age now, we have built up layers of nostalgia—our yearning for the future as much as for the past.

While those of us born at the beginning of Generation Space are in our early fifties and not yet of retirement age, we understand that our time is winding down. We should be saving for retirement and getting our first screening colonoscopies. In the not-too-distant future, when we return to that Astronaut Autograph and Memorabilia Show that we stumbled into at KSC, the Apollo astronauts will be gone and the Shuttle astronauts will take their place as the older generation. The youngest of Generation Space, born as the space shuttle took flight in the early 1980s, are in their mid-thirties, with all the demands of adulthood that entails and no American vehicle ready to take them beyond Earth orbit. The future may be ours—the oldest and even the youngest of Generation Space—to help found now, but it not ours to live out. The two of us will not travel to Mars.

Generation Space—and the two of us right along with it—grew up fascinated by the possibilities of space exploration. We lived in the shadow of Shuttle for thirty years. When we mention the topic of this book to friends or new acquaintances, the response is *me too!* Each of us has a memory, however fleeting or secondhand, an image or a hope. In these last few years—after we moved to California to start our lives anew, while we left certainties behind as the Shuttle program ended—the two of us lost ourselves in order to find ourselves, to find each other and fall in love. We took to the desert of California and to the Space Coast of Florida as a way to understand history, culture, technology, and each other more deeply. The two of us became explorers together—witnesses and investigators—of Generation Space, and this book is our record of this adventure.

Endings are perceptions, ways to parse out time or life, but time is ongoing. Writer Sarah Manguso, in her book titled *Ongoingness*, wrote, "It comforts me that endings are thus formally unappealing to me—that more than beginning or ending, I enjoy continuing." *Atlantis* is still there in Florida, and we see *Endeavour* regularly in California. Anna's mother's death wasn't really an end either. Anna's life went on. We are currently redoing our own backyard, planning a party like the last one that we hosted the night before heading to the Space Coast to see *Endeavour* launch. Space exploration hasn't ended. Endings are a variation of continuing.

Our students—the generation in college now—were born in 1995 or later. They were in elementary school when space shuttle *Columbia* broke apart in the sky on February 1, 2003, and when the rovers Spirit and Opportunity landed on Mars the following year. Children born then, born into an era of roving Mars remotely, are entering high school. Children born today will grow up not doubting that there was and likely is water on Mars.

These are the individuals of Generation Mars. Their grandfathers helped build the Saturn rocket that carried men to the Moon, and their mothers became low-Earth orbiters. If they take up the legacy that Generation Space has bequeathed, these are the humans who can set foot on Mars themselves. The word *generation* comes from the Latin verb meaning *to beget or produce*. Each generation has a responsibility to produce something new and beget the future. We didn't travel to the red planet ourselves. Generation Space begets that future to Generation Mars.

Though travel to Mars seems almost as daunting now as travel to the Moon seemed before the first human-made object was launched into space in 1957, human beings are good at letting our imaginations lead us right along with the science. The thousands of individuals who applied to become astronauts in February 2016 is a signal. Where better than space to really leave one's certainties behind and to allow us to see the world from a very different perspective? How better to understand what we've taken for granted—not just gravity, but our assumptions—and to understand what possibilities exist? Our dream remains for humans to find themselves on our closest planetary neighbor before today's high school and college students retire. We grew up asking for the Moon. May the toddlers of today be able to ask their friends, not as a joke about not fitting in but in all seriousness, *Where are you from—Mars?*

Generation Mars holds the power to renew humanity's wonder and make children again of us all. *Good luck and Godspeed. Go for launch.*

ACRONYMS

ACES	Advanced Crew Escape Suit
AMS	Alpha Magnetic Spectrometer
ANNA	Army Navy NASA Air Force (satellite)
CAPCOM	Capsule Communicator (person on Earth talking to astronauts in space)
COTS	Commercial Off the Shelf
DOD	Department of Defense
DOE	Department of Energy
DSKY	Display and Keypad (as on a computer)
EMU	Extravehicular Mobility Unit
ESA	European Space Agency
ET	External Tank
EVA	Extravehicular Activity
FAA	Federal Aviation Administration
Fermilab	Fermi National Accelerator Laboratory
GPS	Global Positioning System
GRAIL	Gravity Recovery and Interior Laboratory
GUCP	Ground Umbilical Carrier Plate
ISS	International Space Station
IVA	Intravehicular Activity
JPL	Jet Propulsion Laboratory
KSC	Kennedy Space Center

LC	Launch Complex
MOL	Manned Orbiting Laboratory
NASA	National Aeronautics and Space Administration
OMS	Orbital Maneuvering System
OPF	Orbiter Processing Facility
OV	Orbital Vehicle
PEAP	Personal Egress Air Packs
RSS	Rotating Service Structure
RTLS	Return To Launch Site
SCA	Shuttle Carrier Aircraft
SETI	Search for Extraterrestrial Life
SRB	Solid Rocket Booster
STEM	Science, Technology, Engineering, Math
STS	Space Transportation System
SSME	Space Shuttle Main Engine
USA	United Space Alliance
VAB	Vehicle (orig. Vertical) Assembly Building

ACKNOWLEDGMENTS

Too many people to name here answered our questions patiently, placed us in the path of history, and protected us from harm—and many more helped to create the Space Age over more than five decades. We acknowledge all of them in helping us make this book happen.

We are grateful to NASA generally and to all those individuals who welcomed us as journalists to Kennedy Space Center and to Armstrong Flight Research Center and also as guests at the Jet Propulsion Laboratory and several other places. Laurel Lichtenberger approved our media badge requests for KSC, and Allard Beutel, Mike Curie, and the other media relations staff guided us while we were at KSC. Stephanie Stilson got us closer to a shuttle than we ever expected. Gray Creech (Armstrong), Stephanie L. Smith (JPL), and Kevin Rohrer (Armstrong) coordinated NASA Social events that rounded out our experiences with in-depth learning. Merrilee Fellows at JPL first suggested that the way for us to have access to launches at KSC was to become journalists. Also to the astronauts and space workers who shared their insights about the Space Age with us, much thanks.

We are grateful as well to the Kennedy Space Center Visitor Complex, the National Air and Space Museum and its curators Valerie Neal and Margaret Weitecamp, and the California Science Center, especially to its Curator of Aerospace Science Ken Phillips and Vice President of Communications Shell Amega.

To other space writers who preceded us and who will follow us, we are gratified to be in your company. Fellow journalists like Rob Pearlman, Jay Barbree, and Ken Kremer taught us via osmosis, and writer Margaret Lazarus Dean has become a friend.

Anna's poems used within appeared, sometimes in different versions, in the following publications: *Botticelli Review* ("The Visible Universe"), *Queen Mob's Teahouse* ("Trajectory" as "What I Want to Be When I Grow Up"), and *Moonlight Magazine* and *Post Road* (versions of "Google Moon"). "Trajectory" appears in Anna's book *Aperture*, from Shearsman Books.

"Facts About the Moon" is from *Facts About the Moon* by Dorianne Laux. Copyright © 2006 by Dorianne Laux. Used by permission of W. W. Norton & Company, Inc. Traci Brimhall, excerpts from "Saudade" from *Saudade*. Copyright © 2017 by Traci Brimhall. Reprinted with the permission of The Permissions Company, Inc., on behalf of Copper Canyon Press, www.coppercanyonpress.org.

We wrote much of this book during residencies at Dorland Mountain Arts Colony, and we began work in earnest at Ragdale. These and other organizations support writers and artists who seek dedicated time for large projects—that matters to many of us and to the vibrancy of contemporary literature. We participated in the remarkable Santa Fe Science Writing Workshop, garnering tips from George Johnson, Susan Blakeslee, and Robert Lee Hotz, and the eye-opening Launch Pad Astronomy Workshop in Wyoming with the likes of Mike Brotherton, Christian Ready, and other scientists and writers.

Our early readers helped us understand where our words worked and where we needed to work on our words. Thanks to Mary Cantrell (who has been our friend since college), Patricia Grace King, Kim Brown, and Paulette Livers, all of whom read early chapters. Thanks also to Brigid Leahy, Debbie Rindge, and Krista Helvey, who read drafts of the whole book. Many others over the years—teachers and peers at Knox College, Iowa State University, the University of Maryland, and Ohio University—have helped us become better writers, and we thank them.

Chapman University, where we both hold full-time positions, has been supportive of this project from that very first trip to the Space Coast. Thanks especially to Daniele Struppa, Charlene Baldwin, Joanna Levin, Richard Bausch, Jim Blaylock, Tom Zoellner, and Dennis Arp (who vouched for Anna as a journalist). Also, thanks to Megan Scott at Knox College for vouching for Doug as a journalist.

We're grateful to many writer-friends who encouraged our work in large and small ways and to editors who believed in what we'd written. Thanks especially to Leslie Pietzryk for stopping at the Stillhouse Press booth at AWP and then introducing us to editor Marcos L. Martínez. Everyone at Stillhouse has been enthusiastic about this book and about shaping the literary landscape. Angela Bagetta and Jeff Umbro at Goldberg McDuffie Communications have been great resources and advocates as we've moved toward publication. Seth Fischer, the final copyeditor, negotiated Chicago and NASA styles and caught one lingering possessive mistake. Any remaining errors of fact or grammar are ours.

For our families, the most enormous gratitude. Our parents—Rick and Sue Dechow, Andrew and Mary Lee Leahy—instilled in us a curiosity that carries us. Our siblings—Brigid, Richard, Emily, David, Suellen—have put up with us and cheered us on. Maggie Cullen always has our backs and has the loyalty and exuberance of a Cubs fan.

GEN SPACE BOOK CLUB

If your book club or organization is reading *Generation Space*, let Anna and Doug know—send a message to IAmGenerationSpace@gmail.com.

8 FUN FACTS ABOUT ANNA & DOUG

They chose 8 for this book club segment because the figure 8 was the trajectory for Apollo's lunar missions.

They both have bachelor's degrees from Knox College, but Anna graduated before Doug transferred there. Find out how they met in Chapter 10.

They had cats named after scientists (years before Sheldon on *The Big Bang Theory*): Nick (Nicholas J. Schrodinger, for Nick's your buddy and the cat in the thought experiment), Feynman (Richard Feynman), and Oppenheimer (J. Robert Oppenheimer).

For years, they drove Saturn cars, named after the planet and the rocket that propelled humans beyond the bounds of Earth's gravity and on to the Moon.

They moved to California together in 2008 for jobs at Chapman University; Anna landed her position as an English professor, and Doug was interviewed for his librarian position shortly after Anna accepted her job.

They eloped in Las Vegas on 11/29; both the month and the year are prime numbers. Read Anna's accounts of their wedding at OZY.com and in "Marrying Absurd," the essay that won the 2016 *Ninth Letter* literary award in creative nonfiction.

Neither Doug nor Anna read *Moby-Dick* until they had started following the end of Shuttle, pursuing their own white whale of sorts.

They held a joint fellowship at the American Library in Paris, where they copyedited *Generation Space*, and a joint residency at Dorland Mountain Arts Colony, where they did the final proofreading on this book.

8 DISCUSSION QUESTIONS FOR *GENERATION SPACE*

1. This book defines Generation Space as those born between 1957, when Sputnik launched, and 1981, when the shuttle first took to space. Are you part of Generation Space? If so, how do you think not knowing a world without space exploration distinguishes you from generations who came before? If you were born before 1957, what perspective can you offer those who are growing up now? If you were born into the Shuttle era, do you think Generation Mars is a good way to describe you?

2. Chapter 1 talks about Sputnik, Chapter 2 cover Yuri Gagarin and Alan Shepard, and Chapters 3 and 4 talk about the Apollo missions to the Moon. The Soviet Union launched the first satellite and the first human into space, and the United States launched the first and only human beings to the Moon. Now, as Chapter 5 points out, the International Space Station is a collaborative effort and a habitat where both Russian and English are spoken. Which nation won the Space Race? What can we gain from cooperative projects like ISS?

3. In Chapter 4, Doug recounts his first conscious memory: watching the Apollo 11 Moon mission on television. For Anna, trips to the Museum of Science and Industry in Chicago and watching *I Dream of Jeannie* on television when she was four years old shaped her early ideas about space. What are your first memories of living in the Space Age? *You can share your personal memories and dreams of the Space Age at www.generation-space.com/IAmGenSpace.*

4. In Chapter 6, Anna interviews former astronaut Mike Coats and comes up with her go-to question about great or greatest shuttle. In Chapter 10, several astronauts answer that same question. What three questions would you most want to ask an astronaut? Of the astronauts Anna and Doug met or others you know about, which one would you most want to talk with?

5. On numerous occasions while they were following the end of Shuttle, Anna and Doug were faced with delays. Would you have handled these unexpected circumstances the same way? How is hurry-up-and-wait sometimes part of your own life?

6. Would you travel to the International Space Station for six months with no way to get back home until your scheduled return, even if some tragedy struck your family? In Chapter 11, Anna ponders under what circumstances she might and might not leave Earth for an extended time, if she had the chance. Going to Mars will be an even longer commitment with more unknowns. What would make it worth the risk for you to go to Mars?

7. Chapter 15 explores the relationship between technology and nature by chronicling the Merritt Island National Wildlife Refuge as well as NASA's role on the Space Coast in Florida. What do you think is the best balance between technology and nature? When should one take precedence over the other?

8. Chapter 20 posits that robotic missions are important for space exploration. Do you think robotic missions can or should make manned missions unnecessary in the future? Or do you agree with Doug when he says, at the end of Chapter 21, "I want a person—thinking, thoughtful, feeling—to step onto the surface of Mars"?

8 ONLINE SPACE AGE RESOURCES TO CHECK OUT

Spot the Station (offers email/text alerts for ISS passes):
http://spothestation.nasa.gov

NASA Image Archive:
www.nasa.gove/multimedia/imagegallery

Universe Today (for up-to-date space news):
www.universetoday.com

Space.com (for timely space stories):
www.space.com

The Mars Generation (and Astronaut Abby):
www.themarsgeneration.org

National Science Foundation Astronomy & Space Classroom
Resources:
www.nsf.gov/classroom/astronomy.jsp

National Air & Space Museum Educator Resources:
www.airandspace.si.edu/educator-resources

Lofty Ambitions blog by Anna & Doug:
http://loftyambitions.wordpress.com

See www.GenerationSpace.com for more information. Share your memory or story of the Space Age at www.generationspace.com/IAmGenSpace. Follow @GenerationSpace and use hashtag #IAmGenerationSpace.

Anna Leahy and Douglas R. Dechow work and teach at Chapman University in Orange, California. They have written the *Lofty Ambitions* blog together since 2010.

Anna is the author of the poetry books *Aperture* (Shearsman, 2017) and *Constituents of Matter* (Kent State University Press, 2007), which won the Wick Poetry Prize. Her nonfiction book *Tumor* is forthcoming in Bloomsbury's Object Lessons series in 2017.

Doug is the co-author of *SQUEAK: A Quick Trip to Objectland* (Addison-Wesley Professional, 2001), *Intertwingled: The Work and Influence of Ted Nelson* (Springer, 2015), and *The Craft of Librarian Instruction* (American Library Association, 2016).

This book would not have been possible without
the hard work of our staff.

We would like to acknowledge:

Marcos L. Martínez, Managing Editor

Scott W. Berg, Editorial Advisor
Douglas J. Luman, Art Director
Marcos L. Martínez, Editorial Director
Meghan McNamara, Media Director

Editors

Justin Lafreniere
Evan Roberts
Hailey Scherer
Michelle Webber

Our Donors

Anonymous
Therese Howell
Dallas Hudgens
Wayne B. Johnson
William Miller

stillhouse
press

CPSIA information can be obtained
at www.ICGtesting.com
Printed in the USA
FFOW02n1848180317
33497FF